ADVANC

This path-breaking book brings together an international list of contributors to collectively articulate a vision for the field of youth work, sharing what they have learned from decades of experience in the training and education of youth workers. Carefully designed evaluation and research studies have legitimized the learning potential of youth programs and non-school organizations over the last twenty years, and recent attention has shifted towards the education, training, and on-going professional development of youth workers. Contributors define youth work across domains of practice and address the disciplines of knowledge upon which sound practice is based, reviewing examples of youth practitioner development both in and outside of academia. Raising critical questions and concerns about current trends, *Advancing Youth Work* aims to bring clarity to the field and future of youth work, visioning youth work as a fundamental necessity to positive youth outcomes.

Advancing Youth Work will help youth work practitioners develop a common language, articulate their field in one voice, and create a shared understanding of similarities and differences. This book is also an invaluable resource for higher educators, researchers, and students involved with youth work.

Dana Fusco is Associate Professor of Teacher Education, York College, City University of New York.

ADVANCING YOUTH WORK

Current Trends, Critical Questions

Edited by Dana Fusco

Routledge
Taylor & Francis Group

NEW YORK AND LONDON

First published 2012
by Routledge
711 Third Avenue, New York, NY 10017

Simultaneously published in the UK
by Routledge
2 Park Square, Milton Park, Abingdon, Oxon OX14 4RN

Routledge is an imprint of the Taylor & Francis Group, an informa business
© 2012 Taylor & Francis

Library of Congress Cataloging in Publication Data
Advancing youth work : current trends, critical questions / [edited by] Dana Fusco.
  p. cm.
  Includes bibliographical references and index.
  1. Youth workers. I. Fusco, Dana.
  HV1421.A38 2011
  362.7—dc22
  2011011017

ISBN13: 978-0-415-89045-8 (hbk)
ISBN13: 978-0-415-89046-5 (pbk)
ISBN13: 978-0-203-82976-9 (ebk)

Typeset in Bembo and Stone Sans
by EvS Communication Networx, Inc.

Printed and bound in the United States of America on acid-free paper
by Edwards Brothers, Inc.

SUSTAINABLE FORESTRY INITIATIVE
Certified Fiber Sourcing
www.sfiprogram.org

CONTENTS

TABLES AND FIGURES

Tables

Figures

FOREWORD

President Obama, similar to his predecessor, is urging college students to become classroom teachers, especially in the areas of science, math, and technology. College students are rarely urged to become youth or community workers. This is surprising, given President Obama's experience as a community organizer. It is also surprising because youth workers are increasingly fundamental to the success of public schools. Consider, for example, the Bruce Randolf School in Denver, Colorado. Bruce Randolf is often highlighted by the president as a national model for success, in large part because it has successfully brought together teachers, parents, students, and nonprofit organizations to work together with common purpose.

But who is it that brings disparate stakeholders together as partners? Who does the heavy lifting necessary to keep the partnerships together and sustain the common purpose with shared energy? It is youth workers in most cases. Moreover, it is the youth workers who instruct, care for, and are available for the young people when the school day is done. Yet, in policy speeches and in youth policy, the role of youth workers becomes conspicuous only by its absence. There is little mention of the sophisticated skills that youth workers can bring to the table, and almost no mention of how the United States can prepare and support the next generation of exemplary youth workers. *Advancing Youth Work* is an important volume because it challenges this status quo.

I am a strong supporter of President Obama. That said, a conventional focus on schooling limits discourse and policy making regarding young people diminishing the salience and importance of issues such as child poverty and vulnerability, community, contribution, civic engagement, collective deliberation and action, human development, empowerment, leadership, out-of-school opportunities, relationships, and youth–adult partnerships. This salience is picked up here in *Advancing Youth Work*. In exploring the current trends within the field of youth work, this volume helps to raise up youth workers and to demonstrate the many ways that they are critical to youth development and community well being in the United States.

★★★★★

Advancing Youth Work details the lessons learned from exemplary youth workers and from the most thoughtful trainers, educators, and technical assistance providers. It raises the bar, and helps set new standards for excellence. There is much in this volume that cannot be found elsewhere. The editor, Dana Fusco, has brought together an expert group of scholars and practitioners who write with clarity, feeling, and understanding. The authors are adept at integrating research, practitioner wisdom, and observation. In reading this volume, one walks away with vivid images of exemplary youth work, and equally important, with cogent analyses and case examples of effective strategies for youth work education.

For front-line practitioners and supervisors, *Advancing Youth Work* analyzes what it means to be an exemplary youth worker. It describes the strategies through which youth workers connect to the developmental and academic needs of youth. It highlights the ways that youth workers maintain the emotional engagement of young people. Further, this volume details the dynamic nature of youth work, and the ways that youth workers respond to the strengths and rhythms of young people and their communities. It shows the ways that youth workers are able to build relationships and deliver course content simultaneously. In brief, both the science and the art of youth work are explored in this volume.

For policy makers and funders, this volume details the current structure of the field, with attention to both its strengths and weaknesses. It offers particularly cogent analyses of contemporary models of professional development, both within higher education and in community organizations. In analyzing these systems, the authors explore the components of staff development: core competencies, credentialing rubrics, ladders of advancement, community collaboration, field experience, and accountability mechanisms. They draw on observations not only from the United States but from other countries as well.

★★★★★

Youth work is what logicians call an "essentially contested concept." That means that are there are multiple conceptualizations that accurately define exemplary youth work and effective professional development. The task facing the policy maker or youth worker is to choose among those conceptualizations that have the strongest theoretical integrity, empirical support, practical utility, *and* which fit best with local conditions. This is a difficult calculus. The power of this volume is it forces us out of our comfort zones. It forces us to grapple with the challenges of reconciling research, practice, and setting. *Advancing*

Youth Work does not provide easy answers but it does provide a sturdy foundation for all of us to make informed decisions.

Far too many youth workers enter the field with inadequate preparation. They are forced to sink or swim. The fact that many learn to swim, proficiently and with grace, is a testimony to the workers themselves, not to our support of them. As documented in this volume, there is no perceived imperative among policy makers or funders to prioritize professional development for youth workers. Almost all of the professional development systems highlighted in this volume are operating largely on soft monies. Like many of the youth they serve, youth and community workers are themselves in a fragile situation.

It is beyond time for public agencies and foundations to build the capacity and reach of the field. Until there is sustained movement toward infrastructure creation, we will continue to lose exemplary systems as quickly as we can build them. The challenge is not only more money. While current stereotypes about youth work are not overtly tarnished, they are ambivalent. Underlying this ambivalence is a fundamental lack of understanding about the profession. We need assertive and highly strategic campaigns to create the public idea that youth work is essential to youth and to their communities.

★★★★★

In the early 1990s, such an effort was made. Multiple funders including the Wallace Foundation and the Office of Juvenile Justice and Delinquency Prevention supported intensive collaboration among experts across fields to document the youth development approach and the essential roles of youth workers. As the lead author of *Advancing Youth Development: A Curriculum for Youth Workers*, circa 1993, I was responsible for integrating these diverse voices and perspectives into a single document. In reading this volume, I was pleased to see that the curriculum is being used widely in community and school settings in ways that I never imagined. At the same time, it became clear how far the field has progressed. The current volume, that which you now are perusing, reflects the collective expertise and experience that has been gathered over the past twenty years. It is time for funders to affirmatively support public campaigns, the strengthening of professional development systems, and new curricula that incorporate these lessons.

Isolation from opportunity and support is a constant in the lives of hundreds of thousands of youth in the United States. More often than not, youth workers are the ones who, with skill and creativity, are best able to connect with these young people. Exemplary youth workers know how to help young people build from their own strengths and become prepared for adulthood. Youth workers know how to promote positive development, confidence, and compassion among young people. In brief, it is youth workers who know how to prepare young people for the challenges and joys of life, in addition to preparing youth to do well in school. It is beyond time to invest in these workers.

My recommendation is that you acquire *Advancing Youth Work*. Realize, however, that most youth workers will not have easy access to it. So, I also encourage you to find ways to share the insights with your colleagues. If everybody does this, the information will quickly be disseminated across the country. And if somebody could arrange it, it would be great for the First Lady, Michelle Obama, to give an abstract of this volume to her husband as a simple reminder that the preparation of exemplary youth workers is of equal importance to the preparation of exemplary teachers.

Shepherd Zeldin
Bascom Rothermel Professor of Human Ecology
University of Wisconsin-Madison

PREFACE

While youth programs and other non-school organizations have long ago discovered the potency of learning opportunities that can take place under their auspices, the past twenty years has legitimized their discoveries through carefully designed evaluation and research studies. Much of the 1990s focused on researching the quality of those programs for promoting positive youth development. In addition to showing that youth programs can lead to a range of positive developmental outcomes for young people, consistently revealed was that staff effectiveness was the single most important variable for producing those outcomes (Little, Wimer, & Weiss, 2008; Mahoney, Parente, & Zigler, 2009; Metz, Bandy, & Burkhauser, 2009; Phelan, 2005; Smith, Peck, Denault, Blazevski, & Akiva, 2010). Unfortunately, this finding is juxtaposed to the reality that staff retention is a major challenge for many community agencies serving youth. As a result, the past decade has shifted its attention to the development of the workforce with the hope of creating a stable and prepared pool of youth workers.

Interest in youth work and workforce development has been high and investments significant with support from national foundations such as The Wallace Foundation, The Annie E. Casey Foundation, and The David and Lucille Packard Foundation; intermediaries like the Forum for Youth Investment; professional associations like the National Institute for Out-of-School Time and the National After-School Association; and institutions of higher education across the country. Each group has contributed to field building in distinct ways. State and national networks have been formed to help connect initiatives, promote conversations, and bridge roadblocks. In 2008, the Association for Child and Youth Care Practice (CYC-P) launched the first national credential in the field. The last decade alone has been birth to journals and research forums designated to out-of-school time and youth development. The Robert Bowne Foundation launched the *Afterschool Matters* journal in 2000; a peer-reviewed online journal published the first issue of the *Journal of Youth Development* in 2006; and one year later, an Out-of-School Time Special Interest Group was formed within the American Educational Research Association. Many initiatives at building competency frameworks for youth workers also have emerged: the North American Certification Project published competencies for professional child and youth work practitioners in 2001; the National 4-H Headquarters developed a set of Professional Development Standards in 2005; and in 2009, the Next Generation Youth Work Coalition produced a review of Youth Work Core Competency frameworks.

Further, the government has engaged the issue for the first time in over thirty years, though much of the focus is on afterschool education. In March 2006, members of the bi-partisan Congressional Caucus on After School Programs endorsed a letter to expand funding for 21st Century Community Learning Centers that link school and non-school learning. In 2009, the U.S. Department of Education sponsored a three-day web dialogue that centered on 21st Century Community Learning Centers. Day Two focused solely on the professional development needs of the program staff and Day Three centered on the challenges to providing professional development to youth workers. In 2010, "extended learning time" made its way into the narrative of the reauthorized Elementary and Secondary Education Act, though the implication of refocusing youth work (and its resources) as solely educational is not to be missed.

Higher education is also a key player. There has been an upsurge in the development of university training programs and institutes for youth workers such as Arcadia University, Bank Street, City University of New York, John Hopkins University, Rutgers University, University of Wisconsin, University of Pittsburgh, University of California, University of Minnesota, and University of Indiana, among others. In addition, the Advancing Youth Development (AYD) curriculum developed by the Academy for Educational Development continues to be offered in partnership with colleges and extension programs throughout the country each year with other localities adapting AYD to meet local needs and award credentials. Collectively, thousands of youth workers receive some sort of training annually and thousands more do not.

Some of these workforce efforts are explicitly aimed at advancing youth work to the status of a "profession" akin to teaching or social work; for others, professionalization might be an unintended consequence. Some of these efforts are working in tandem with each other; others are running along on parallel tracks with little opportunity for collision. Others still are in direct tension with each other raising critical questions and concerns about the field and the future of youth work. Has youth work become synonymous with afterschool education? Are credentials the way to support staff stability? What might be the unintended consequences of requiring credentials and degrees for youth workers? Will institutions of higher education support the growth of the discipline and the profession even when enrollment fluctuates? Needed is a way to frame these workforce efforts so that we can consider how each uniquely and collectively puts us in a position to advance youth work.

The purpose of *Advancing Youth Work: Current Trends, Critical Questions* then is twofold. First, the book aims to bring into one view some of the current trends (and tensions) in advancing youth work. Each initiative on its own tells a story of how it arrived and where it aims to go. Brought into one view, the set of initiatives helps us collectively add to a field-building narrative, an aim perhaps no one story on its own is able to accomplish. The second goal is to critically question and reflectively examine these current trends in order to more purposefully set our sails. It will be important to lay the groundwork for this volume here such that individual chapters, with value on their own, are also read with this broader purpose in mind. The chapters to follow do not sit neatly next to each other. In fact, they are at times juxtaposed; each offering a different way of seeing youth work and youth work education. This volume is explicit in aiming to face those tensions and asks the reader to observe the tensions not with the need to resolve them necessarily, but with the purpose of examining them in relation to the broader mission of advancing the field.

To guide the reader, the volume reviews three current workforce trends: competencies, credentials, and curriculum. The trends are introduced in Chapter 1 in a conversation with Ellen Gannett. Having worked in the field for almost thirty years, Ellen has been witness to and participant in many of the trends now underway. Her perspective is insightful and offers the reader a broad vision of the current state of the field. Having laid the framework for the volume in Chapter 1, Section I will move into rich narratives around the trends of competencies and credentials. In Chapter 2, Sarah Jonas will present how within the context of her work at Children's Aid Society, competencies played a role in designing and implementing a series of professional development workshops for the staff giving them a guidepost to think about and reflect on their practice with young people. In Chapter 3, Dale Curry, Andrew J. Schneider-Muñoz, Frank Eckles, and Carol Stuart, discuss the recent implementation of the National Child and Youth Certification exam that was designed based upon an agreed upon set of competencies in child and youth care work. In Chapter 4, Joyce Walker and Kate Walker present an alternative view of practitioner development that relies on expertise, rather than competencies. They provide examples of professional development that support reflective practice through analysis and discussion. Similarly in Chapter 5, Judith Bessant describes how competency frameworks sit in contrast to university training in Australia and are more aligned to vocational education, a theme picked up later in Chapter 9 by Dana Fusco. Collectively, the chapters in Section I help us to view two of the current trends, competencies and credentials, from multiple angles and frames of reference.

The focus of Section II is on the third trend area: curriculum, and specifically the role of higher education in youth work education. Section II highlights several successful programs in higher education as well as presents the challenges in forming a legitimized discipline in academia. Pete Watkins, in Chapter 6, and Michael Heathfield in Chapter 7, present two models developed in collaboration with their respective institutions of higher education that have each become a respected asset in their urban communities. Presented here are the histories of those programs, the disciplinary base deemed important to quality youth work education, and the lessons learned. The chapters also point to some larger contextual shifts that are impacting youth work education, e.g., decreased funding for youth programs and professional development overall and more targeted funding for practitioners focused on skill development. The authors express concern about the move away from the deep, probing and questioning-stance more likely, though not exclusively, found in college classrooms.

One way to express the concern is in the question: Do we need a legitimized professional education akin to that of nursing, teacher education, social work *before* funders and agencies recognize the importance of the development of practitioners or does the funding and the demand need to be in place before higher education responds? In Chapter 8, Camille Williamson reflects on her journey to becoming a youth worker, highlighting the path through and between various degree programs within a university system. She not only articulates a vision for Youth Studies programs but envisages such training for the multitude of professions that interact with young people including doctors and police officers. In Chapter 9, Dana Fusco argues that it is the development of the youth work discipline that is a necessary next step in advancing the field. She unpacks how higher education legitimizes bodies of knowledge rendering them necessary to the field and urges us to consider an inclusive and broad body of knowledge that spans youth populations, programs, contexts, and disciplines. In Chapter 10, Ross VeLure Roholt and Michael Baizerman question whether higher education will remain a necessary partner in the future of youth work. While recognizing the importance of preparing the next generation of professoriate, they argue that youth studies and youth work are contested spaces with the university and the community. In Chapter 11, Jacqueline Davis-Manigaulte describes in detail how practitioners are impacted by learning environments that create communal spaces for dialogue and feedback outside of a university setting. Collectively, the chapters present many perspectives on viewing youth work education. They help us to see the necessary features of quality learning environments for youth workers but do less in helping us to determine the "what" or the content of the curriculum. Currently, there is no agreed upon body of knowledge for youth studies, as Fusco in Chapter 9, reminds.

Section III then attempts to address the question: Is youth studies one discipline or many? The hope is that by understanding youth work across its varied contexts we can better design a model of youth work education (and the discipline/curriculum of Youth Studies) that is broad and inclusive. Several contexts of youth work were already presented in earlier sections. Chapter 2 focuses of competencies in out-of-school time and afterschool programs; Chapter 3 emerges from child and youth care work; and Chapter 11 focuses on a professional network of practitioners in various community-based youth programs. Section III aims to bring into the mix some additional contexts of youth work practice from which we can ask: What is youth work? Is there an essence across contexts? Is it too varied to be encompassed under one disciplinary umbrella? In Chapter 12, Helen Jones describes youth work in England. The ideals presented in this chapter were critical to the formation of youth work in the United States and thus help us to situate current youth work in our own history of Boys and Girls clubs and settlement houses. In Chapter 13, Ross VeLure Roholt presents a brief description of civic youth work and Judie Cutler describes youth work on the reservation. These briefs are combined in this chapter to highlight the vast differences of youth work in different cultural milieu. In Chapter 14, the same dialectic is attempted in bringing together two additional distinct practices: recreation and child and youth care. Jim Sibthorp and M. Deborah Bialeschski describe the playground movement beginning with early settlement house reformers such as Jane Addams. The roles of play (and later recreation and leisure) have become pivotal to current understandings of youth work. Later in the chapter, Carol Stuart and Jack Phelan describe the deep and layered practice of child and youth care work in Canada helping us to capture the youth worker who is available in-residence, round the clock to those who need him/her. Finally, in Chapter 15, Joel Nitzberg presents yet another perspective on youth work as community education. Here we see that the playground worker might also be the community educator. While these vast contexts of youth work seem disparate, they also each aim towards the development and growth of young people. In the final section, we ask some critical questions and maybe answer a few. In Chapter 16, Jane Quinn relates the current dialogue to the 1991 recommendations of the Carnegie Council on Adolescent Development. Here Jane helps us to situate the present in history and evaluates the advances already made. In Chapter 17, Dana Fusco reviews the current dialogue through a futuristic lens. She draws out the meta-themes of the volume's narrative and uses them to launch a set of questions for thinking about the future of the field. In an effort to think about discipline of the field more broadly, she puts forth a typology that maps several principles of youth work across several contexts of practice.

In this book, twenty-three authors from around the globe with experiences in youth work that span three generations have come together to collectively articulate a vision for the field, and to individually share what they have learned from their experiences in the training and education of youth workers. Some of us work within higher education rooted in academic departments; some within extension programs and continuing education; some of us work for intermediary agencies conducting training across cities and states; we teach and we conduct research. We agree in the essence and power of youth work in supporting youth development. We observe, and have taken part in, the recent flurry of activity in youth work training and education. We anticipate a long-awaited future where all children and youth have access to professional mentors and guides during out of school time.

References

Little, P., Wimer, C., & Weiss, H. B. (2008). *Afterschool programs in the 21st century: their potential and what it takes to achieve it.* (Issues and Opportunities in Out-of-School Time Evaluation Brief No. 10). Cambridge, MA: Harvard Family Research Project.

Mahoney, J .L., Parente, M .E., & Zigler, E. F. (2009). Afterschool program in America: Origins, growth, popularity, and politics. *Journal of Youth Development,* 4(3).

Metz, A., Bandy, T., & Burkhauser, M. (2009). *Staff selection: What's important for out-of-school time programs? Research-to-results brief.* Washington, DC: Child Trends.

Phelan, J. (2005). Child and youth care education: The creation of articulate practitioners. *Child & Youth Care Forum, 34,* 347–355.

Smith, C., Peck, S.C., Denault, A.S., Blazevski, J., & Akiva, T. (2010). Quality at the point of service: Profiles of practice in after-school settings. *American Journal of Community Psychology, 45,* 358–369.

INTRODUCTION

1

A CONVERSATION WITH ELLEN GANNETT

Dana Fusco and Ellen Gannett

This Introduction chapter will present an overview of three trend areas: competencies, credentials, and curriculum, through a conversation with one of the leaders in the field, Ellen Gannett. Ellen is Director of the National Institute on Out-of-School Time (NIOST) at the Wellesley Centers for Women at Wellesley College, Wellesley, Massachusetts. As the director of NIOST, Ms. Gannett ensures that research bridges the fields of child care, education, and youth development in order to promote programming that addresses the development of the whole child. She has contributed to the writing and development of ASQ: Assessing School-Age Child Care Quality, School Age and Youth Development Credential (SAYD) as well as the Afterschool Program Assessment System (APAS), and is currently working with the National Afterschool Association (NAA) on a set of core competencies for staff. Here I introduce the workforce trends in conversation with Ellen. The original interview took place on January 29, 2010 and was conducted over the telephone. The chapter was produced collaboratively by editing the transcript to correct and elaborate on the content. Content was again updated closer to the publishing of this volume. Dana Fusco served as the interviewer guiding the questions in relation to the framework of the book, around Current Trends and Critical Questions. The decision to begin the book "in conversation" is intentional in helping to frame the book in both content and style as dialogic and participatory.

Setting the Stage

Ellen, where are workforce issues situated in the overall mission of NIOST?

Workforce development is a very important and vital issue to what we are going to be able to do, if we are going to advance the field, if we are going to make any headway in reaching positive outcomes for kids. I think we have determined both from our own research and looking at others that the quality of the practitioner is critical to helping young kids succeed in school and life. We have to do everything we can to strengthen the workforce as the critical component of quality and helping kids do better.

We have been focused on workforce issues now in a really intentional way for a good 20 years. Progress is being made but it is slow going. I often get discouraged because we backtrack again and again trying to balance limited resources with what is really important. When times are tough, professional development and workforce issues take a backseat to direct service. For vulnerable kids it's hard to argue that direct service is not important or that we need to think about serving kids *before* we invest in professional development but I think this is a faulty argument. We will never get out of this cycle of mediocrity and poor quality if we don't address the issue. It is not either/or. We have to make sure that at the same time we are focused on quality programming, we also are focusing on quality staff. It is part of the same solution and the investments need to be targeted as such. We cannot keep backing off on our commitment to professional development and workforce every time we have a funding crisis.

Starting with Competencies

It seems that a critical first step in the workforce development initiative has been defining the core competencies for youth work practitioners. Tell me about your work defining and studying core competencies.

This work has been a long time coming. We have been looking at core competencies for many years but since my involvement in the Next Generation Youth Work Coalition (Next Gen), it has taken more of a focus and very recently we had a couple of things happen. Number one, the National Afterschool Association in giving up its leadership around accreditation has strategically decided that workforce issues including professional development will be their priority for the next number of years. Given what is going on at the city and the state level in terms of professional development system building, NIOST has put a high priority on helping. Judy Nee, even though she has resigned as president of NAA, will continue as a board member focusing on professional development. Judy and I co-presented (in Summer 2010) at various national conferences including the Beyond School Hours Conference sponsored by Foundations, Inc., the 21st Century Community Learning Centers Summer Institute, and the NIOST Summer Seminars on the topic of nationally recognized core competencies and credentials.

The second thing that happened is the State of Washington contracted with Next Gen to compile and analyze core competency frameworks across the country. Nicole Yohalem, from the Forum for Youth Investment, Betsy Starr, my colleague, and myself wrote a paper, which is now on our websites (see Starr, Yohalem, & Gannett, 2009). The paper summarized 14 state and organizational sets of core competencies and brought to life some of the most commonly cited competencies. Further work supported by NAA, Florida Afterschool Network, Pennsylvania Keys, Child & Youth Care Certification Board and NIOST has produced a draft document, *Nationally Recognized Core Competencies for Afterschool and Youth Development Professionals*. Following a field review and pilot during the spring of 2011, we hope that NAA will recognize and endorse this set of core competencies as a way to inform what higher education, programs, directors and trainers can do with them and how they might drive credentials at multiple levels.

Are you focused now on afterschool then given the collaboration with the National After-school Association?

No, our work at NIOST is very broadly defined to include all of the different subfields of youth development, not just afterschool. Our work includes school age care and youth work, people who work with adolescents, people who work in summer camps, people who work in a variety of settings, including school-based programs.

Do you see the youth work core competencies cutting across those sectors?

We try to look at core competencies across settings that cut across the full continuum of ages, so we were very intentional in identifying sets of competencies that didn't stop just at age 12. We wanted to look at the ones that were very intentionally broadly defined, that would range from as young as five all the way up to age 18 or 21 and we were able to collect a number of those frameworks. The other important criterion we used was that the frameworks cut across various settings and auspices. It wasn't just about afterschool; it wasn't just about licensed programs. We didn't want to pigeonhole any of this work or perpetuate silos. The strength of this field has got to be that we think of ourselves in a very broad-based way.

People who work outside of formal classrooms take on a lot of different roles. Some of them work in libraries; some of them work in museums; some of them work in cultural institutions; they work in youth serving agencies, school based settings. It is so much bigger than just afterschool and I think that the terminology keeps tripping me up because I always end up flipping and flopping between my words. When I talk about afterschool somebody inevitably asks—what about before school? What about summer, evenings, vacations, holidays? So it is a complicated field because of its diversity but I am pushing a broad-based definition. It's about what the practitioner does, not who pays their paycheck or where they work.

What makes them core and is there another list on "noncore?"

As you get more and more specific to the setting, you find yourself moving away from the core, and it's pretty hard to decide where is the line in the sand and where is the boundary. I am working with a committee from the Association of Child and Youth Care Practice on the revisions of the Competencies for Professional Child and Youth Work Practitioners. What they are trying to do is even more challenging because they are taking a set of competencies that had been previously written with residential and foster care in mind, client-based youth prevention programs. Their aim is to expand those core competencies to include afterschool age care and youth development programs. They have gone through a number of different versions of it but they have made a decision that they are ready to make their core competencies as core as possible so it applies to the full diversity of the youth work field. In order to do that we went line by line looking at each one of the core competencies statements replacing words like client with child and youth or family; replacing words that have been more clinical and more treatment oriented toward development. It was a very painstaking process and took a long time but the committee ultimately created a set of core competencies that could in fact pull together all the different subsets of the field, including the residential group and the foster care group and the treatment groups with everybody else.

The goal is to have different implementation guides, targeted to the particular sectors with indicators and examples of practice that will take that particular core statement and bring life to it. The interpretations that will follow will be more specific but at the core level we are talking about practices that should be non-setting specific and that build on youth's well being and empowerment in general.

This may be a semantic distinction but when I hear the word "competencies" I think of skills and I wonder if that's an intentional choice of language. Why not capabilities, for instance?

I don't know if it is intentional because I often find myself wanting to or needing to define it. What is a core competency and should it stop at a skill level? I think not. There's the need for understanding our body of knowledge. To the extent that core competencies are often defined as something that can be observed and documented, whereas a body of knowledge is more theoretical and conceptual. A core competency for many states, especially at the entry level, involves not only skills but it also involves attitudes, values and different attributes and the demonstration that you know something. My definition is a lot broader and integrates skill with knowledge. The state of Illinois, on the other hand, very clearly differentiates between body of knowledge and core competencies and has been working diligently on the core body of knowledge level first. Their next phase of work will be around the competency level.

Let me share my concern with the language from the perspective of someone who sits as a dean that oversees professional programs in health, education, occupational therapy, and youth studies. There is kind of an interesting tension in academia as to where youth studies resides and I worry that the language of competencies doesn't serve us well. It doesn't serve us well in helping to move youth studies into the core of academia. It keeps us in the mindset of a trade. [See Chapter 9 for a more in-depth discussion of the tensions within academia.]

I am well aware of that tension. In fact, I have sat in on higher ed conference calls where a group of faculty, instructors and deans of various colleges have been meeting together around this conversation. For many of them the terminology of competency was very much a word that they didn't want to align themselves with. Interestingly, the American Camp Association, which has been doing some work around professional development, very carefully chose not to use the word "competency" and instead they have decided to use, and I like it, what they call KSAs (knowledge, skills and abilities). I know the folks at University of Minnesota tend to shy away from competency terminology as well and I am completely fine with that. I think in the end as a framework it works just as well and I think they can be interchangeable. Often people want to be able to demonstrate knowledge through formal observations, portfolios, interviews and other kinds of data collection as a way to validate what that person knows and can do.

From Competencies to Credentials

Let's say we have a list of KSAs, competencies, or whatever language we are going to opt for. Now what?

What I think we have learned is that if you use core competencies strictly for the establishment of certifications and credentialing, then you are barking up the wrong tree. The use of core competencies or KSA needs to be embedded in organizational life. I think this is what we have missed in our excitement for building professional development systems that worked so well in early childhood education. We spent much time trying to see if we push these systems developmentally, and we used the same infrastructure of using core competencies and credentials and registries, would it work in youth work? Increasingly I think we are learning that earning a credential is not going to make a difference in what goes on in a program day to day or ensure we reach really strong positive youth outcomes for kids. It is not a silver bullet. It is not something that in and of itself will make a difference for children and youth. We have to be working at the system level but we can't forget what is happening in programs, in organizations and how the staff is being supported or not. Whether you earn a credential, or a certificate, or get a college degree, you bring it back to your organization, and there may be a huge disconnect between what you have learned in training or in higher ed and what you may find in terms of your practice. I think it is very important that we pay attention to that level and that we use core competencies not only for driving course work, training work, credentialing work; they have got to drive what happens at the organizational level as well.

It's very interesting because I think as people are coming together from different disciplines, they are bringing with them the lessons learned from those areas like teacher education and there is this kind of "Medici Effect" that's happening. So it's really fascinating.

We look to the teaching field as a great example of how certification alone is not enough. There is more and more attention being paid to coaching, mentoring, and the support that new teachers need. Teaching certification has in no way shown the quality of practice that we would expect. The same sort of thing is happening in organizations often caused by the lack of supervision, guidance, coaching, and mentoring around common quality standards. Staff, while they do tend to leave because of the lack of benefits and low compensation, one of the major reasons for the turnover in youth work, as we are seeing from the research, is that they are not sufficiently supervised. They are not supported; they don't know what their job is, what is expected of them, and how they are supposed to learn their craft.

This could be a fascinating study: Why is it that a credential does not predict success on the job? I have some theories about that and I think some of it is the way that we approach professional education in academia.

It's the United States of America, and we are very conscious of credentials in terms of professionalism. In medicine you wouldn't go to a doctor that didn't go to medical school and didn't have a MD. That's the first thing that you look for but that doesn't make that doctor, a good doctor. So in every field it may be one of the first areas that the public will look for. Okay, so you have taken the courses, you have the core competencies, you got the credential, now what?

What do we need to do to make sure that earning the credential is actually enough? So that once the credential is earned we can put some stock in that credential and that to me is the work of higher ed.

That is one of the reasons that online learning or online credentials make me very nervous because there is typically no relationship with a mentor. Is it only a paper and pencil test? Is that enough to show that the person knows his/her craft? I think not, except in some rare cases. That is one of the reasons I like the CDA [Child Development Associate] model because it is very hands on. There are opportunities for people to work with their supervisor/instructor over time so that they get the support they need. These courses lead to the credential. The cohort model is so powerful where practitioners get to earn their credential together taking courses, discussing, and reflecting on their practice. All of this is the most important aspect of some of the credentials that I really appreciate here in our state in Massachusetts. We have what's called the School Age and Youth Development (SAYD) credential, and it was a wonderful experience for people mainly because of that cohort model and because of the idea that each participant works alongside of a group of 10 or 20 people discussing their work and reading and going on field trips together. It didn't get funded again, but the model itself is terrific and was recently adapted by Massachusetts as the Professional Youth Work Credential for youth workers who work primarily with adolescents.

From Credentials to Curriculum

What role do you see higher education playing in all of this?

I think higher education has a very important role to play in legitimizing the field and helping to put a stamp on the fact that this really is a career. It's a profession, and, once higher ed makes a commitment to it, I think we are going to see a lot more opportunities emerge. At the moment higher ed has not stepped into this arena in the way it could have, and I have a theory about that. I tend to take the long view and I see peaks and valleys of higher education's interest in all of this. Higher ed acts like a business before it makes a commitment to a new audience. Will people come forward if we establish a discipline, a new discipline in youth work or afterschool or whatever it is? Will people come? You need a stimulus. What is going to stimulate people to enter a field that is under resourced, under paid, abysmally unsupported, where the turnover rate is 40–60 percent a year and there is no clearly defined career track that has been articulated for people as they move into the field at the entry level? Where are they going to go next?

I worked in a school-age program and I know that the only place to go in a lot of afterschool programs is to kill off the director! That's it—you go from line staff to director and there is no other role for promotion. There needs to be a policy direction that will motivate and stimulate higher ed to get involved. There was some traction before the 21st Community Learning Centers took off, but then I noticed a waning of interest. I think it is because classroom teachers began to enter the field in large numbers. They already had credentials and teaching certificates. So the question then is okay, well, here you have afterschool programs in greater numbers being staffed quite intentionally with classroom teachers, why make an investment in a youth worker who you know is going to leave anyway, who is being so unfairly paid to the teachers who gets 20 or more dollars an hour compared to the youth worker who can barely eke out 10 dollars an hour? You've got to see a whole different dynamic in terms of motivation and policy development that I think would have been terrific and could have really inspired a lot of higher ed institutions to step up because we needed to build a workforce. Now who is the workforce? We haven't even quite figured it out and now another policy development is unfolding before our eyes which is "extended learning time." This may again change the landscape. Youth development, youth workers—will there always be a place for them? I think in the end there will be, but to so many people in our country they are invisible. They are out there running camps, libraries, museums; they are doing all kinds of things and are working in all kinds of interesting settings that are informal by design. But the youth workers in these settings are mostly invisible to most of us in the public and they know that the public is not supporting them. Are youth workers completely dispensable and will it matter if they stick around or not? These kinds of questions have their own value. In many ways we have to begin with the youth workers themselves, the advocacy that they can play on their own behalf to demonstrate how vitally important they are to the development of kids and to define the identity of the field.

One of the things that I love to do is meet with people in the field and to have this conversation about what is the unique identity of their work, how is it different and complementary to other educational settings. People are so grateful for the opportunity to discuss it and to shine a spotlight on the value of their work as a unique contribution to the development of kids— not to replicate or duplicate what happens in a classroom, but to bring other great opportunities for kids that they wouldn't get elsewhere around the social and physical and artistic domains—the things that schools may not be doing anymore. That's why I am so thrilled you are doing the international chapters because there are other countries that really value the youth worker, the UK and other places where they understand that youth work plays an important role in the development of children and youth.

This was a recent realization for me—when I was looking at where in our government youth development resides, and it's really kind of tucked away under the Department of Health and Human Services, almost invisible.

That's another reason why higher ed hasn't stepped up: they can't find the funding source. Where does it come from?

Where does it come from? If you look at New Zealand, for instance, that has a Ministry of Youth Development, an entire ministry devoted to youth development this to me says, "This is what we value as a country."

In the United States, so much is driven by education. I think this book has a lot of potential. You have the potential to do a lot of mind changing for people to get their mind away from it only being an educational line item. Here is the other thing that makes this work so complicated—California is trying to develop multiple pathways between youth work and other professions and seeing youth work as a pipeline to classroom teaching. I don't know if you will raise that or not, but it does question whether this work is just a temporary job.

I think it's one of those pivotal tensions. I mean it's certainly not where I would want to see the field going. I hope that by virtue of the fact that I am bringing together people across youth work sectors, I think that will address the issue without specifically addressing it.

The tension over the last decade has been very difficult for youth workers and practitioners. They are being pushed toward the academic agenda at the exclusion of so many other developmental needs that children and youth have—emotional and psychological and mental health and trauma and it's upsetting. I hope that we are seeing a rebalancing of this because we have to rebalance it. We do need to acknowledge that youth work is different than the role of the education.

Now, there are some good things on the horizon—things I think we need to build on. Clearly, the work around quality assessment tools that are increasingly looking at program specifications, but looking at staff practice as well for promoting continuous program improvements. I think we are going to be in better shape to help programs work on improving their practice. But they can't do it alone. It's just too hard for organizations to do it alone and that is why higher ed has to step up. Not in the traditional way. We cannot expect people to show up on campuses. I think what higher ed can do is take on roles at the community level and help to support good solid practice. That should happen on site as much as possible. That is the kind of exciting higher ed models that I love to see; when it's community-based and faculty show up at the doorstep of practitioners, as opposed to the other way around. If higher ed faculty like yourself and others can be more supportive and engaged with practitioners at the practice level, it will be great.

Where do you see workforce development for youth practitioners in 5 years? Twenty years?

I hope we have figured it out by then, and that there will be a discipline of youth work and development. The good news is I think it will be a multidisciplinary approach. It will be a very exciting field as higher education gets more and more interested in finding a home for this work. Where do you nest it? I would say everywhere and anywhere, wherever there is interest, the School of Social Work? So be it. If it is in the School of Education, that's fine too. If it is in Child Development, okay. If it is in Human Development, that's good too because in the end this work is so exciting and so multidisciplinary it can be anywhere, but it needs to reach out into this different kind of learning that is not pigeon holed into one discipline or the other.

When you think about youth work, I see opportunities for an unbelievably exciting career. One where people can move from many different settings as they advance over time because youth work will be embedded in so many different great employment opportunities. With a degree under your belt and experience working with children, many institutions and organizations will want to employ youth workers. The field will offer a very diverse and exciting career—it could be fantastic. I do think we are going to be okay. I really do think that higher ed is going to play an important role in legitimizing the field in ways that no other institution can do—otherwise it may be viewed as a trade. And we will continue to struggle with the question—is youth work a vocation or a profession?

Well, here's the one caveat I would offer. If we don't produce a professoriate for youth studies, we are not going to get anchored here. I agree with you; I think it is an interdisciplinary discipline, and where it's housed, I don't think, is the issue but who teaches it and who leads it in academia is still kind of in the mix because we don't have professors of youth studies and so what we have are people who, like myself, were youth workers, hold a PhD, and could teach some youth work courses. And, that's almost the best-case scenario.

I wonder if we have to grow our own. NIOST and the National Writing Project, with support from the Robert Bowne Foundation, is sponsoring the Afterschool Matters Practitioner Fellowships in cities across the country, in Philadelphia, Minneapolis, Seattle, and we are starting two more in New Orleans and Pittsburgh next year. These are practitioners, mid to advanced; they typically don't have masters or PhDs but they are working on writing papers for submission in academic journals. There are also people who have their eye on higher education and want to move into advanced degrees because of the excitement of asking questions and writing about their practice. I think overtime we may end up having many people who grow into these roles of professors of youth development or of youth work because of opportunities like that.

Conclusion

This chapter illuminates the ways in which current workforce development trends have taken prominence in the field. It also underscores some of the central tenets that are being formed. Namely, that the strength of the field is in its breadth; that credentials are necessary but not sufficient; and that higher education while involved remains an uncommitted partner in many cases. The introduction sets the stage for the upcoming chapters to explore in greater depth the successes and challenges in pursuing various field-building activities and helps us identify next steps in Advancing Youth Work.

Reference

Starr, B., Yohalem, N., & Gannett, E. (2009, October). *Youth work core competencies: A review of existing frameworks and purposes*. Seattle: School's Out Washington & Next Generation Youth Work Coalition. Retrieved October 25, 2010, from http://www.nextgencoalition.org/files/Core Competencies Review, October 2009.pdf.

SECTION I

Competencies and Credentials

2

EMBEDDING AND SUSTAINING YOUTH WORKER CORE COMPETENCIES IN OUT-OF-SCHOOL TIME PROGRAMS

Sarah Jonas

In the spring of 2007, the Children's Aid Society (CAS) embarked on the process of creating agency-wide core competencies for youth workers, and a corresponding system of professional development for its 28 school- and center-based afterschool programs. The project was initiated by COO, Dr. William Weisberg, who describes the work as "changing the culture of our agency." It was about spelling out, in clear and consistent language, exactly what we expected our youth workers to know and be able to do with the young people we serve. We had a good foundation from which to start. As New York City's oldest and largest family and youth serving agency, CAS had over 150 years of experience running quality programs to support young people's physical, social, emotional and cognitive development. We provided centralized training to our 300 part-time youth workers at After School Staff Days twice a year, and site-based training through orientation and regular staff meetings. Our training topics were varied, and included everything from homework help strategies to behavior management to cooperative games. Most of the time, staff reported finding the content to be helpful and relevant. However, we continued to find that the quality of staff varied widely from site to site, and even within sites. Like many community-based organizations running afterschool programs, CAS staff were mostly young, college-aged men and women with little to no teaching experience. They were relying on CAS to tell them what they needed to know in order to do the work well and to help them learn to do it. And we realized we were not doing a very good job of communicating to our youth workers the "big ideas" behind all the programmatic training topics. While it was useful to staff, for example, to learn fun games to play with youth during the transition from one activity to another, we were not always making sure that every staff person knew how to structure a basic activity so as to engage youth and retain their interest. Similarly, theme-based arts and crafts projects would get staff only so far if they were unable to modify the projects for the particular age group with whom they were working. Bottom line, we needed to articulate a coherent set of core knowledge and skills for our youth workers, and a corresponding system of professional development, which would ensure our staff would be providing a high quality experience for our youth.

Creating the Core Competencies and Delivery System

We began by forming a CAS core competencies committee, led by Dr. Weisberg, and consisting of youth development and afterschool "experts" from across our agency. Among the group were the Director of Education Services and a group of supervisors and program directors from our community schools and "City and Country" (community centers and camps) divisions. Reflecting the comprehensive reach of our agency, the group included social workers, educators and youth development practitioners. We reviewed the small set of existing youth worker core competency frameworks, brainstormed our own lists of "big ideas," and compared this to research on best practices from the fields of youth development and out-of-school time. Ultimately, we settled on six CAS youth worker core competencies (CAS YWCC): build caring relationships, cultural competence, manage behaviors, understand stages of development, structure activities, and youth workers as community resources. Initially, we discussed safety and professionalism. However, we decided not to include these in the core competencies because we felt that safety was more about policies and procedures (and could be covered in the site-based staff orientation) and that professionalism cut across all six areas.

Our list of core competencies began with *build caring relationships* because we knew that the quality of a young person's experience in our programs was largely determined by the extent to which he or she felt connected to and supported by staff. Accordingly, *build caring relationships* would focus on strategies for creating affirming, trusting relationships with young people and promoting a spirit of collaboration within peer groups. *Cultural competence* was deemed critical in order for our youth workers to engage effectively with our diverse youth population. This competency would stress the importance of staff being conscious of their own beliefs, values and traditions and the expectation that they would create an inclusive environment where youth could explore and celebrate their own cultural identities. *Manage behaviors* was the training topic most requested by our staff, who, despite being well-meaning and talented, were often unable to engage the young people in their groups due to poor management skills. This competency would offer strategies for positive discipline, and help staff learn to set clear expectations, be consistent and, whenever possible, engage youth in problem solving. Being an effective manager wasn't enough—*structure activities* emphasized that in order for our staff to maintain high levels of engagement and provide enriching learning experiences, they needed to design activities that were well-organized, fun and helped youth develop new skills. *Stages of development* would add another dimension to youth engagement by introducing the concept of the five developmental domains (physical, social, emotional, cognitive, and moral), exploring the intersection between a young person's biological age and his or her developmental level, and presenting tools and strategies to help staff design developmentally appropriate activities that would capture youth interest. Finally, we wanted to make sure our youth workers understood what it meant to work within the context of a multi-service agency that sought to address the needs of the whole child. *Youth workers as community resources* encouraged staff to get to know each individual child in their care and to acquaint themselves with the many resources offered by CAS (and the surrounding community), so that they might serve as a bridge between the two.

For each competency, we developed an introductory workshop module that would expose staff to the core knowledge and skills for that particular competency, and provide them with basic strategies they could apply and continue to develop back at their sites. It made sense to deliver the core competency curriculum through Afterschool Staff Day, which was a structure we had in place for over ten years, consisting of two Saturdays of professional development, one in October and the other in March, for all part-time afterschool staff and full-time program directors. By working within an existing agency training structure, we could focus more on content and delivery and less on the logistics of creating and introducing a new event to our staff. The committee agreed to make the core competency training mandatory for all staff as a condition of continued employment (for future staff, this would be discussed at the time of hire) and pay our part-time staff to attend. This would provide an added incentive to complete the core competency course, and send a strong message to staff that the agency valued professional development and was serious about the core competencies. We also discussed the possibility of paying staff to complete the full competency curriculum (either through a stipend or salary increase), but realized this would not be sustainable over time. Instead, we decided to expand our Part-Time Excellence Awards, an existing structure for recognizing outstanding afterschool staff with a small monetary award and framed certificate, to be targeted to staff who truly exemplified the core competencies.

Our next step was to think about how to roll out the sequence of core competency modules over the two Afterschool Staff Day events. Based on our best thinking about what staff needed right away to begin working with youth, we decided the competencies we would cover in October would include build caring relationships, manage behaviors, and understand stages of development and, in March, cultural competence, structure activities, and youth workers as community resources. In order to create the curriculum for the core competency workshops, we turned to groups of "in house experts," who would generate the content and training design for each module and also, in some cases, serve as the first year trainers for some of the modules. These experts were CAS practitioners with years of experience, both in direct youth service and in training and supervision of youth workers and program managers. The project of putting together the curriculum was to be managed by the CAS full-time Director of Education, whose job was to support and monitor program quality for all of CAS' afterschool and summer camp programs. The Director of Education would also be responsible for pulling in the latest research on best practices in the afterschool and youth development fields. The value of using our own CAS staff to develop the curriculum is explained by Dr. Weisberg in the following way, "We wanted the competencies curriculum to be rooted not just in theory but in experience." This approach of using in-house experts to design and deliver the training had the added benefit of creating buy-in across the agency for this new system. Using in-house, full-time, salaried staff for the trainers also helped with the sustainability of the system, since the agency would not have to pay outside consultants.

In addition to making sure the content of each module was sound, accurate, and relevant, we also wanted to ensure that the design of each module was consistent, engaging, and clear, so that it could be well implemented by any trainer. The training design we came up with consisted of a 90-minute session including a warm-up activity, a discussion of core content, and an application activity. The warm-up would introduce the topic and get people interested in hearing more. The content discussion would draw on and add to what the participants already knew about the topic, and the application activity would allow the staff to try out what they were learning about the topic through an interactive experience. The application activity was key, as feedback from our own staff (and basic research on effective training practices) indicated that activities such as role-plays and case studies were the most effective learning tools. Finally, each core competency workshop would include a handout with the "big ideas," or most important concepts about the particular competency, which would form the basis for the discussion and application activity, and be something the participants could walk away with at the end of the session.

One issue that emerged almost immediately was the interdependency among the various competencies. For example, we knew that in order for staff to effectively manage behaviors, they would need a solid understanding of stages of development. Likewise, in order to build caring relationships with youth, staff would need to be culturally competent. This resulted in there being some redundancy in the final CAS YWCC document, with some of the competencies being cross-referenced. We viewed the duplicity as a strength of the document in that it made explicit the connection among the individual competencies as being part of a coherent, larger set of knowledge and skills. Staff would be able to see that as they grew more competent in one area, it would strengthen their skill in other areas.

We also developed a parallel training module for afterschool program directors that would introduce them to the content their staff were receiving and help them to learn strategies for supporting their staff's ongoing development of the core competencies. The design of the program directors' workshop included having the group review and summarize each of the six core competencies, and then work in small groups to discuss how they would incorporate the core competencies into staff supervision and coaching. The module would be delivered by the Director of Education, would be mandatory for all program directors, and would take place during Afterschool Staff Day, while the youth workers were in their training sessions.

Implementation and Effectiveness

For the first year that CAS implemented the core competencies, all staff, from inexperienced to veteran, were required to take the training modules. Going forward completion of the six core competency modules would be a requirement for continued employment with the agency. As we planned for the October 2007 Afterschool Staff Day, our energy was spent on securing trainers. We had 300 youth workers in total and needed 12 trainers (four each to focus on each of the three core competencies for that day). Each trainer would need to repeat his/her module three times. In order to make the day easier on the trainers, who were volunteering their time, we made it a priority to do as much of the preparation work, as possible, for them including sending out electronic copies of the final modules and handouts, and having copies of the handouts (including sign-in sheets and evaluation forms) ready for them, so that all they would have to do was show up ready to implement the training. Many of the trainers told us after the event was over that they really appreciated having all the "leg work" done centrally.

To help gauge the effectiveness of the modules, we created evaluation forms for participants to fill out after each session. In addition, the Director of Education debriefed with all of the trainers about how their sessions had gone. We gathered a great deal of interesting data about what worked and what did not, and made adjustments to the training modules as necessary. For example, for stages of development, we asked small groups of staff to generate an arts and crafts activity that would meet the developmental needs of the age group they work with, using a handout on ages and stages as a reference. However, many groups got stuck on coming up with an activity, bypassing the correlation to the ages and stages. One of the trainers made the excellent suggestion to have the youth workers reflect back instead on an activity done during the prior week at their sites, analyze how developmentally appropriate the activity had been, and generate ideas for how to make it even more engaging for the age and stage of the youth in their groups. With the revised activity, the participants would have a critical opportunity to reflect on their own practice and to connect it to the stages of development. Based on agreement from the other trainers that this would be a good adjustment, we changed the module to include the revised activity. Even though one of our goals from this project was to have "permanent" training modules so that future trainers would not have to reinvent the wheel, it was clear that we needed to go back and review the modules from time and time, and always remain open to feedback from our trainers and staff.

Another piece of feedback we received from trainers and program directors was that, in the future, we should provide Level II courses, designed to build on the introductory level core competency courses. This would keep more experienced staff engaged and give staff a chance to probe more deeply into some of the topics. In response, we developed Level II courses in the areas of behavior management, stages of development and youth leadership, which were open only to staff who had taken the introductory course in each topic. The Level II courses were designed to offer greater opportunities for discussion, sharing of best practices among staff, and the chance to participate in several, varied role plays.

Embedding Competencies More Deeply in the Organization

Supports for Program Directors

While the first year implementation of the CAS YWCC training was largely a success, it was immediately clear that we needed to pay attention to what happens after and beyond After School Staff Day, which only provides an introduction to the core competencies. We knew that the degree to which staff developed their skills in each competency would depend mainly on the quality of supervision and support they received back at their sites. That meant that we needed to focus on supporting the afterschool program directors by providing training and tools designed to help them to support their staff. We created a two-hour training module that provided staff with a brief introduction to all six core competencies. The Director of Education facilitated this workshop at the various sites the first time, but required that the program directors and education coordinators (teachers who worked part-time for CAS, helping us to align our afterschool programs with the schools' curriculum) participate in the training sessions as a train-the-trainer opportunity. We soon added a similar mini-module to include in the afterschool orientation that all sites provided to their youth workers before the start of each program year.

Another strategy to assist program directors was integrating the core competencies into our monthly program directors meetings. We focused these sessions on how supervision could be used to support core competency development, and invited more experienced program directors to do supervision "best practice" presentations for their peers. Program directors shared strategies such as highlighting a particular core competency at each weekly staff meeting and offering recognition to staff who exemplified a particular competency. In recognition of the fact that much of the responsibility for training line staff falls on program directors, we also offered them a train–the–trainer workshop, in which they created core competency mini-modules that could fit into the timeframe of a 45-minute staff meeting.

Tying the Core Competencies to the Performance Management System

As we focused more on the link between supervision and core competency development, we realized that if our aim was to create a cohesive system, we needed to align our performance management system with the core competency work. We began by updating the part-time afterschool staff biannual evaluation forms to include the core competencies. After getting feedback from supervisors on the best way to do this, we decided to create a section that listed each of the six core competencies with space to rate whether or not the staff person had achieved satisfactory, needs improvement, or outstanding status in each. The core competencies would then become part of the conversation between supervisor and group leader that took place twice a year during the formal evaluation process—a conversation that included a discussion not only of the ratings themselves, but also of strategies for growth and improvement.

As the core competences were introduced into the performance management system, individual sites made their own contributions. One site, for example, created a youth worker reflection sheet. During the evaluation process, staff used the sheet to write about their strengths, challenges and need for support in each of the core competencies. The program director would review the sheet with the staff member and continue to refer to it during subsequent supervisory meetings. The reflection sheet template and process were shared with all of the program directors during a monthly program directors meeting. Another director at one of our community centers suggested creating a poster of the CAS core competencies to make them more visible at the sites. This would provide another tool for program directors to keep the competency language front and center when working with staff, and also serve to introduce our school and community partners to our youth worker professional development system. Our COO supported the idea of creating a poster and made funds available for the project. We designed an attractive color poster that listed all six core competencies and their indicators as well as photos of staff working with youth. A letter-size version of the poster was also made available, electronically, to all sites. This was to be used during the interview and hiring process, to introduce prospective employees to the core competencies, and to make clear to them the expectations that CAS has for its youth workers.

Connecting the Core Competencies to Program Quality Assessment

We also created a system to monitor the impact of the core competencies at the program level. Three times a year (November, February, and May), assistant division directors would observe the afterschool programs and rate them on how well they were doing on each of the CAS YWCC. The November and April observations would follow the October and March After School Staff Day events and would gauge how well sites were implementing what they learned. We decided to pilot the program observations at a small group of sites, following our first year of implementing the core competencies. One interesting result of the pilot was that supervisors realized that not all of the core competencies could be directly observed, and that measuring the degree to which they were present required deeper probing, such as interviews with the program directors or discussions with youth participants. While we all agreed that it was essential to tie the core competencies to the program observation and monitoring conducted by division directors, we also needed to recognize that the individual program directors and their teams were busy conducting their own program assessments using the New York State Afterschool Network Quality Self-Assessment tool (NYSAN QSA). To avoid framework fatigue, we felt it was essential to make explicit the overlap between the CAS core competencies and the NYSAN QSA. We worked with the program directors to identify the sections of the NYSAN QSA which reflected the CAS core competencies (such as the "Relationships" section, which echoed much of our *build caring relationships* competency), and agreed that sites would take into account the level to which their staff were proficient in the CAS core competencies when determining how highly to rate their programs on these sections of the NYSAN QSA.

Challenges

Budget Constraints

Growing budget constraints have put strain on the CAS core competency initiative. In 2009, the Director of Education was promoted to another position within the agency, and the decision was made not to immediately fill the vacancy. While part-time youth workers continue to get trained in the core competencies through Afterschool Staff Day, some of the systems for support at the site level have suffered. Leaner budgets mean that program directors find it difficult to pay for their staff to attend training outside of normal work hours, and therefore have to rely almost exclusively on weekly staff meetings to cover the bulk of professional development. These meetings are frequently short and rushed, taking place at the end of the program day. To meet this challenge, program directors have become adept at creating microtraining modules— sometimes no more than 15 minutes in length—to help staff explore and share best practices tied to the core competencies. Another strategy has been to focus on a common core competency each month, and use program directors' meetings to share best practices on how to coach staff in that particular competency.

Keeping Veteran Staff Engaged

As all sites have a mixture of less and more experienced staff, it can be a challenge to keep the core competencies "fresh" for veteran staff. Staff who feel that they are already skilled in the core competencies can become frustrated at having to participate in training with their less experienced peers. One solution to this problem is to have veteran staff at each site create and facilitate an updated version of the core competency overview workshop, offered during afterschool and camp orientations. Program directors would, of course, offer their expertise and guidance in the creation of these modules and assist with training, as needed. The modules would look different at each site, and could even be shared among sites, so that sites would be able to offer a "new" core competency overview workshop each year. In addition, veteran staff would be gaining new skills as trainers, which would add to their own professional growth and keep them interested and motivated.

Program directors have also requested that the agency develop a wider array of specialized training modules to be offered at Afterschool Staff Day for staff who have already taken the basic core competency workshops. For example, they've asked for a series of courses on working with adolescents, behavior management geared towards elementary, middle and high school, and more support for staff on working with youth with special needs.

Aligning the CAS YWCC with the School Day Philosophy

For the CAS afterschool programs that operate within community schools (partnerships between CAS and the New York City Department of Education, in which CAS offers a range of support services to young people and their families), an ongoing challenge has been the disconnect youth sometimes feel between the school day and afterschool environments. While directors share the CAS YWCC with school principals and teachers (who are pleased to know that we have a clear set of standards for afterschool staff), they find that the school staff do not always operate under a similar set of expectations for staff/youth interactions. This has been most apparent in the area of managing behaviors, where the school's approach to discipline may not always reflect the approach advocated in the CAS core competencies. For example, in some schools, the focus is on the punitive, whereas CAS afterschool staff are taught to work with youth who have acted inappropriately, and help them to come up with their own solutions for making things right. While there is no easy fix, there is a clear need for continued dialogue between the program directors and school partners around this issue. One promising practice that has emerged from several sites is having CAS staff conduct training for teachers on positive youth development and positive behavior management.

Lessons Learned

Create a Sustainable System

By drawing on in-house expertise to design, deliver, and revise the core competency curriculum, CAS was able to avoid the costs associated with paying outside consultants. Through creating standardized, easy to follow training modules, that could be used over and over again, we ensured that we wouldn't have to reinvent the wheel each year and could cycle new groups of trainers in and out, with minimal preparation. However, the willingness of agency staff to donate their time as trainers, and their attitude towards this role, was largely shaped by how easy we made it for them. This included not only having the curriculum already designed, but getting them the training materials well in advance of Afterschool Staff Day, so that all they had to do was show up on the day of the event, ready to train. In order to keep this system running smoothly over time, it was essential that we kept all the training materials in a well-ordered electronic filing system, in a central location, so that the staff in charge of organizing the training event could easily access it for years to come.

Another mechanism for keeping the core competencies alive and well, beyond training, was to link them to our performance management system. By including the core competencies in our part-time staff evaluation forms, we helped to ensure that they would remain a focus of staff supervision. Most critical, we built in supports for program directors, such as site-based training tools, train-the-trainer opportunities and best practice sharing through program directors meetings that would assist program directors in effectively coaching and supervising their staff to develop their core competencies.

Assign a Project Manager to the Initiative

A key feature of the success of the CAS core competency initiative was the agency's decision to assign a lead staff person—the Director of Education—to launch, manage, and coordinate the project. This was important not only in terms of making sure the work got done, but also in terms of ensuring the resulting system of training and supervision would be a coherent whole. It helped to have a project manager with a background in education, as well as in training, who could create curricula that were of high quality, both in content and design. The Director of Education received critical support not only from dedicated administrative staff, who oversaw many of the logistics of the training events, but also from the agency's Afterschool Staff Day committee, made up of afterschool program directors, who provided key input and feedback.

Training Is Not Enough

Although CAS initially focused on Afterschool Staff Day to introduce staff to the core competencies, and the event continues to be a key feature of our professional development system for part-time youth workers, it was clear that much more was needed in order for the competencies to truly impact staff practice and behavior. The areas of ongoing training, supervision and performance management systems all need to be addressed if an agency expects staff to continue to develop their knowledge and skills over time. For CAS, this included creating additional training modules to make it easy for program directors to deliver year-round training to staff in the core competencies and providing train-the-trainer support. Through our monthly program directors' meetings, we devoted time to building the capacity of our program directors to effectively supervise staff and to incorporate the core competencies into supervision. The best method for accomplishing this was through peer-to-peer sharing of best practices and problem solving. We changed our part-time staff evaluation forms so that staff would be rated explicitly on the core competencies and also created a system whereby assistant division directors would observe programs and give feedback to program directors on how well program staff were implementing the core competencies.

Find Ways to Recognize Staff for Their Growth

While CAS determined it could not afford to give staff additional compensation for the completion of the core competencies, the agency does pay part-time staff to attend training. In addition, the agency created part-time staff awards, which include a framed certificate as well as a small monetary award, which are announced at the March Afterschool Staff Day event. Each cycle, sites nominate one staff person for this award, and between four and six awards are given out each season. These awards provide a way to formally recognize staff who exemplify the core competencies and reinforce the organization's commitment to the core competency framework. The awards are a source of pride to the winners as well as to the program directors of the nominating sites. Recognition can also be fun and informal. Our COO started a tradition, at the October Afterschool Staff Day, of offering a dinner for two to the first youth worker who can name all six CAS YWCC.

Support of Agency Leadership Is Critical to Success

The Children's Aid Society's top leadership initiated the youth worker core competency effort, and its ongoing support has been the essential ingredient in growing and sustaining the project across two major agency divisions. Our COO has committed time and agency resources to the initiative—everything from assigning staff to manage the project, to identifying the in-house experts who would create the training modules, to approving funds for the core competency posters. Throughout, he has included agency staff in the design of the system, been responsive to staff feedback about what is working and not working, and been receptive to ideas for improvement. By consistently attending and participating in Afterschool Staff Day, Dr. Weisberg has sent a strong message to our youth workers that the agency is deeply serious about the core competencies and committed to helping all staff excel. The commitment of our executive leadership is echoed in that of our division heads, who readily agreed to adapt the part–time staff evaluation and program observation processes to focus on the impact that the core competencies were making on staff and program quality. With support from division leadership, program directors have worked to link their supervision of staff to ongoing core competency development.

The CAS Youth Worker Core Competency effort is still a work in progress, but with the consistent support of our top agency leadership, the core competencies have become part of the culture of our agency, and permanently changed the way we think about youth program quality.

3

ASSESSING YOUTH WORKER COMPETENCE

National Child and Youth Worker Certification

Dale Curry, Andrew J. Schneider-Muñoz, Frank Eckles, and Carol Stuart

Child and youth work (CYW) has been described by many as more art than science. Krueger and Stuart (1999) link competence with context emphasizing the importance of learning how to recognize, change and create context. Krueger (2007) describes CYW as complex, developmental, interpersonal, intersubjective, and contextual. The following quote by Gerry Fewster (2004) perhaps captures the thinking of many leading CYW professionals:

> Good child and youth care isn't brain surgery—it's much more difficult. No educational courses, training programs or text books can give you what you need in order to be with, understand and guide a young person through the fear, pain, chaos and anger once these demons are at work … Being in relationship means that we have what it takes to remain open and responsive in conditions where most mortals-and professionals-quickly distance themselves, become "objective" and look for the external "fix."

(p. 3)

Such statements and views might be seen by some as presenting a difficult challenge for enhancing the development and status of the profession using some of the more standard professional indicators such as formal education and training linked to professional exams and/or certification of competence. The authors considered that to take that view would be to miss an opportunity to bring the art and the science of youth work into mutual purpose. Since research indicates that staff competence is a primary factor in the quality of care and service outcomes for children and youth (Burchinal, Howes, & Kontos, 2002; Cost, Quality, and Child Outcomes Study Team, 1995; Curry et al., 2009; Gable &

Halliburton, 2003; Knoche, Peterson, Pope, Edwards, & Jeon, 2006; Miller & Hall, 2007), the assessment and development of CYW practitioner competence is an essential task. The further fact that the U.S. child and youth care workforce could be larger than all of the other human service populations combined (perhaps as many as 5.5 million child and youth workers, including part-time) (Annie E. Casey Foundation, 2003) elevates further the importance of having a highly competent CYW workforce serving children, youth and families.

The assessment of competence through recognized professional processes such as exams, internships, and supervisory assessments would lend credibility to CYW amongst other professionals with whom they interact daily. At the same time, these professional processes must be seen as credible from inside the profession. We recognize the role of complexity in practice with children, youth and families. Finding ways to accurately assess child and youth worker competence that captured both the art and the science was arguably the most important challenge for CYW leaders involved in the North American Certification Project (NACP). This chapter will provide background information on the NACP and an introduction to the certification program administered by the Child and Youth Care Certification Board. Information pertaining to the large scope of the child and youth work field, a delineation of essential underlying competencies and ethical standards common across various practice settings, and strategies for assessing these competency areas will be discussed.

Broad Scope and Competencies of Child and Youth Work Practice

Recent discussions across the varied fields of child and youth work practice have led to the recognition that the broader field consists of a common core of knowledge, skill, and value base. Most professions develop because of this commonality and not based upon the setting in which work is conducted, the age group of who receives services, or characteristics of the type of population served (e.g., mental health, child maltreatment) (Curry, Eckles, Stuart, & Qaqish, 2010). CYW leaders in the areas of after school, residential treatment, juvenile justice, child welfare have recently identified common essential workforce competencies necessary for these fields of practice and have begun to initiate certification efforts at the local and state levels (Eckles et al., 2009; Gannett, Mello, & Starr, 2009; Hall & Gannett, 2010).

The scope of CYW practice is described as including a focus on "infants, children, and adolescents, including those with special needs, within the context of the family, the community, and the life span" and the competencies also broadly defined to encompass:

> ... the optimal development of children, youth, and their families in a variety of settings, such as early care and education, community-based child and youth development programs, parent education and family sup-

port, school-based programs, community mental health, group homes, residential centers, day and residential treatment, early intervention, home-based care and treatment, psychiatric centers, rehabilitation programs, pediatric health care, and juvenile justice programs. Child and youth care practice includes assessing client and program needs, designing and implementing programs and planned environments, integrating developmental, preventive, and therapeutic requirements into the life space, contributing to the development of knowledge and practice, and participating in systems interventions through direct care, supervision, administration, teaching, research, consultation, and advocacy.

(National Organization of Child Care Worker Associations, 1992, p. 83)

It was on this broad base of understanding that the North American Certification Project began its work. The professional certification program, administered by the Child and Youth Care Certification Board (CYCCB) and sponsored by the Association for Child and Youth Care Practice (ACYCP) is the result of years of work by many North American Child and Youth Care Professionals. In 1992, seventy international representatives from associations, education programs and child and youth serving organizations gathered at the University of Wisconsin Milwaukee and established the International Leadership Coalition for Professional Child and Youth Care (ILCPYC). A second meeting of the ILCPYC with additional leaders from the field of youth development in 1999 and a third meeting in 2003 resulted in the development of a plan to develop a certification process.

During a seven-year period (2000–2007), the Association for Child and Youth Care Practice, a national organization that promotes professional child and youth care practice in the United States, brought together international leaders in a variety of child and youth work areas to study and address workforce needs focusing on certification at the professional level across practice environments. Focusing on the inter-relatedness of the various settings in which work is delivered, a major task was to identify the fundamental principles that underlie child and youth care practice. Guiding this effort was a belief that professions emerge from the common body of knowledge, skills and values rather than by the setting (after school/community-based or out-of-home), age of child/youth, or population (e.g., mental health, child welfare, homeless).

The competency development process involved a meta-analysis of the fields' articulation of competencies that also included the development of new competencies where gaps were identified. The competencies incorporated what workers currently value, know and do as well as what best practice standards indicate that they *should* value, know, and do. Determination of the list of competencies involved several work groups and several years of discussion and refinement. The competencies are organized into the following five domains: (1) professionalism, (2) cultural and human diversity, (3) applied human development,

(4) relationship and communication, and (5) developmental practice methods (Curry et al., 2009; Eckles et al., 2009). The reader is referred to Mattingly, Stuart, and VanderVen (2002) for a more detailed description of the competency development process.

The Certification Program

The certification program has been implemented on a national scale since 2008. Following a pilot study which focused on assessing the validity and reliability of a situational judgment exam as well as piloting two additional assessments in order to comprehensively assess all the competencies developed by the NACP; a new non-profit organization, the Child and Youth Care Certification Board, Inc. was incorporated to implement the certification program. A CYW professional who is interested in becoming certified must first complete a written exam. Once the exam has been passed, the professional has one year to submit an application. The application includes several items:

*   Evidence of training and/or education in the five domains (minimum of 250 hours with 100 hours occurring in the last 5 years).
*   A supervisory assessment of a sub-set of competencies.
*   An electronic portfolio created by the candidate that addresses a set of questions designed to measure a different sub-set of competencies.
*   Two reference letters from peers in the field.

The certification program requires rigorous attention to the competencies defined for the field and a strong commitment to being a professional. It is time-consuming and extensive. The members of the NACP and the board members of the CYCCB believe that this is necessary for the development of the profession into one that is recognized by others, but still maintains the relational, contextual nature that is inherent in youth work. The following sections describe the development and initial validation of the assessment procedures. There is still work to be done but the CYCCB believes that credible professional development on a national scale requires the rigor outlined in the following sections.

Assessment Strategies

Since the field has not yet discovered a "silver bullet" assessment tool or strategy that can adequately measure the varied facets of competence involved in child and youth work across practice settings, a multi-measure approach was implemented. In addition to obtaining professional references and background information pertaining to an applicant's professional memberships, employment history, education and training, assessment strategies used in the national certification program predominantly emphasize three approaches: (1) situational judgment exam, (2) portfolio assessment, and (3) supervisor performance assessment. The identification of broad cross-field competencies led to the development of an assessment plan that included a process to identify the most appropriate assessment measure (supervisor assessment, portfolio, or exam) for each competency. There was an attempt to assess as many competency areas as possible via the certification exam. Six panel members made independent recommendations for assigning each of the competencies, of which there are over 100, to one of these methods of assessment. After discussing areas of disagreement, the panel members came to consensus on the most appropriate method for assessing each competency. Once the competencies that could be assessed by a situational judgment exam were identified, the expert panel was asked to independently prioritize the competencies according to importance. The panel determined the number of items for each competency (one, two, or three items) based on the importance of the competency in the field of practice. The panel's responses were averaged to determine the number of items for each identified competency.

Portfolio and supervisor assessment teams developed instruments focusing on the competencies that could be more appropriately assessed using those evaluation tools. For instance, the competency, "practitioner is a positive representative of the organization as evidenced by personal appearance," and behavior could not be assessed by exam or portfolio but best by supervisor assessment whereas "incorporating wellness practices into one's own lifestyle" was best assessed in the portfolio with a statement of philosophy.

Situational Judgment Exam

A situational judgment exam was developed that requires practice judgments from the examinee based on case scenarios. The scenarios were developed from case studies of actual incidents elicited from the field from a variety of practice settings. A situational judgment approach (SJA) to assessment emphasizes the use of realistic scenarios, typically asking test-takers to identify the best alternative among the choices offered. The most correct answer for each item is determined by a panel of subject matter experts. The SJA was used because research has determined that SJA tends to have a high level of face and content validity, less adverse impact by gender and ethnicity, can measure a variety of constructs including interpersonal competencies that are crucial in child and youth work settings, are relatively easy to administer in bulk (paper and pencil or online) and typically have acceptable validity correlations with job performance (Chan & Schmitt, 2002; Clevenger, Pereira, Wiechmann, Schmitt, & Harvey, 2001; McDaniel, Morgeson, Finnegan, Campion, & Braverman, 2001). Finally, situational judgment was felt to be a means of addressing arguments of those who resist exams as being poor indicators of competence. Situational judgment can present complex situations and multiple questions to assess the candidates' ability to deal with complexity and make independent decisions based on theory as well as context (see Table 3.1 and 3.2).

Although these examples are not actual cases or items included in the certification exam, they provide examples of the types of cases and items and illustrate the potential usefulness of SJA. The development and pilot administration of the exam involved ongoing review by national and international child and youth worker experts as well as extensive statistical item analysis by the research team. Seven hundred and seventy-five participants from 29 community-based and out-of-home care practice sites in six states and two Canadian provinces were administered the exam during the pilot testing validation study in 2006. Findings from the pilot study indicated that the exam was reliable (Cronbach's alpha = .90), correlated with supervisor assessment of performance on the job ($r = .26$), and had face validity.

The low correlation between SJA and on-the-job performance is comparable to findings in other studies considered to underestimate the true strength of the relationship between the exam score and on-the-job performance. The relationship is underestimated due to range restriction (e.g., very poor performers tend to be weeded out; thus limiting the range of performance assessed) and there is little variability in the supervisory assessments. According to Sackett, Borneman, and Connelly (2008), both range restriction and criterion unreliability, typical of efforts correlating exam scores with supervisor ratings of

TABLE 3.1 Sample Test Item for Competency I.B.4.c

Apply specific principles and standards from the relevant Code of Ethics to specific problems.

You are a practitioner working in an emergency shelter that primarily serves homeless youth who are 14 to 21 years old. Legally, in this state, runaways under the age of 16 must be reported to authorities. One evening a young-looking female youth comes in and makes inquiries as to the services available in the shelter. She tells you she is 18, but you strongly suspect she is much younger, possibly 13 or 14. As you interview her, she reveals that she ran away from home about a year ago and has been working as a prostitute for the past 6 months. She refuses to tell you her real name or where she is from. When you ask her what she needs from the shelter, she tells you that she could use a place to stay overnight.

As a practitioner, you:

a) Have a legal obligation to talk her into staying at the shelter until a longer-term program can be worked out or she can be reconnected with her family. You have no obligation to contact the authorities.

b) Have a legal obligation to make the shelter services available to her and check to be sure she is aware of the risks involved in her lifestyle.

c) Have a professional obligation to contact the appropriate authorities if she leaves the shelter.

d) Have no legal or ethical obligation beyond making services available to her that she has specifically asked for.

TABLE 3.2 Sample Test Item for Competencies I.B.6.c and I.B.6.e

IB6c. Describe the rights of children, youth and families in relevant setting/s and systems
IB6e. Describe and advocate for safeguards for protection from abuse including institutional abuse

Lisa (a 13 year old female in residential treatment) became angry during an individual counseling session with Social Service Manager (MH) and cursed at the staff member. Lisa was escorted to "off dorm" time out due to disrupting the milieu. While in time out, Lisa continued to use profanity toward staff members, urinated on the floor, and said "maybe I should pimp again and make some money..." After communicating several expectations and after Lisa refused to calm down, staff member (JT) began to physically escort Lisa to seclusion when Lisa became physically assaultive, hitting staff member JT. Staff members JT and SR physically restrained Lisa and eventually removed her to the seclusion room. Within 30 minutes, Lisa regained physical control of herself and agreed to a plan to maintain the safety of Lisa and the staff members. Lisa cleaned the seclusion room and the time out room.

Choose the best answer:

1. Lisa's rights were <u>not</u> properly protected in this situation.

2. The physical restraint, as explained in this case study was justified and proper.

3. An alternative intervention such as having the staff member (JT) switch off with another staff member should have been tried.

4. Lisa was just seeking attention and should have been ignored by staff.

---

worker performance lead to an underestimation of validity. Clevenger et al. (2001) estimate that typical SJA validity correlations in the .20 to .40 range to be significantly higher, among the best validity coefficients when compared to personnel selection approaches.

Face validity was found as participants who took the exam in the pilot study overwhelmingly indicated that it accurately assessed important aspects of child and youth work across practice settings. For example, 90% of respondents in the pilot study perceived that the items in the exam accurately assess important aspects of CYW and the case examples provide realistic samples of CYW. This provides additional evidence that the exam measures essential elements of child and youth work. The reader is referred to Curry et al. (2009) for additional information pertaining to the reliability and validity of the certification exam.

Portfolio Assessment

A more qualitative approach to assessment was used to best determine proficiency in certain competency areas. Use of portfolios is becoming an increasingly prevalent tool for learning and assessment in a variety of fields (Driessen et al., 2006; Gearhart & Osmundson, 2009; Sickle, Bogan, Kamen, Baird, & Butcher, 2005). Portfolios are intended to provide an individual the opportunity to exhibit samples of efforts and achievements, as well as provide evidence of an individual's reflection on learning and practice (Paulson, Paulson, & Meyer, 1991). Project team members also recognized that a portfolio approach could be adapted to permit practitioners to provide evidence of competence within their respective practice settings.

The competency-based electronic portfolio assessment used by the CYCCB allows the candidate to reflect on his or her own practice and determine how specific competencies are expressed. Each portfolio item is based on a required competency listed in the CYCCB competency document that has not been assessed by another method (i.e., exam or supervisor assessment) (Curry et al., 2010).

The portfolio activities are divided into seven sections across the five domains and at least one item must be completed in each section. Some sections have multiple activities from which one may be chosen. An example from one of the sections is below. The criteria for review are provided for both the applicant and reviewer within the electronic portfolio form. An applicant's portfolio is reviewed by two previously certified reviewers. If disagreement exists regarding the completeness of the portfolio, an assessment from a third reviewer is provided. Table 3.3 is an example of the portfolio format and instructions. The reader is encouraged to visit the website of the Association for Child and Youth Care Practice (www.acycp.org) and the Child and Youth Care Certification

TABLE 3.3 Sample Portfolio Assessment for Competency I.B.1.d

I.B.1.d. Contribute to the on-going development of the field

Instructions: If you are a current member of a local, regional, or national youth work related organization, list the organization, describe your participation (such as offices held or committee memberships), any trainings you have presented, courses you have taught, research in which you participated, governmental committees representing child and youth care, and articles you have published (relating to the practice of child and youth care work).

Assessment Criteria:

- Includes membership in an appropriate group
- Includes list of contributions
- Lists minimum of (1) contribution

Activity B-1

Organization	Activity

Board (www.cyccertificationboard.org) to further explore the electronic portfolio approach to assessment.

Supervisor Performance Assessment

Project members recognized the importance of including assessment information regarding on-the-job performance. Supervisory assessment of worker performance is one of the most frequently used measures of employee performance. Although the research has noted limitations of its effectiveness (e.g., leniency bias, halo effect, inconsistency between supervisors), when combined with other indicators of performance, it is an important measure to include in an overall assessment of the worker's on-the-job competence, especially when direct assessment is not feasible (Dohrenbusch & Lipka, 2006; Gonsalvez & Freestone, 2007; Larson, Day, Howarth, Clark, & Vogel, 2003). Since direct observation of worker performance is very labor intensive and often not practical or cost efficient on the scale of national certification, project staff decided that it was essential to include a supervisor's assessment of a workers performance. Involvement of supervisors in the certification process can also lead to other benefits (e.g., support for the certification program and ongoing worker development). The supervisor assessment consists of a series of competency statements from the certification program with a five-choice rating scale, ranging from "consistently demonstrates this competency" to "does not demonstrate this competency." The form is to be completed by a supervisor who has extensive and direct knowledge of the applicant's work with youth. Examples of several assessment items pertaining to competencies in Domain V (Developmental Practice Methods) may be seen in Table 3.4.

TABLE 3.4 Sample Items from Supervisor Assessment

Practitioner supports a healthy and safe environment by participating in emergency procedures specific to practice setting and carrying them out in a developmentally appropriate level. (Competency V.B.2.a.1)

Practitioner demonstrates an ability to employ appropriate infection control practices. (Competency V.B.2.d.3)

Practitioner demonstrates the ability to teach skills in several domains of activity e.g., arts, crafts, sports, games, and music. (Competency V.B.5.b.)

5	4	3	2	1
Consistently demonstrates this competency		Inconsistently demonstrates this competency		Does not demonstrates this competency

Comments: _____

_____

_____

_____

Putting it All Together

This chapter has provided a summary of a major assessment initiative, a component of a national credentialing program, that is the result of the efforts of numerous committed child and youth work professionals from various practice settings in North America. The authors have emphasized the importance and complexity of assessing child and youth worker competence in context across practice settings. Given the complexity of assessing child and youth worker competence, a multi-measure approach is being used by the CYCCB. Although the certification exam has received the most scrutiny from the initial research, all three assessment methods are considered essential by the CYCCB to obtain a more accurate assessment profile of worker competence. Additional research is necessary to document the impact of the full credentialing program. Preliminary findings indicate that higher scores on the certification exam are associated with better on-the-job performance, according to supervisor assessments (Curry et al., 2009; Curry et al., 2010). In addition, a comparison of those who completed the entire certification process (including the full supervisory assessment and portfolio) with those who did not complete in the pilot study indicates that completion of the certification process is predictive of worker performance beyond what is accounted for by the certification exam alone. This provides some empirical evidence that including the supervisor and portfolio assessments adds to the validity of the credentialing program beyond the use of the exam. Unfortunately, findings from the pilot study also indicate that many eligible workers do not complete the certification process (only 27% completed the full certification process).

Efforts must be undertaken to identify barriers to completion and support worker efforts toward obtaining the national credential. A few promising in-progress activities include the development of a certification preparation manual and training program focusing on all three assessment measures. Certification mentoring and coaching appears to be an effective strategy in some locations (e.g., Indiana youth worker cohorts).

The NACP and ongoing work of the CYCCB has made a significant contribution to the establishment of a practical, reliable and valid assessment approach and credentialing program that is currently being implemented on a national scale to promote higher standards of care for children, youth and families. The competency framework can be used in a variety of ways to promote higher standards. For example, educators and trainers can ensure the relevancy of coursework provided to current and future practitioners. It can provide a framework for child and youth work-specific concentrations and degree programs to be established in higher education. As an example, the Kent State University program in Human Development and Family Studies has recently adapted its youth development concentration to better align with the national competencies and certification program. New courses were developed and others dropped or adapted to make the coursework more meaningful and better prepare students for certification and child and youth work practice. Content from the CYCCB electronic portfolio is now included in coursework. Upon completion of their degree, students are eligible to take the national certification exam at Kent State University and potentially receive Provisional Certification from the CYCCB, thus making the students more marketable in the child and youth work job market. Other university programs are also using the competency and certification program to develop and/or strengthen existing CYW programs (e.g., University of Pittsburgh, Indiana University).

Ongoing research and development pertaining to the credentialing program as well as other workforce issues must continue. The CYCCB recently partnered with Kent State University in establishing a research center focusing on the CYW workforce (International Institute for Human Service Workforce Research and Development). This newly established institute can facilitate discussion pertaining to workforce issues and resources as well as collaborate with and support the efforts of others interested in CYW workforce research.

Since one of the most important factors affecting the care of children and youth is the quality of the CYW staff, a much greater emphasis must be placed on the recruitment, education and training, career development, and the retention of competent practitioners. The assessment and credentialing program administered by the CYCCB can potentially impact millions of workers, thus improving the lives of significantly more children, youth, and families.

References

Annie E. Casey Foundation (2003). *The unsolved challenge of system reform: The condition of the frontline human services workforce.* Baltimore, MD: Author.

Burchinal, M., Howes, C., & Kontos, S. (2002). Structural predictors of child care quality in child care homes. *Early Childhood Research Quarterly, 17,* 87–105.

Chan, D., & Schmitt, N. (2002). Situational judgment and job performance. *Human Performance, 15,* 233–254.

Clevenger, J., Pereira, G. M., Wiechmann, D., Schmitt, N., & Harvey, V. S. (2001). Incremental validity of situational judgment tests. *Journal of Applied Psychology, 86,* 410–417.

Cost, Quality, and Child Outcomes Study Team. (1995). *Cost, quality, and child outcomes in child care centers public report* (2nd ed.). Denver: University of Colorado at Denver.

Curry, D., Eckles, F., Stuart, C., & Qaqish, B. (2010). National child and youth care practitioner certification: Promoting competent care for children and youth. *Child Welfare, 89,* 57–77.

Curry, D., Qaqish, B., Carpenter-Williams, J., Eckles, F., Mattingly, M., Stuart, C., & Thomas, D. (2009). A national certification exam for child and youth care workers: Preliminary results of a validation study. *Journal of Child and Youth Care Work, 22,* 152–170.

Dohrenbusch, R., & Lipka, S. (2006). Assessing and predicting supervisors' evaluations of psychotherapists—an empirical study. *Counseling Psychology Quarterly, 19,* 395–414.

Driessen, E. W., Overeem, K., Van Tartwijk, J., Van Der Vleuten, C. P., & Muijtjens, A. M. (2006). Validity of portfolio assessment: Which qualities determine ratings? *Medical Education, 40,* 862–866.

Eckles, F., Carpenter-Williams, J. Curry, D., Mattingly, M., Rybicki, M., Stuart, C. (2009). Final phases in the development and implementation of the North American Certification Project (NACP). *Journal of Child and Youth Care Work, 22,* 120–151.

Fewster, G. (2004). Editorial. *Relational Child and Youth Care Practice, 17,* 3–4.

Gable, S., & Halliburton, A. (2003). Barriers to child care providers' professional development. *Child and Youth Care Forum, 32,* 175–193.

Gannett, E. S., Mello, S., & Starr, E. (2009). *Credentialing for the 21st CCLC staff: An overview of the benefits and impacts.* Wellsley, MA: National Institute on Out-of-School Time, Wellesley Centers for Women, Wellesley College.

Gearhart, M., & Osmundson, E. (2009). Assessment portfolios as opportunities for teacher learning. *Educational Assessment, 14,* 1–24.

Gonsalvez, C. J., & Freestone, J. (2007). Field supervisors' assessments of trainee performance: Are they reliable and valid? *Australian Psychologist, 42,* 23–32.

Hall, G., & Gannett, E. (2010). Body and soul: Reflections on two professional development credential pilots in Massachusetts. *Afterschool Matters, 10,* 13–21.

Knoche, L., Peterson, C. A., Pope Edwards, C., & Jeon, H. J. (2006). Child care for children with and without disabilities: The provider, observer, and parent perspectives. *Early Childhood Research Quarterly, 21,* 93–109.

Krueger, M. (2007). Four areas of support for child and youth care workers. *Families in Society: The Journal of Contemporary Social Services, 88,* 233–240.

Krueger, M., & Stuart, C. (1999). Context and competence in work with children and youth. *Child and Youth Care Forum, 28,* 195–204.

Larson, L. M., Day, S. X., Howarth, S., Clark, M. P., & Vogel, D. L. (2003). Developing a supervisor feedback rating scale using outside observers. *Measurement and Evaluation in Counseling and Development, 35,* 230–238.

Mattingly, M., Stuart, C., & VanderVen, K. (2002). North American Certification Project (NACP) competencies for professional child and youth work practitioners. *Journal of Child and Youth Care Work, 17,* 16–49.

McDaniel, M. A., Morgeson, F. P., Finnegan, E. B., Campion, M. A., & Braverman, E. P. (2001). Use of situational judgment tests to predict job performance: A clarification of the literature. *Journal of Applied Psychology, 86,* 730–740.

Miller, B., & Hall, G., (2007). What counts in after school? Findings from the Massachusetts Afterschool Research Study (MARS). *Journal of Youth Development, 55*(3), Article No. 603RS001.

National Organization of Child Care Worker Associations. (1992). The international leadership coalition for professional child and youth care. *Journal of Child and Youth Care Work, 8,* 69–83.

Paulson, L. F., Paulson, P. R., & Meyer, C. A. (1991). What makes a portfolio a portfolio? *Educational Leadership, 58,* 60–63.

Sackett, P. R., Borneman, M. J., & Connelly, B. S. (2008). High-stakes testing in higher education and employment: Appraising the evidence of validity and fairness. *American Psychologist, 63,* 215–227.

Sickle, M. V., Bogan, M. B. Kamen, M., Baird, W., & Butcher, C. (2005). Dilemmas faced establishing portfolio assessment of pre-service teachers in the southeastern United States. *College Student Journal, 39,* 497–509.

4

ESTABLISHING EXPERTISE IN AN EMERGING FIELD

Joyce Walker and Kate Walker

Linda was the primary youth worker for Sisterhood, an all-female youth group that focused on mutual support and exploring issues determined by the youth, often issues of identity and gender. On Friday, Linda left Sisterhood exhausted. Self-questioning filled her mind and the myriad of dilemmas she faced with the young women flashed before her eyes. First, there was Chandra and the fundraising money. The group was selling candy to raise money for their upcoming retreat, and the girls had jointly decided that each member should raise the same amount of money in order to attend. Chandra tearfully told Linda that she had sold the candy, but her family had to use that money to pay their utility bill and now she didn't know what to do or say to her friends. Then there was the persistent question of when to share personal information with the girls. Linda worked hard to create a space where the girls felt comfortable sharing their experiences and opinions, and they often asked Linda personal questions. Just this week in a discussion about the upcoming prom, they asked how Linda had dealt with pressure to have sex on her prom night. Linda wanted to build rapport and trust with the youth, but she also knew she had an obligation to set appropriate boundaries on what she shared. To top it off, Linda's new co-leader, Natasha, was upset and offended by the girls' cursing. But the girls themselves were miffed when Natasha tried to impose a new rule—a "curse jar" for the girls to put a quarter in every time they cursed—when they had collectively created the rules for their space prior to Natasha joining their group. Linda struggled to respond to these various dilemmas in ways that balanced the diverse considerations at play while keeping youth and their needs at the center.

As this vignette illustrates, daily youth work practice is complex and dynamic. It is riddled with situations that are layered and require dealing with multiple considerations and changing circumstances. Recent research by Larson and Walker (2010) describes the range of dilemmas youth workers face in their daily practice (including those from the opening scenario). The dilemmas that Linda faced involve addressing tensions between the program and youths' outside lives, maintaining consistency and professionalism in leaders' interactions with youth, and accommodating different leadership styles and philosophies among staff. These practice dilemmas represent the knotty situations that even experienced practitioners face every day and for which there is no formula or manual to point the way. Youth workers need to understand and effectively respond to these individual and group dilemmas in order to restore conditions where learning and positive development can occur.

In this chapter we explore a tension around adequately accounting for the relevant knowledge needed to respond to this real world complexity. Following the thinking of some prominent social scientists (Flyvbjerg, 2001), psychologists (Ericsson, Charness, Feltovich, & Hoffman, 2006), educational theorists (Eisner, 2002; Schon, 1983) and the classic philosopher Aristotle, we propose that practitioners like Linda need to develop "practitioner expertise" which draws on a combination of knowledge, skills and, in particular, judgment. We suggest that in efforts to understand and promote quality youth work practice, there has been a tendency to default to scientific knowledge and technical skills and neglect the practical judgment to apply knowledge and skills in making sound, ethical choices in specific situations like those Linda faces in her daily work with young people. Following a discussion of expertise with particular attention to the virtue of practical wisdom, we examine professional development strategies compatible with developing practitioner expertise and offer several case examples of professional development opportunities that aim to foster the practical wisdom, critical thinking and reflective practice fundamental to our understanding of youth worker expertise.

Practitioner Expertise

In recent years, considerable efforts have been made to guide and standardize practice through the creation of frameworks of core competencies to develop and support an effective youth worker workforce (Astroth, Garza, & Taylor, 2004; Starr, Yohalem, & Gannett, 2009). Many of these efforts are modeled on the field of early childhood, social work or residential care and are seen as a foundational piece of professionalizing the youth development field. A core competency is a basic skill, knowledge, or attitude in a specific domain. Youth work core competencies articulate what it is that adults working with youth need to know and do in order to deliver high quality programs. For example, common content areas across various youth work competency frameworks include curriculum; professionalism; connecting with families; health, safety and nutrition; child and adolescent development; cross-cultural competence; guidance; professional development; connecting with communities; and environment (Starr et al., 2009).

These competency frameworks typically have sub-categories, with indicators detailing observable behaviors reflecting that competency seen in one's practice. For example, the competency content area of "connecting with families" might have sub-categories such as engaging, supporting, and communicating with families. The content area of "health, safety and nutrition" regularly includes items concerning CPR and first aid procedures; risk management, such as the number of chaperones required for group outings; and healthy eating habits. These frameworks tend to focus on the operational, more measurable units of practice.

However, the tendency to reduce youth work practice to measurable terms risks reducing youth work to a purely technical skill. Deconstructing practice to the most measurable units can lead to a fragmented focus and one that attends less to significant elements such as the role of judgment (Smith, 1996). By whittling down practice to the ability to undertake specific tasks, it becomes largely stripped of its social, moral and intellectual qualities (Smith, 1996). It is important to consider whether the dominant competency frameworks adequately encompass the relevant kinds of knowledge practitioners need to do youth work well.

Different Types of Knowledge

Perhaps in the classic conversations of Aristotle we can find the language and concepts that define expertise as it applies to the social practice of youth work. According to Flyvbjerg (2001), Aristotle discussed three intellectual virtues: *episteme, techne,* and *phronesis*—generally translated as scientific knowledge, technical knowledge, and practical knowledge. *Episteme* is science or scientific knowledge. It concerns universal, invariable, and context-independent principles assumed to apply to all situations one encounters. Consider the reality of gravity or in youth work, the basic tenets of adolescent development. *Techne* refers to technical skills or craft. It is the application of concrete, variable, and context-dependent knowledge which produces things. Just as the surgeon knows how to perform a procedure, a youth worker knows how to facilitate a group. Finally, Aristotle's third and most important virtue, *phronesis,* is practical knowledge. The concept of *phronesis* goes beyond scientific and technical knowledge and involves value judgment and ethical decision making in social practice. "The person possessing practical wisdom (*phronesis*) has knowledge of how to behave in each particular circumstance that can never be equated with or reduced to knowledge of general truths" (Flyvbjerg, 2001, p. 57). This wise, practical reasoning is the sustained, cultivated ability to recognize and make sound, ethical choices in specific situations. Doing so requires an interaction between the general and the concrete. According to Eisner (2002):

> Practical reasoning is deliberative, it takes into account local circumstances, it weighs tradeoffs, it is riddled with uncertainties, it depends

on judgment, profits from wisdom, addresses particulars, it deals with contingencies, is iterative and shifts aims in process when necessary. Practical reasoning is the stuff of practical life. It is not the stuff of theoretical science. It is not enduring and it is not foundational. Its aim is to arrive at good but imperfect decisions with respect to particular circumstances.

(p. 375)

Reflect back on youth worker Linda's dilemmas. While she may have excellent negotiation skills, she must make a judgment about whether to negotiate, decide herself or let the young women decide, or some combination. She makes this decision based on her practical wisdom, her circumstances and the goals she is trying to achieve in her program. For the youth worker, *phronesis* represents the kind of wisdom required to appraise the diverse problems and situations encountered in daily practice, the thoughtful deliberation of the merits of differing paths of action, and having the strategic skills to respond to these situations in ways that achieve the desired ends—in this case, to facilitate young people's learning and positive development.

Other practice fields have argued that in addition to the rational analysis of scientific inquiry and the value of the measureable technical skills, highly relational work with human beings relies as well on properties such as judgment, context, practice, experience, common sense and intuition (Flyvbjerg, 2001). In the field of youth development, priority has been placed on the enumeration of core youth worker competencies and on the value of evidence-based practice leading to measureable youth outcomes. The scientific knowledge and technical skills of youth work have dominated the landscape and eclipsed the value and understanding of the role judgment, or practical wisdom, plays in the work. The framework of practitioner expertise we propose aims to integrate these three kinds of knowledge and elevate the role of practical wisdom.

Expertise in Youth Work Practice

What we refer to as practitioner expertise is the sum, interaction and application of the three intellectual virtues of scientific knowledge, technical skill and practical wisdom. Expertise involves not just "knowing that" but "knowing how": it involves knowledge and skills for both understanding and action (Sternberg et al., 2000). Moreover, it involves practical know-how or making sound choices in particular situations. Expertise is oriented to an active praxis wherein knowledge, skills, activities, and context are joined in situations. "Expertise in this sense is an active integration of knowledge, activities, skills and moment that together are necessary to do the job that has to be done at high levels of quality and consistency" (Baizerman, 2009, p. 88). Whereas competencies tend to focus on particular skills or discrete attributes, expertise is a broad capacity or understanding to engage in an activity or practice. It is more than the demonstration of competencies; it is the ability to orchestrate multiple competencies into a full range of response necessary for effective practice that is highly relational, group situated and individual centered. This understanding of expertise is premised on the situated nature of knowledge and builds on Schon's (1983) move away from a rational dualism where knowing is separate from doing; rather, it views "practice" as a way of handling knowledge (Blank, 2007).

Expertise is earned through prolonged practice (Baizerman, 2009), a feature that distinguishes the expert from novices and less experienced people. Recently, a small study compared the considerations and strategies that expert and novice youth workers use in appraising and responding to dilemmas of practice (Walker & Larson, 2011). Its findings suggest that experts tend to (1) see more complexities and identify more nuances and considerations; (2) see more possibilities and have a larger repertoire of possible responses; (3) generate multi-pronged responses which take into account, address, and balance multiple perspectives and considerations; and (4) generate youth-centered responses that give youth and their developmental needs and interests focal importance. Similar to the literature on expertise in other fields, this study found that expert responses reflected more complex, multi-dimensional understandings of the issues which emerge in practice and generated more creative, flexible solutions, while novice responses reflected a more declarative understanding of the issues and generated more rigid and less nuanced solutions. Research finds that experts see more nuances and possess a wide repertoire of tactics than novices do (Ross, Shafer, & Klein, 2006). Further, the ability to take a pluralistic perspective and address multiple demands has been identified as a feature of expertise (Fook, Ryan, & Hawkins 2000; Levin, 1995). These findings suggest that it may be important to train youth workers to attend to the complexity of the real world of daily practice, and for developing the capacity to balance diverse and often competing considerations while keeping youth at the center (Larson, Rickman, Gibbons, & Walker, 2009).

Professional Development of Expertise

The idea that expertise is acquired through experience and developed through habit suggests that it is individual, organic and even serendipitous. Yet education for work in the field and continued training for professional development address the deliberate and systematic exposure to the scientific knowledge, technical skills and practical judgment required, in combination with everyday work experience, to develop expertise associated with high quality performance achieved by knowing what is required and how to do it well. Three decades of research on expertise across a wide range of disciplines—from surgery to chess—suggests that beyond sheer years of experience or even natural ability, it is ongoing deliberate practice with feedback that appears to matter most in developing and maintaining expertise (Ericsson, Charness, Feltovich, & Hoffman, 2006). Deliberate practice is defined as taking on tasks that are appropriately challenging and chosen with the goal of improving a particular skill. Practitioners learn when they have ongoing opportunities to engage with the full range of challenging problems associated with their practice and receive authentic feedback. In other words, it is not about going through the motions, but having ongoing opportunities to work at addressing some of the most difficult problems in one's field with coaching, questioning and critical reflection.

The question arises about how practitioner expertise can be intentionally fostered, nurtured and stimulated. In terms of education and training for professional development, what kinds of activities, strategies and experiences contribute to the development of practitioner expertise? Many educational, training and professional development experiences promote the knowledge of current research and standards of professional practice as well as the core skills required in everyday youth work practice. In academic settings, learning strategies typically include lectures, readings, analytical papers, skill-focused trainings, well-supervised field experiences, internships, participatory seminars and observations. It is not uncommon for professional development to be offered in sporadic, unconnected segments through half-day workshops, conference presentations, skill trainings and subject matter hot topics. Some of these approaches appear to be more effective than others in intentionally sharpening practical wisdom, honing values and judgment, and assessing the context of everyday practice dilemmas to sort out the preferred and ethical solution. Based on our growing understanding of expertise, we postulate that youth workers (1) benefit from work on real world problems where they can practice solving dilemmas from multiple perspectives and apply multiple considerations to achieve the most appropriate end given the context and ethical framework; (2) benefit from peer group interactions that press them to reflect critically on their practice verbally and in writing and to pose questions that stimulate new solutions and approaches to the work; (3) grow in confidence and understanding when they can articulate the historic and philosophical roots of youth work in the language common to established researchers, writers and scholars in the field; and (4) rely more confidently on their judgment and practical wisdom when it is grounded on a clear, principled and reasoned ethical stance to guide their work.

When practitioners were asked to describe positive learning environments that worked best for them (Walker, 2003), experienced youth workers consistently credited the following features as fundamental to engaging them in learning in ways that transformed their thinking about themselves and their work. They feel most challenged, stretched and engaged when dealing with real world situations while supported by people with actual work experience in the field. The knowledge that instructors have been in the trenches doing youth work generates mutual trust, openness and respect. They highly value a cohort of peers with whom they can share and learn, develop professionally and be encouraged to think in new ways. They appreciate a reciprocal learning environment where it is clear instructors are learning from them just as they learn from the instructors; many experience this kind of reciprocity with the young people in their programs.

We examined professional development programs, trainings and fellowship opportunities within our own university that seem congruent with the pursuit of expertise, that focused intentionally on the inclusion of scientific, technical and practical knowledge, and that participants described as personally and professionally transformative. Examples are illustrated in the three cases that follow with an emphasis on the attributes of learning experiences that promote practical wisdom and judgment. Following the examples the shared features of these three models will be discussed.

Youth Development Leadership M.Ed. Program

This interdisciplinary professional graduate degree program is designed to promote leadership for the field and within organizations and to infuse expertise and scholarship into the practice of experienced youth workers. Each year 10–20 graduate students form a Youth Development Leadership (YDL) cohort to pursue a 30-credit M.Ed. program comprised of four core courses in education, self-designed seminars and a field experience plus ten elective credits taken anywhere in the university. The graduate studies are intentionally combined with full or part time work in the field thus establishing the cycle of doing, inquiring, applying and critically reflecting, an approach that often parallels their work with young people. The program opens doors to the career potential and possibilities in youth work and can lead to new roles such as researcher, scholar, teacher and policy analyst.

The YDL Program invites experienced youth workers into a two-year program of work and study with an emphasis on integrating and applying: (1) theory, concepts and knowledge; (2) skill building; (3) critical inquiry and reflective practice; (4) action research; and (5) peer learning strategies (Stein et al., 2005). It is a "high touch" program where the give and take with faculty and peers in seminars and small classes allows practitioners to argue and parse out options to problems and dilemmas of all sorts. Faculty advisors familiar with the university and the metropolitan community become mentors, coaches and "systems guides" as practitioners experiment with new roles and ideas. Many youth workers choose an international work experience for their field experience and faculty work to help make these placements possible. These international experiences enrich the cohorts by exposing them to the dramatically different contexts of youth work in other nations.

Ongoing contact after graduation allows the program to follow the career paths of graduates who are now directors of community centers and youth agencies, principals of schools, candidates for public office, doctoral students at leading universities, leaders in informal learning at places like the National Science Foundation, within the museum learning community, in community education and the Beacons movement as well as within the settlement house movement in a major city. Students frequently comment on how acquiring the language and theory of youth development empowers them and increases their value to colleagues.

> The language has had an impact on me. When you are in a clinical field you use a clinical language and that language revolves around fixing people ... When you're in the youth development field, I could hear the language here was that of development which certainly gave me a new sense of what working with youth is all about.
>
> (Madzey-Akale, 1996, p.15)

An article describing the YDL Program (Stein et al., 2005) quotes former students on the value of having practical and intellectual colleagues and on the changes in the principles and beliefs that now shape their practice. Two graduates expressed it this way:

> YDL took me to a new level of consciousness of humanity. I am a new person because of this experience: more grateful, more connected, more focused ... The relationships I formed ... confirmed the essence of a youth worker and what it entails: a passion for respect, recognition and relevance of youth.
>
> (p. 319)

> As a youth development leader, I have a responsibility now, a moral obligation, to use the knowledge and skills gained through this program to advocate for the creation of organizations, institutions, and policies that create a healthy atmosphere for today's youth. This I am committed to. I believe I have arrived at my destination.
>
> (p. 320)

After School Matters Practitioner Fellowship

The second example, the After School Matters Practitioner Fellowship is a professional development and leadership initiative for mid-career professionals designed to inform program quality and improve practice through reflection and inquiry. Writing and action research are central to this model, which is designed to promote reflective practice, critical inquiry, practice wisdom and field building for a small cohort (10–12) of practicing youth workers. The fellowship is supported by a partnership that includes the National Writing

Project, a local nonprofit agency, and the National Institute on Out-of-School Time (NIOST). Writing is a tool for reflection and the means for turning an action research project into a publishable article which contributes scholarship for the field. The fellows meet for half a day, 15 times over the year in addition to a writing retreat and concluding Public Roundtable. The Twin Cities Afterschool Matters Fellowship (Minneapolis) is co-facilitated by an experienced writing teacher and an experienced local youth worker. At each meeting they write, share writings, respond to the writings of colleagues, and study exemplary examples of inquiry and reflection by scholars. They practice writing assignments and plan a final project of action research based on their own observations, surveys, interviews or other methods within their organization or circle of colleagues. The fellowship explores current theory and literature of reflective practice and critical inquiry in youth work; moreover, it immerses youth workers in the methodology of practitioner research and creates a supportive intellectual community in which the fellows raise and explore their own questions to better serve the people in their programs and communities.

The remarkable aspects of this learning experience are the quality and character of the reflections stimulated by a community of learners and the power of the message to "write to learn what you have to say." The fellows completed some type of action research project and wrote final papers, some of which may be submitted articles for professional journals. The fellows moved beyond their early narrative and descriptive writing to reflective, analytical essays that offered helpful insights into their own practice as well as the practices within their agency. At the end of the fellowship, the fellows articulated the importance of taking time for critical inquiry and reflection and described how the action research and writing led them to a deeper understanding of the complexity of their practice (Walker, 2010). As one fellow wrote:

> By actively engaging in reflective practice and intentionally changing my work as a result of my inquiry stance, I become a knowledge maker. Through this Fellowship my practice improved not because I spent hours reading journal articles and attending workshops, but because I created knowledge directly from my reflections and experiences as a practitioner.
>
> (Minnesota Writing Project & University of Minnesota Extension Center for Youth Development, 2010, p.13)

Deliberate Practice Matters

The University of Minnesota's Youth Work Institute has developed a training program, Deliberate Practice Matters, to cultivate deliberate practice that uses the dilemma scenarios from Larson and Walker's (2010) research. This 18-hour course is available for non-credit or with the option for graduate credit if university tuition is paid. It can be taken as a class or offered on contract for organizational staff at their location. Through experiential activities like collective deliberation of case studies, Socratic dialogue, and mind-mapping of dilemmas, the curriculum hones participants' skills in attending to the complexity of real world practice, and guides them in developing the capacity to address diverse considerations while keeping youth at the center. The dilemmas at the core of the curriculum, like the introductory dilemma at the beginning of this chapter, reinforce critical thinking, creative problem solving and judgment as well as analysis of context, principles of practice and ethical reasoning.

Discussion and analysis of dilemma-based cases can be a useful component of youth work training (Banks & Nohr, 2003). In other fields of practice—education, business, medicine—collective discussions of challenging cases are often used to help trainees understand the real world complexities of practice. Dilemma-based cases might help practitioners think critically about and cope with the situated and complex nature of their work. In the real world of daily practice, decision and actions are typically made "in flight." They are more immediate than deliberative. It can be helpful to practice "sizing up" a situation and developing an appropriate response or plan of action. Deliberation is a way to explore possibilities, consequences, tradeoffs, and it is enhanced by multiple interpretations and perspectives. Returning to those dilemmas, practitioner expertise involves the ability to appraise the diverse problems and situations encountered in one's field, the thoughtful deliberation of the merits of differing paths of action, and the capacity for strategic and practical skills to respond to these situations in ways that achieve the desired ends—in this case, to facilitate young people's positive development.

Pilot tests of the Deliberate Practice Matters curriculum have begun to document impact. Following the training, participants reported that when facing a dilemma they were more likely to (1) take time to reflect before responding, (2) see layers of complexity in a dilemma, (3) have options and choices for possible responses, and (4) feel confident in their response (Walker, 2008). Participants seem to value the deliberation of practice dilemmas to parse out possibilities and discuss judgment and ethical calls with a group of peers. Participants regularly bemoan the infrequent opportunities available to take time to reflect and think about how to respond to the bigger picture and how such opportunities help youth workers to work with more of an open mind and to ask more questions to find out more about a given situation. In an end of session evaluation, one participant wrote:

> This is a very proactive approach to youth development! Scenarios were real, relevant and sticky – PERFECT! We were able to really open up and use each other and what we commonly encounter in our work as resources. Information was relevant and reflecting on others' stories has helped me feel more confident in the decisions I make as a youth worker.
>
> (Walker, 2008, p. 3)

Shared Features

These three cases have several important features in common. First, they cultivate reflective practice as a group, collective or cohort, working together to inquire and process issues. While the words *reflective practice* can suggest some solitary activity or private meditation, it is exceptionally powerful as a collective experience. Whether the group forms for two years or six weeks, the process of working together and offering mutual support seems to be a critical factor in making the learning experience relevant for many of the learners. Second, using real world practice dilemmas or cases from divergent perspectives and value stances provides practice in dialogue and youth involvement while applying professional judgment and practical wisdom that transcend routine application of established rules, procedures or mechanical skills. The field needs professional development that accounts for the complex reality and artistry of everyday youth work practice. Third, the development of practitioner expertise takes time and sustained practice. Each example creates forums for dialogue, debate and conversation that encourage participants to explore research, their own assumptions, and the implications of their decisions on their daily practice. Too often youth workers are not afforded the time and support for this kind of critical reflection. Finally, two of the cases used writing as an effective tool that pushed practitioners to articulate their thoughts and ideas, share the writing with others, and then reflect critically on what was written and one used true stories collected through research. Like writing, being articulate in the language of one's field is essential for expertise because it allows one full rein to say what they know and think. The writing plus the ability to use the language of the field reinforces the idea that practitioner voice and wisdom is as important as the subject matter knowledge and practical skills of the worker. It is summarized by the fellow's comment cited earlier about becoming a knowledge maker.

This review of education, training and professional development that support the development of expertise falls short in two important areas. One is the adoption of guiding principles and an ethical stance that works across allied fields. While youth work has not adopted such a stance nationally (or even locally for the most part), the issue is important because such principles and value statements give guidance for the contextual, nuanced thinking and deciding required of one with expertise. Another is the youth rights issue particularly when the young people are in their teen years and close to assuming adult rights and needs. Here the tough practice issues and dilemmas are grounded not just to age but in values and context, precisely those arenas that require responsive judgment and expertise.

Tensions Associated with the Pursuit of Expertise

This chapter is not an argument to eliminate standards and competencies nor is it intended to be critical of the increasing exposure youth workers have to relevant research and the potential utility of evidence-based practice. Rather, it is a plea not to disregard *phronesis*, the practical wisdom and judgment essential for practitioner expertise, on the grounds that it is not easy to define, not readily amenable to measurement and not convenient to embrace in educational and training environments increasingly pushed to minimize time commitments and personal contact. The many tensions that exist in the emerging field of youth work or youth development are real and they affect receptivity to a concept like practitioner expertise. Models for professionalization of the field are still linked to early childhood providers, childcare workers, school teachers and social workers. These models assume that licensed, credentialed, certified, tested and graded equals qualified. Likewise, models for accountability, driven by both public and private funders, are largely based on measureable outcomes which lean disproportionately toward measuring what happens to individual young people. The model for learning across the age span remains for many the curriculum and instruction model of the school. Finally, the models for practice are increasingly equated with program delivery, an approach that defines and describes youth workers more like instrumental agents of organizations and curriculum rather than professionals with agency to create, engage and work alongside young people to achieve mutually established goals and outcomes.

Given the lively debates about the future of the field, it's a good time to be talking about a wide range of topics and issues that matter significantly to practitioners. One is the idea of practitioner expertise. Another is the proposition that high quality youth work can be a proxy for measureable youth outcomes. Issues of cultural context, different ways of knowing, and different world views held by communities are being raised across the country and around the globe. The youth development field—youth work included—often refers to its interdisciplinary nature and its roots in voluntary participation, volunteer leadership, experiential pedagogy and community-based learning. The field needs to create a new 21st-century model for professionalization that honors its interdisciplinary roots, champions its participatory pedagogy, embraces the rights, engagement, passion, voice and leadership of young people, is open to different knowledge and ways of knowing, and values the interconnection of scientific knowledge, technical skills and practical wisdom.

References

Astroth, K. A., Garza, P., & Taylor, B. (2004). Getting down to business: Defining competencies for entry-level youth workers. In P. Garza, L. M. Borden, & K. A. Astroth (Eds.), *New directions for youth development: Professional development for youth workers* (pp. 25–37). San Francisco, CA: Jossey-Bass.

Baizerman, M. (2009). Deepening understanding of managing evaluation. In D. W. Compton & M. Baizerman (Eds.), *New directions for evaluation: Managing program evaluation: Towards explicating a professional practice* (pp. 87–98). San Francisco, CA: Jossey-Bass.

Banks, S., & Nohr, K. (2003). *Teaching practical ethics for the social professions*. Copenhagen, Denmark: FESET.

Blank, J. (2007). Reflective practices in arts education: A review essay. *International Journal of Education & the Arts, 8.* Retrieved September 30, 2010, from http://www.ijea.org /v8r5.

Ericsson, K. A., Charness, N., Feltovich, P. J., & Hoffman, R. R. (Eds.). (2006). *Cambridge handbook of expertise and expert performance: Its development, organization and content.* Cambridge, UK: Cambridge University Press.

Eisner, E. W. (2002). From episteme to phronesis to artistry in the study and improvement of teaching. *Teaching and Teacher Education, 18,* 375–385.

Flyvbjerg, B. (2001). *Making social science matter: Why social inquiry fails and how it can succeed again.* Cambridge, UK: Cambridge University Press.

Fook, J., Ryan, M., & Hawkins, L. (2000) *Professional expertise: Practice, theory and education for working in uncertainty.* London, UK: Whiting and Birch.

Larson, R. W., Rickman, A. N., Gibbons, C. M., & Walker, K. C. (2009). Practitioner expertise: Creating quality within the daily tumble of events in youth settings. In N. Yohalem, R. C. Granger, & K. J. Pittman (Eds.), *New directions for youth development: Defining and measuring quality in youth programs and classrooms* (pp. 71–88). San Francisco, CA: Jossey-Bass.

Larson, R., & Walker, K. (2010). Dilemmas of practice: Challenges to program quality encountered by youth program leaders. *American Journal of Community Psychology, 45,* 338–349.

Levin, B. B. (1995). Using the case method in teacher education: The role of discussion and experience in teachers' thinking about cases. *Teaching & Teacher Education, 11,* 64–79.

Madzey-Akale, J. (1996). *Master of Education Youth Development Leadership Program: Program evaluation.* Minneapolis: University of Minnesota, Extension Center for Youth Development.

Minnesota Writing Project & University of Minnesota Extension Center for Youth Development. (2010, September). Final Report for the Twin Cities Afterschool Matters Fellowship 2009–10. Minneapolis: Author.

Ross, K., Shafer, J. L., & Klein, G. (2006). Professional judgments and "naturalistic decision making." In K. A. Ericsson, N. Charness, P. J. Feltovich, & R. R. Hoffman (Eds.), *Cambridge handbook of expertise and expert performance: Its development, organization and content* (pp. 403–419). Cambridge, UK: Cambridge University Press.

Schon, D. A. (1983). *The reflective practitioner: How professionals think in action.* New York: Basic Books.

Smith, M. K. (1996). Competence and competency. Retrieved February 1, 2010, from http://www.infed.org/biblio/b-comp.htm.

Starr, B., Yohalem, N., & Gannett, E. (2009, October). Youth work core competencies: A review of existing frameworks and purposes. Seattle: School's Out Washington & Next Generation Youth Work Coalition. Retrieved October 25, 2010, from http://www.nextgencoalition.org/files/Core Competencies Review, October 2009.pdf.

Stein, J. A., Wood, E., Walker, J. A., Kimball, E. M., Outley, C. W., & Baizerman, M. (2005). The youth development leadership experience: Transformative, reflective education for youthwork practitioners. *Child and Youth Care Forum, 34,* 303–325.

Sternberg, R. J., Forsythe, G. B., Hedlund, J., Horvath, J. A., Wagner, R. K., Williams, W. M., Snook, S. A., & Grigorenko, E. (2000). *Practical intelligence in everyday life.* New York: Cambridge University Press.

Walker, J. (2003). The essential youth worker. In F. A. Villarruel, D. F. Perkins, L. M. Borden, & J. G. Keith (Eds.), *Community youth development: Programs, policies, and practices* (pp. 373–393). Thousand Oaks, CA: Sage.

Walker, K. (2008, Fall). *Deliberate practice matters in youth work: Pilot evaluation.* Minneapolis: University of Minnesota, Extension Center for Youth Development.

Walker, K. (2010, August). National afterschool matters practitioner fellowship program: A formative evaluation of the Minnesota 2009–10 fellowship. Minneapolis: University of Minnesota, Extension Center for Youth Development.

Walker, K., & Larson, R. (2011). *Youth worker reasoning about dilemmas encountered in practice: Expert-novice differences.* Manuscript submitted for publication.

5

YOUTH WORK AND THE EDUCATION OF PROFESSIONAL PRACTITIONERS IN AUSTRALIA

Judith Bessant

What is youth work in Australia? At first glance this question appears to be relatively straightforward. Yet, asking a basic question such as that and providing answers to such apparently simple questions is not straightforward. In this case, as with so many other aspects of the social and community services sector, there is complexity everywhere, evident, for example, if we survey the kinds of community-based, non-government organizations (NGOs) where youth workers are employed. There are tens of thousands of agencies across Australia where youth workers are employed. They offer a large array of services that include: child welfare and child protection, employment services, housing services, youth justice, supported accommodation for people with a disability, legal services, education, probation services, health services (including drug and alcohol), individual and family relationship counseling, and community activities, information and referral services. Added to this we should note that the NGOs offering these services are shadowed by services provided by statutory agencies managed and funded by national, state and local governments. There is also a smaller burgeoning quasi-private sector offering youth services of various kinds. While there is a case for distinguishing between statutory agencies and NGOs, Australian governments at all levels have moved over the last three decades to formalize partnerships with NGOs. The result is that many NGOs have become front-line government agencies fully funded by, and accountable to governments. Finally, in many cases state-run agencies, like the NGOs, employ paid and fully qualified youth workers as well as volunteer and/or untrained youth workers.

Apart from this organizational complexity, Australian youth workers are employed in an array of positions involving different kinds of practice skills. This complexity is evident if we look at the brief of a union like the Australian

Services Union (ASU), which provides industrial protection for social and community service workers (SACS) including youth workers, welfare officers, social workers, counselors and child care workers. The ASU recognizes that youth workers may work in services like youth refuges, women's refuges, family support services, disability services, community legal centers, employment and training services, Aboriginal organizations, community or neighborhood centers, family day care centers, community transport services, home and community care services, environmental organizations, or migrant or ethnic services and aid agencies. The specific job positions youth workers are employed are as varied as: Advocate Case Manager or Caseworker, Professional Social Worker, Community Development Worker, Recreation Worker, Community Educator, Counselor, Disability Support Worker, Family Support Worker, Family Therapist, Social Educator, Group Worker, Indigenous Child Protection Worker, Vocational Educator, or Youth Worker.

Australian youth work exhibits many of the features that can typically be found in Australia's human service sector. Like welfare officers, child care workers, community workers and social workers, youth workers are employed in everything from very large bureaucratic agencies to quite small one or two person units. They may be employed on a paid or volunteer basis. They also have various education, training and skill levels: some may have no formal qualifications, while others have postgraduate qualifications. Youth work in Australia currently is subject neither to specific, legally mandated professional requirements regarding skill or education levels nor to a national professional body specifying that people employed as youth workers must possess a certain level of prescribed education or training. Perhaps the only thing that can be said with any confidence is that in Australia youth workers work predominantly with young people ages 12 to 25.

This chapter attempts to explain the inchoate character of contemporary youth work by sketching its historical trajectory. In doing so, I suggest that it is not possible to produce a value-free history. What I am arguing for is one that does more than rely on the testimony of the more powerful historical actors at the expense of the less powerful whose voices and experiences have tended to be written out of many accounts of our past. An inclusive view of history would inform how we can best characterize current youth work, especially the quality of education provided, and begin to explore a very big question: what might constitute "good" youth work education?

Australian Youth Work: A Brief Historical Overview

Child Saving

Any historical account of Australian youth work will point to a wide range of styles of practice and intervention. Having said that, what is clear is that it's a history that can be best described as a major "governmental" project (Foucault 1973, 1982, 1991; Garland 1992). By that I refer to the numerous and diverse ways modern states, NGOs (and associated institutions like hospitals, schools and clinics) along with a range of human service professions, and the intellectually-trained, have developed and used a range of disciplinary knowledge (e.g., psychology, sociology, criminology, statistics, clinical science) as well as practices (e.g., teaching, counseling, budget advice, etc.) to manage people and to have people manage themselves. The idea of governmentality does not however imply that it all works in a smooth and integrated way. Indeed, Foucault and writers influenced by him (Dean, 1994) have pointed to the often fragmentary, incoherent and even contradictory array of techniques and interests operating in a project that Foucault (1991) called the "objectification of subjects." This typification can be applied to youth work and most of the human service sector originating in the late eighteenth and early nineteenth centuries and the project of "child-saving" (Garland, 1992).

Child-saving is one part of the larger and more complex history both of childhood (Ariès, 1973) and of adolescence (Kett, 1977). A primary and explicit interest of "child savers" was to ensure that children and young people had a childhood. While that was promoted as a positive, it entailed that children and young people develop within a *habitus* that engendered their subordination, dependency and vulnerability. In that context, childhood and adolescence were defined in reference to characteristics antithetical to the essential characteristics of adulthood like autonomy, rationality or responsibility to say nothing of such activities as working, having sex, gambling, drinking or smoking. The child savers moved to ensure that children be protected from these adult activities and dispositions. They also worked to design new institutional practices and spaces that helped reshape the lived experience and identity of children and young people. In short, a key feature of the child movement was to extend the infantilization of children and young people by representing and rendering dependent, cohorts of young people who historically had been relatively independent and competent. Motivated by a Christian ethos, philanthropic activists produced a series of legislative reforms to prevent child abuse, child labor and sexual exploitation and establish exclusions zones in which children could be safely housed and their childhood protected. It was a move that also occurred in places like Australia and the United Kingdom, which saw a flow of legal and policy innovations and the establishment of mass compulsory primary education, Children's Courts and child protection systems. These were accompanied by institutionalized interventions organized through the activities of volunteers and later by professionals who moved into the homes and on to the streets of working-class children. The interest was to help by better managing their lives, courtesy of an increasing network of religious, community and sport clubs (Chinn, 2008). The child savers did much to create and popularize the modern ethos and idiom of paternalism, which claimed then, and continues to claim, the ability to identify the "best interests" of the child or young person. It was argued that this could be achieved, in part, by locating childhood and adolescence in a trajectory of human development said to occur in stages that begins in infancy and proceeds to childhood.

This historical narrative spoke of stages which paralleled the already well-established account of social development constructed by earlier theorists of civil society (e.g., Comte's law of three stages), which played an important role in the development of scientific racism. In these human development stories, each person recapitulated the larger history of civilized society from primitivism to mature rationality. This provided a basis for later scientific accounts by psychologists like Piaget, Kohlberg and Erickson in the twentieth century of the appropriate age-based stages of development of the child's moral, psychological, social or cognitive abilities. Well into the 1970s, the dominant interpretative framework used in histories of Australian child and youth welfare viewed the motives and the accomplishments of the child savers and welfare policy makers as naturally altruistic and beneficial. By the 1980s this approach to child welfare was subjected to serious critique (van Krieken, 1992). In Australia, revisionists like Roe (1983), Kennedy (1989) and Watts (1987) drew on a growing body of international scholarship with neo-Marxist (Offe, 1984), feminist (Wilson, 1977) and/or Foucauldian provenances (Dean, 1994; Foucault, 1973; Greenblatt, 1999). The result was a body of scholarship that produced a new picture of youth welfare. Much was made, for example, of the discovery of the systematic practice of removing children deemed to be neglected, illegitimate, orphaned or "half-caste" from their families. That revisionism in turn provoked a strong reaction from defenders of the policies and practices of child welfare. For revisionists like Howson (1999), for example, understanding the removal of children, and specifically indigenous children, was best done by seeing it as a case of the state "doing the right thing" by bringing Aboriginal people into the modern age. The same argument was made for intervention into the lives of the poor. The history of child welfare/protection soon became part of the "culture wars."

Australia's Colonial Legacy

Given the colonial pattern of modern Anglo Australian history, it is not surprising to discover that the history of Australian youth work points to a significant British legacy, which has more or less shaped Australian youth work from the mid-nineteenth century into the present. Early forms of youth work involved what some historians (Roe, 1983; van Krieken, 1991a, b) describe as a class-based project driven by "respectable fears" about "social degeneration" and social order with an interest in pacifying the urban poor. As mentioned earlier, child saving was part of a larger movement dedicated to solving new social problems like delinquency denoted in Australian terms as "larrikinism" (van

Krieken, 1991a, b). Classic expressions of the importation of British models included the Sunday School movement, the YMCA and its network of sporting facilities or the spread of the Boy Scout movement. The continuing influence of the British connection was signified in 1941 by the Commonwealth government's passage of the National Fitness Act and in the role of first generation youth work educators who offered to staff the youth work courses. This kind of youth work emphasized various styles of organized group work, a strong ethos of physical health, fitness and educational programs designed to secure the objectives of racial hygiene. It rested on a presumption that young people, and particularly young men, needed to be kept occupied, off the streets and on the straight and narrow. In a second wave, youth work for girls was brought into the fold with the establishment of Christian-based organizations like the Girl Guides, or the YWCA. Youth work of this kind had its origins in Britain (Hamilton-Smith & Brownell, 1973).

At this point it is worth noting that like most indigenous cultural practices, indeed entire populations, the rich array of local Aboriginal practices used to raise children and young people were seriously damaged. In their place we saw the forced removal of Aboriginal children from their families and communities and their placement in homes and missionaries. It was not until recently that we saw a revival of local Aboriginal ways of working with young people and a move to incorporate them into mainstream youth work practice (Collard & Palmer, 2006; Palmer, 2006). Until the 1970s, most youth work in Australia was done by untrained volunteers, many with Christian affiliations. Much of that work emphasized organizing and socializing young people through structured activities that included games and organized leisure. The explicit interest was in the governance of young people, and securing what was seen as the precarious transition from adolescence to adulthood, a phase in the life cycle generally recognized as particularly risky. For much of the twentieth century following G. Stanley Hall's (1905) intervention, modern adolescence was understood scientifically as a time of storm and stress, a troubled, troublesome and high-risk stage in the human life-course that required very close monitoring. Hall's work on modern adolescence is a salutary reminder of how youth work in Australia has been indebted to British ideas, ways of imagining youth and institutional forms. Having said that, it is also important to note how the theoretical vocabulary and frames produced by American sociologists, psychologists and criminologists writing on "youth culture," delinquency, gangs and youth development, were also very influential (Cloward & Ohlin, 1960; Cohen, 1955; Parsons, 1964).

Australia's Recent Policy and Political Context

The 1970s was a watershed for Australia as it was for many other Western nations. In that decade many hitherto "settled" patterns of cultural, economic, political and social development began to be challenged and undone. Australian political commentator, Paul Kelly (1994), used the term the "Australian settlement" to describe a policy consensus that lasted from 1901 to the mid-1970s characterized by a commitment to "White Australia," a regulated economy, full employment, industrial regulation and "cultural protection." All these were gradually undone from the 1970s as Australia, like other developed countries, saw the resurgence of economic liberalism, a shift away from secondary industry and towards a service economy while also increasing investment in education (Bessant, 2008).

The function of welfare, which had been valorized as a source of social cohesion in the 1960s, was challenged in the 1970s and 1980s by Marxist (Blackburn, 1972) and feminist (Orloff & Skocpol, 1984) critiques of "social control," which came to be understood as techniques for reproducing systemic social oppression. Other critiques saw human service work in its various guises as contradictions of the welfare state that worked to prevent people who were oppressed becoming aware of their subjugation (Habermas, 1974). By the 1990s Foucauldian style critiques of governance (Fraser, 1997; Lemke, 2001) also came to the fore.

On the ground, the community services sector struggled to cope with an increasingly diverse and often incoherent agenda characterized by an excess of policy objectives designed to punish "welfare dependency," while at the same time promote human rights, identify and address risk, advance empowerment of the disadvantaged, remedy social exclusion, promote strong communities, invest in "social capital" while also being effective and accountable to governments. Youth work in the field of human services entails a variety of different interests and practices; it's a highly contested field characterized by paradox and contradiction between "control *and* cure" or "regulation *and* emancipation."

At the same time, universities had become sites of debates and intellectual exchange. By the 1980s some youth work education was being located in universities which opened the possibility it would entail more critical reflection. Advocates for a more democratic approach drew on the broader intellectual movement involving neo-Marxists, feminists and, from the mid-1980s on, post-structuralists who challenged traditional youth work theory and practice by highlighting the politics and power relations embedded in modes of regulation that characterized traditional forms of youth work. While this was happening in some quarters, other youth workers went in the opposite direction, by continuing to promote an overtly anti-intellectual sentiment by arguing that there was no need to educate practitioners by exposing them to ideas and various academic disciplines. It was not uncommon, for example, to hear claims that education was indulgent and pretentious and that good intentions, altruism, experience and a commitment to young people were all that was needed.

Australian Youth Work Today

Contemporary Australian youth work now faces a serious crisis. Certain decisions and actions are currently being made that run the risk of having a major negative impact on youth work practice and education. It's a crisis that relates to the issue of identity, power and the status of youth work as a profession. What would help defend youth work is clarity about its professional identity. That, in conjunction with the establishment of a professional association and a more regulated sector, will go some way towards securing the future for youth work practice and youth work education. Without the protection of a healthy professional association that is prepared to defend decent wages and conditions and educational standards, the future will not be as strong as it could be.

Having acknowledged that, there are a few hindrances to achieving clarity about youth work identity, which is an essential precondition for the development of a professional association. To begin, there is no solid body of academic research or professional literature in Australia that offers an agreed-on description of youth work. This, in part, may reflect the fact that youth workers are employed in a diverse range of organizations and deploy a wide array of practice modes (from community development, counseling, outreach, advocacy, case management to group work). It reflects too the fact that practicing youth workers draw on a wide range of academic disciplines like sociology, psychology, criminology, education, organizational studies, economics and youth studies, to say nothing of a larger body of unexamined and often tacit religious interests, and ethical traditions along with any number of social prejudices about young people. It also reflects the fact that on the current best evidence most practicing youth workers do not have formal youth work qualifications (Chew, 1995). This feature is an impediment to developing a consensus about its identity and status as a profession.

There is also no national or state-level legislative framework that regulates entry into youth work at either the national or sub-national level in the ways that legislation currently regulates entry into other relevant professional groups like teachers, psychologists and nurses. For this reason also there is value in establishing a national network of state- and territory-based professional association/s or institute/s that set practice and educational standards and which are actively involved in accrediting professional education programs. (While there are some fledgling state-level professional bodies, Australia does not have a national body with such a brief). This absence is frequently explained by reference to the disparate, over-worked, under-resourced and un-credentialed character of the youth sector (Bessant, 2004; Sercombe, 1997). There is not an agreed on structure for identifying the ethical frameworks that might be used to describe good youth work practice. While various state-level peak bodies have worked to develop codes of practice for youth workers, what resulted were statements about doing good that were based on compositions of incompatible philosophical traditions. Given all this, it is not surprising to find that the current education and training of youth workers in Australia is similarly diverse.

Youth Work Education or Job Training

In Australia, universities and Tertiary and Further Education (TAFE) colleges provide most youth work specific education and training. There are currently higher education youth work specific bachelor degrees in four universities. There are also many TAFE sector certificates, diplomas and advanced diplomas in youth work. While it sounds like a rich educational basis, the future provision of youth work education and training is highly volatile. There is evidence of increasing numbers of applicants enrolling in university-based youth work degrees which typically build on a foundation of social science and arts subjects along with youth work specific subjects and some workplace based supervised training or fieldwork. Entry into the youth work field is also possible for graduates in social work, community development, psychology, or generalist social science degrees. There is also evidence that the failure to adequately fund Australia's universities by successive national governments combined with economic liberal thinking is resulting in closure of programs that are small and deemed to be uncompetitive.

The less expensive and more instrumentally oriented competency-based frameworks used in TAFE are seen as an attractive option for those interested in cutting costs. This, in conjunction with the retractions of such offerings in higher education, highlights how the future of youth work education is at risk. More generally, the development of TAFE-based job training has taken place in the context of a general push for more instrumental education oriented towards specific, narrow skills said to be necessary for particular components of youth work practice. It's also worth considering this in the context of recent government policy aimed at creating a seamless dual sector that connects higher education (university) with TAFE. It's a context in which we have seen limited debate about the value of education. It's a development that has seen an almost unquestioning acceptance of a utilitarian approach to education and that has produced a pedagogy of force-feeding of nationalized standards determined by market demands as opposed to the more humanistic, active learning, Socratic and not-for-profit approach (Bills, 2009; Grubb & Lazerson, 2004; Nussbaum, 2010). In short, the risk is that youth work education will become job training in the narrow behaviorist sense of the word as opposed to a more humanistic approach to practitioner education. Added to this is the potential stratifying effect of such vocational training. In other words, job training of the kind that characterizes the competency-based approach runs the risk of reproducing if not exacerbating socio-economic and educational inequalities. As Bills explains (2009), analysts have been concerned about disproportionate placement of minority groups and students from lower socio-economic marginalized groups in such lower status vocational tracks. This is not a new issue; rather it has been a long standing assumption that lower achieving students are and ought to be counseled into vocational training track rather than higher education which conflicts with the ideals of education for a democratic society in which all students are given opportunities for higher education (Stone, 2009). While TAFE can provide pathway to higher education and a ladder out of "constrained life chances," the question is, particularly given the prevailing fiscal context whether the former will replace the later.

All this is reason for concern for those with an interest in youth work becoming a fully fledged profession, characterized by decent wages and conditions, oriented to high standards of practice, and reliant on well-designed university-based educational offerings. The lack of a clear professional-occupational identity is one problem. The absence of a professional association in the prevailing context is another, because without a professional body the job of securing and sustaining quality youth work education falls on educators. Without an accrediting body that has the power to specify basics like requisite core youth work subjects, or minimum contact hours, or the nature and duration of practicum, or staff to student ratios, or the amount to be spent per student on library resources etc, youth work education becomes an easy target for university managers on the look-out for "efficiencies." It is to the educational aspects of the current crisis facing youth work that I now turn.

Competency Framework

Any shift from university-based education to TAFE training reliant on a competency model of training is not likely to enable the kind of valuable educational experience leading to the intellectual and practical capacities typical of highly effective youth professionals. While I cannot offer a comprehensive or critical analysis of the competency framework here, I can briefly indicate some of the limitations with competency-based training. (For a more comprehensive critical reflection see Edwards & Nicoll, 2006; Grant, 1999; Iverson, Gergen, & Fairbanks, 2005; Jordan & Powell, 2007; Lum 2004.)

The competency framework adopted by the Australian TAFE system in the early 1980s involves training primarily informed by a "technical rational" interest. Habermas (1971) identified the human interests that inform human action, and in doing so he asked what kinds of knowledge we seek when we act with various intentionalities. In specifying his analytic theory of human and knowledge constitutive interests, Habermas identified three kinds of knowledge and their respective constitutive interests. He suggested that human engagement is oriented towards achieving one of the following interests, i.e., a technical interest vested in domination and control; a practical interest in understanding; and an emancipatory interest in achieving some form of freedom or emancipation. In turn each of these interests has an elective affinity with a particular style or mode of knowledge. Habermas' analytic can be seen schematically in Table 5.1.

If we apply this typology to youth work, the *technical interest* involves practitioners seeing and treating young people as *objects* to be managed, dominated or controlled. While this might sound like a negative interest, that is not always the case. It is worth remembering that without some interest in domination and control we could not be self-preserving. At a most basic level, we would not, for example, be able to work with young people in ways that require organization and administration. Having said that, the question remains as to how such an interest is expressed and whether its pursuit is in the interest of the young person. *Practical interest* is critical for appreciating the human and social dimensions of practice. Youth work that is informed by a practical interest entails constructing shared meanings based on ethical ideas about, for example, why we act in particular ways towards young people. Outcomes of this interest can be seen in the establishment of styles of interaction, rituals and ethical ideas. In these ways we can give effect to a life lived through ideas of what is good. The final interest Habermas (1971) identifies is *emancipatory interest*. This entails work oriented towards freeing young people and youth workers from deceptions, delusions, or social constraints that inhibit their freedom. A youth worker with an emancipatory interest may, for example, work in ways that identify age-based prejudice through critical reflective practice and act to have that recognized and challenged (Emslie, 2009). While we may have an orientation toward one particular interest, it is common for us to operate with more than one interest in mind. Indeed it is even possible to draw on all three within the one activity or project.

Habermas' (1971) model is useful because it helps identify the primarily technical interest that informs a lot of vocational competency-based training and in doing so points to the dangers and limitations of an instrumentalist approach to practice. Competency-based training emphasizes efficiency, replicability and simplicity, the hallmarks of the technical. It is used to certify fitness to practice in measurable, behaviorist and detailed ways. The specification of the relevant competencies is derived from first identifying and then analyzing activities

TABLE 5.1 Habermas' Analytic Framework

Types of Human Interest	Kinds of Knowledge	Research methodologies
Technical > Calculative predictions	Instrumental > causality	Positivism, empirical methodology
Practical > Interpreting and understanding	Practical understanding	Hermeneutic methods
Emancipatory > Critique and liberation	Emancipation > reflective	Critical social theory/ science

assumed to be essentially technical into sub-sets of skills and behaviors said to constitute a given job performance. It is a model that assumes a certain technical capacity associated with repetitive, routine, replicable activities based on following a set of instructions to achieve a predetermined objective. The identification of competencies also works on the principle that there are minimal requirements or standards determined by governments and employers rather than by the professional practitioners themselves based on complex interpretation and judgment that change according to the context. Checklists are common forms of assessment tools, and are popular because they offer a simple, quick and "objective" way of determining whether the objective has been achieved. Assessment of a set of competencies is typically achieved by assessing a given set of desirable behaviors using a binary criterion, i.e., competent or not competent.

While competency training plays a useful role in all professional education, whether it is designed to prepare medical practitioners, carpenters or youth workers, it is not enough on its own. TAFE competency-based training offers an excellent pathway to university education where that initial training is then built on and extended by programs informed by graduate attributes. Competency-based training can produce highly proficient technicians possessing both novice and beginning level capacities who are able to follow instructions. It does not do so well if we are looking for reflexive and critical professionals able to decide when rules need to be adapted or broken (Dreyfus & Dreyfus, 1986).

Youth work in common with other forms of modern human service work, requires the capacity to make good judgments, to design and engage in complex and often diverse social interventions. It is multi-faceted, dynamic, messy, and unpredictable work that requires expertise that cannot be rote learned by following rules or instructions. It is also work that is not amenable to being divided up into distinct subsets of prescriptive behaviors. While it is critical for practitioners to be able to perform certain skills like making referrals or using a psychometric instrument to determine levels of risks, this is not enough for good professional practice. This is because amongst other things, the skills and knowledge that make up good practice cannot be separated from the ideas, knowledge and interest that inform them. As youth workers themselves testify, their practice cannot be broken down into separate elements that can be detached from context (Bessant, 2009; Foundation for Young Australians, 2010) Youth work students need to be exposed to all the various types of knowledge. They need to recognize the value of the various interests that inform their work and the work of others, as well as the different kinds of research drawing respectively on the empirico-positive, hermeneutic and critical traditions. This matters if we are interested in reflective practice.

If competencies have a beginning role to play, but do not on their own offer a secure enough framework, what might we aim for when designing a good education? I suggest that what is required is an enlarged sense of professional capabilities understood as the abilities a capable, reflective professional youth worker will demonstrate. This is the challenge of good university youth work education.

Youth Work Education in the University

The task of educators and the curriculum needs to be understood as equipping people to be professional. This entails a combination of intellectual training as well as professional development. Designing a curriculum of this kind begins with the specification of the key capabilities associated with being a youth work professional which would include the following:

- Being cognitively well-equipped to distinguish between what is true and what is not.
- Being able to mix, in an informed way, research styles, and appreciate the value of each for research with and for young people.
- An ability to engage in critical reading, listening and thinking.
- An ability to understand where key frameworks in policy, casework, politics, and economics come from.
- An understanding of the vocabulary and theoretical frameworks that have shaped Youth Work.
- An appreciation of the role and power of language.

In contemporary higher education, teachers begin by identifying graduate capabilities and then attempting to align the curriculum, learning activities, teaching activities and assessment activities with those capabilities. Typically, they include both generic capabilities as well as youth work specific attributes. It is critical for educators to be clear about graduate attributes, skills and knowledge (i.e., self-knowledge about one's own interests, dispositions and capacities, and the ability to lead a life as a professional and individual they have reason to value). There are also a range of specific technical skills and knowledge needed to equip graduate youth workers. Too often however such capabilities run the risk of ending up as little more than wish lists or bland and empty statements akin to corporate mission statements (Watson, 2009). Even with the best intentions, it is difficult to guarantee the quality learning in the context of modern universities characterized by managerialism and serious underfunding.

It is also important that students are ethically skilled and oriented to cultivate principles or virtues like prudence and courage and integrity. This would translate into capabilities like:

- Having an ethical vocabulary and the confidence and skill to use it.
- Being able to distinguish instrumental goods from ultimate goods.
- Being able to engage in phronesis which entails being adept in making good judgments generally, and in appreciating the need for case-by-case-based judgments informed by theoretical/ethical insight.

- An appreciation of a virtue ethics' framework both for themselves and for the young people they work with, and a sense of how it is applied or operationalized.
- Being reflexive and context sensitive (e.g., able to read and operate in complex social contexts).
- Able to communicate across a range of registers with a variety of people, organizations, and styles of discourse.
- Self-reflexive (e.g., able to understand their motivations/interests).

This identity of the professional reflective youth worker in turn permits the design of a youth work professional intellectual curriculum project. It provides a basis for a good youth work education. A key test in determining the quality of youth work education is whether it equips student to make good judgments in different situations about where they face tensions or contradictions. More specifically this means being able to identify the desirable "golden mean," the point between two extremes, which or what is often mistakenly described as presenting a dilemma or tension in youth work. In what follows I explain why it is a mistake to see this as a dilemma. On the one hand, we have the guardian-ship approach that emphasizes the need to protect the young person and which assumes the adult professional/carer is in a better position to know what is in the interest of a young person than does the young person herself. On the other hand, we have the libertarian or empowerment approach. The extremes of this later approach promotes the idea that young people ought to be free agents, to decide what is in their own interest and to be supported to act accordingly. A good education helps clarify the confusion that exists about this dilemma or puzzlement. The confusion refers to the way a "duty of care" is frequently mistaken for the popular idea that young people need close management given they are "inherently troublesome" or incompetent (i.e., morally, socially, phys-ically under-developed). That is, given the innately unruly character and rela-tive incompetence of young people, they cannot be trusted to know what is in their best interest and to act accordingly. Guardians, on the other hand, do. They are more knowledgeable and more experienced and know better what is in the interest of the young person more than that person himself or her-self. For this reason, adults as guardians contend that they have a duty of care to exercise their authority by making decisions for, and often without even consulting with or gaining the consent of the young person. Put differently, a tension is said to exist between a young person's right or positive freedom (i.e., freedoms to do X or expect Y) and an adult's duty of care to protect them from harm (a negative freedom). Moreover, the idea that young people have the same human rights as adults is often considered dangerous because it is said to prevent or constrain adults from performing their duty as guardians. This thinking confuses the issue because the proposition that young people ought to be accorded the same rights and the same moral consideration as adults does not imply that young people should be treated in the same way as adults. If a young person is less able, because, for example, they are physically smaller or less experienced than older people, then that point of difference places an obligation or duty of care on others to ensure the young person is supported in ways that make it possible for them to exercise their rights. This point can be clarified if, instead of a young person, we consider a person who has a chronic illness or another disability, like mental illness or quadriplegia. Because that person is not physically able to exercise his right (e.g., to make decisions about matters that affect them) does not mean his freedoms, like being able to chose to be the kind of person they value or to do what they value, should be made by someone else? People with disabilities that affect their capacities are still generally recognized to have a right to exercise freedoms because they have a moral status that derives from the fact they are a person. However, it is because they have such a right that they should not be just left to go it alone, because they can't. In other words, equal rights do not necessarily mean equal treatment. Indeed, a just and fair society is one in which young people's well-being is secured by opportunities to exercise freedoms, to make informed choices, and to be supported in achieving what they choose. It is because young people are not always able to do X or Y on their own that others, namely youth workers, have an obligation or duty of care to assist.

In short, a critical test of a good youth work education is whether it helps equip graduates to exercise good judgment about where on the continuum between the paternalistic approach typically expressed as the need to override a young person's human agency and the need to support them to make their own choice and then to have the capacity to know what kind of support they need to achieve what they chose to do or be. I am talking about an education that pays close attention to the role of age-based prejudice and that teaches reflexive and critical thinking in ways that encourage graduates to question common-sense knowledge, including scientific claims at work in their *habitus*. This means being able to tell the difference between myth and truth and, when they are one of the same, between good science and scientism. It also means being able to recognize how young people change not only in respect to what they can do and know, but also what their community permits them to do, that is what they may do. In short, a clear indicator of whether a graduate has the potential to determine the golden mean between an overly paternalistic and an overly libertarian approach can be seen in their ability to see how certain classes of persons have certain rights and obligations to display what they can do, while others, namely children and young people, regardless of their state of knowledge, are forbidden to make public use of them (Harre, 1979).

Conclusion

This chapter provided an account of youth work in Australia as it is practiced in its various forms and sites. A cursory historical overview suggested why contemporary youth work still struggles to reconcile the tensions between its commitment to a governmental project grounded in an ethos of paternalism and a commitment to a rights-based practice oriented to conceptions of freedom, well-being and a flourishing life. I argued that while the disparate character of youth work has certain strengths, it also leads to some difficulties. It has impeded the development of a strong collective professional identity. The need for a consensus around core practices and the consolidation of an agreed on knowledge base are further impediments in the way of developing such an identity, both of which are prerequisites for professionalization. In the final section of the chapter, I addressed the question of professional youth work education and the respective merits of embedding youth work education in competency-based training and capability-based higher education. In arguing against a sole reliance on competency-based training, I argued that a higher education framework is more likely to ensure that graduates achieve the requisite intellectual, ethical and practical capacities associated with being a well-grounded and highly effective professional. Amongst the graduate capabilities that constitute a good education is the ability of graduates to both recognize their own dispositions and to nourish them, as well as being able to do the same in regard to the young person with whom they are working.

References

Ariès, P. (1973). *Centuries of childhood: A social history of family life.* Harmondsworth, UK: Penguin.

Bessant, J. (2004). The Loch Ness monster and youth-work professionalism: Arguments for and against. *Youth Studies Australia, 23*, 26–33.

Bessant, J. (2008). The end of certainty: Policy regime change and Australian youth policy – 1983–2008. *Youth and Policy: The Journal of Critical Analysis, 100*, 27–40.

Bessant, J. (2009). Aristotle meets youth work: A case for virtue ethics. *Journal of Youth Studies, 4*, 423–438.

Bills, D. (2009). Vocationalism. In A. Furlong (Ed.), *Handbook of youth and young adulthood* (pp. 127–134). London: Routledge.

Blackburn, R. (1972). *Ideology in the social sciences.* Glasgow, Scotland: Fontana.

Chew, P. (1995). Report of the Minister of the training of youth workers in Victoria to the Minister Responsible for Youth Affairs, The Hon Vin Heffernan, August. Melbourne, Australia: Victorian Government.

Chinn, S. (2008). *Inventing modern adolescence: The children of immigrants in turn-of-the-century.* New York: Rutgers University Press.

Cloward, R., & Ohlin, L. (1960). *Delinquency and opportunity.* New York: Free Press.

Cohen, A. (1955). *Delinquent boys.* New York: Free Press.

Collard, L., & Palmer, D. (2006). Kura, yeye, boorda, Nyungar wangkiny gnulla koorlangka: A conversation about working with Indigenous young people in the past, present and future. *Youth Studies Australia, 25,* 25–32.

Dean, M. (1994). *Critical and effective histories: Foucault's methods and historical sociology.* London: Routledge.

Dreyfus, H., & Dreyfus, S. (1986). *Mind over machine: The power of human intuition and expertise in the era of the computer.* New York: Free Press.

Edwards, R., & Nicoll, K. (2006). Expertise, competence and reflection in the rhetoric of professional development. *British Educational Research Journal, 32,* 115–131.

Emslie, M. (2009). Researching reflective practice: A case study of youth work education. *Reflective Practice: International and Multidisciplinary Perspectives, 10,* 417–427.

Foucault, M. (1973). *The order of things: An archaeology of the human sciences.* New York: Vintage Books.

Foucault, M. (1982). *Discipline and punish: The birth of the prison.* London: Penguin.

Foucault, M. (1991). Governmentality (pp. 73–86). In G. Burchell, C. Gordon, & P. Miller (Eds.), *The Foucault effect: Studies in governmentality.* Hemel Hempstead, UK: Harvester Wheatsheaf.

Foundation for Young Australians. (2010). What works. Retrieved August 15, 2010, from http://www.fya.org.au/what-we-do/research/what-works.

Fraser, N. (1997). *Justice interruptus: Critical reflections on the "postsocialist" condition.* New York: Routledge.

Garland, D. (1992). Of crimes and criminals: The development of criminology in Britain. In M. Maguire, R. Morgan, & R. Reiner (Eds.), *The Oxford handbook of criminology* (2nd ed., pp. 11–56). Oxford, UK: Clarendon Press.

Grant, J. (1999). The incapacitating effects of competence: A critique. *Journal Advances in Health Sciences Education, 4,* 271–277.

Greenblatt, S. (1999). *Marvelous possessions.* Cambridge, UK: Cambridge University Press.

Grubb, W., & Lazerson, M. (2004). *The education gospel: The economic power of schooling.* Cambridge, MA: Harvard University Press.

Habermas, J. (1971). *Knowledge and human interests.* Boston, MA: Beacon Press.

Habermas, J. (1974). *Legitimation crisis.* Boston, MA: Beacon Press.

Hall, G. (1905). *Adolescence: Its psychology and its relations to physiology, anthropology, sociology, sex, crime, religion and education.* New York: D. Appleton and Company.

Hamilton-Smith, E., & Brownell, D. (1973). *Youth workers and their education.* Melbourne, Australia: Youth Workers Association of Victoria.

Harre, R. (1979). *Social being.* Oxford, UK: Blackwell.

Howson, P. (1999). Rescued from the rabbit burrow. *Quadrant, XLIII,* 10–14.

Iverson, R., Gergen, K., & Fairbanks, R. P. (2005). Assessment and social construction: Conflict or co-creation? *British Journal of Social Work, 35,* 689–708.

Jordan, R., & Powell, S. (2007). Skills without understanding: A critique of a competency-based model of teacher education in relation to special needs. *British Journal of Special Education, 22,* 120–124.

Kelly, P. (1994). *The end of certainty.* Sydney, Australia: Allen & Unwin.

Kennedy, R. (1989). How liberal welfare history constructs reformist poor. In F. Kennedy (Ed.), *Australian welfare: Historical sociology* (pp. 399–407). Melbourne, Australia: Macmillan.

Kett, J. (1977). *Rites of passage: Adolescence in America, 1970 to the present.* New York: Basic Books.

Lemke, T. (2001). The birth of bio-politics — Michel Foucault's lecture at the Collège de France on neo-liberal governmentality. *Economy & Society, 30,* 190-207.

Lum, G. (2004). On the non-discursive nature of competence. *Educational Philosophy and Theory, 36,* 485-496.

Nussbaum, M. (2010). *Not for profit: Why democracy needs the humanities.* Princeton, NJ: Princeton University Press.

Offe, C. (1984). *Contradictions of the welfare state.* London: Hutchinson.

Orloff, A., & Skocpol, T. (1984). Why not equal protection? Explaining the politics of public social spending in Britain, 1900–1911 and the United States, 1880s–1920. *American Sociological Review, 49,* 726–750.

Palmer, D. (2006). Going back to country with bosses: The Yiriman Project, youth participation and walking along with elders. *Children, Youth and Environments, 16,* 317–337.

Parsons, T. (1964). *Essays in sociological theory* (Rev. ed.). Washington, DC: Free Press. (Original work published 1949)

Roe, M. (1983). *Nine Australian progressives: Vitalism in Australian bourgeois thought: 1890–1960.* St. Lucia, Australia: Queensland University Press.

Sercombe, H. (1997). The youth work contract: Professionalism and ethics. *Youth Studies Australia, 16,* 17–21.

Stone, J. (2009). Keeping kids on track to successful adulthood: The role of VET in improving school outcomes. In A. Furlong (Ed.), *Handbook of youth and young adulthood* (pp. 135–143). London: Routledge.

van Krieken, R. (1991a). *Children and the state: Social control and the formation of Australian child welfare*. Sydney, Australia: Allen and Unwin.

van Krieken, R. (1991b). The poverty of social control: On explanatory logic in the historical sociology of the welfare state. *Sociological Review, 38,* 1–25.

van Krieken, R. (1992). *Children and the state: Social control and the formation of child welfare*. Sydney, Australia: Allen and Unwin.

Watson, D. (2009). *Bendable learnings: The wisdom of modern management*. Sydney, Australia: Random House.

Watts, R. (1987). *The foundations of the national welfare state*. Sydney, Australia: Allen and Unwin.

Wilson, E. (1977). *Women and the welfare state*. London: Tavistock Publications.

SECTION II
Curriculum

6

A DECADE OF EDUCATING YOUTH WORKERS AT AN URBAN COMMUNITY COLLEGE

Pete Watkins

Traditionally, youth workers in the United States have not been viewed as professionals, and youth work has not been viewed as a profession. Rather, youth workers have operated on intuition and instinct or have had training in a related profession such as social work or education. In 1999, as part of the national movement towards professionalization of the field occurring in the U.S., two local youth serving agencies partnered with the Community College of Philadelphia (CCP) to develop a credit-bearing certificate in youth work. While developing the program, CCP faculty and local youth work professionals wrestled with difficult questions such as where to house the program, who the target audience was, how to entice youth workers to participate, how to get employers to recognize the new credential and how to create degree paths for those students who chose to go beyond the certificate. As the program evolved, answers to these questions slowly emerged. When the certificate program was launched, youth work was a nascent profession without an established knowledge base of its own. There were few books written specifically for youth workers and almost no instructional materials designed for use in college level youth work classes. Faculty teaching the first youth work courses had to create lessons using a variety of sources. In the ensuing years, hundreds of students have completed youth work courses at CCP including experienced youth workers looking to develop themselves professionally, mid-life career changers, and young adults seeking to enter the field of youth work. The certificate program has served as an entry point into the field and helped attract new talent to the profession. Here I review the successes, the challenges and the lessons learned from a decade of youth worker education in Philadelphia, a large city in the northeastern United States.

Program Overview

Over the past decade, there have been various efforts around the country to create organized systems for the professional development of youth workers. In Philadelphia, the local community college has been an integral part of these efforts. The Community College of Philadelphia (CCP) offers two Certificates in Youth Work. The first is a nine-credit Proficiency Certificate in Youth Work comprised of three core courses—Foundation of Youth Work, Family and Community Engagement, and Critical Issues in Youth Work. The second is a 33-credit Academic Certificate in Youth Work, which in addition to the three core courses includes a 156-hour practicum in a youth serving agency, and general education and elective courses. Completion of the Proficiency Certificate indicates knowledge and understanding of basic principles of youth development and mastery of essential skills necessary for working with youth. The Academic Certificate also indicates a level of proficiency in other areas including math and English.

The Proficiency Certificate is understandably more appealing to many students since it can be completed in one semester even while working and will open the door to entry level jobs. The Academic Certificate can be completed theoretically in one year, but for many students takes considerably longer especially since many students need to take remedial math and English courses as part of the program. Surveys of students completed in 2003 and again in 2010 indicated that over half of the students in the program are part-time, defined as taking less than 12 credits during the semester in which the survey was conducted. Even many full time students take more than one year to complete the 33-credit Certificate because they may be required to take developmental courses in English and mathematics. Many students who go as far as the Academic Certificate go on to earn an Associate's Degree. Courses from the Proficiency Certificate all count towards the Academic Certificate and courses from the Academic Certificate can be applied towards an Associate degree usually in Human Services, but also in Liberal Arts or Justice.

The Certificates have been carefully designed not to be terminal credentials, but rather to form the first step on an educational ladder. Many youth work students have gone on to earn Bachelor's and Master's degrees. Having a viable transfer path is critical to attracting students. At CCP, and likely at other community colleges, ambitious and academically well-prepared students avoid and are advised to avoid terminal programs which are viewed as limiting and "vocational." The fact that students can continue on to a baccalaureate and graduate programs has been critical to the program's success.

Table 6.1 presents a grid showing the coursework required for the Academic Certificate. As stated, very few students progress through the program in two semesters. Most students attend part-time and, it takes more than two semesters to complete the program.

TABLE 6.1 Youth Work Academic Certificate Curriculum

Course Number and Name	Credits
FIRST SEMESTER	
YW 101—Foundations of Youth Work	3
ENGL 101-English Composition I	3
YW 110-Family and Community Engagement	3
CIS 103-Applied Computer Technology	3
Directed Elective Choose One	
BHHS 101-Introduction to Behavioral Health and Human Services	
BHHS 105-Introduction to Group Dynamics	
BHHS 111-Introduction to Helping Skills	
BHHS 151-Child Abuse and Family Violence	
JUS 171-Juvenile Justice	
PSYC 101-Introductory Psychology	
PSYC 115-Parenting	
PSYC 201 Child Psychology	
PSYC 215-Developmental Psychology	3
Math 118-Intermediate Algebra or higher	3
SECOND SEMESTER	
YW 115-Critical Issues in Youth Work	3
ENGL 102—English Composition II	3
Directed Elective-Choose one from list above	3
Directed Elective-Choose one from list above	3
YW 196-Practicum in Youth Work or BHHS 195-Practicum in Human Services	3 or 4
MINIMUM CREDITS NEEDED TO GRADUATE	33

History

In 1996, two Philadelphia organizations, the Pennsylvania Council of Children Youth and Family Services (PCCYFS) and the Federation of Neighborhood Centers (FNC), became involved in the Building Exemplary Systems of Training (BEST) initiative. The BEST initiative, funded by the Wallace Reader's Digest Foundation, sought to improve young people's lives by professionalizing the field of youth work and creating systems for training youth workers. PCCYFS and FNC are both intermediary organizations that provide training and support to member agencies who in turn work directly with youth across the region. The member agencies range from small neighborhood-based programs to large multi-site human services agencies and campus-based residential treatment programs. As part of the BEST initiative, these two organizations began providing workshops for youth workers using the Advancing Youth Development (AYD) curriculum developed by the National Training Institute for Community Youth Work (NTI). In 1999, NTI encouraged service agencies to partner with their local community colleges to create a youth work program. NTI believed that creating college-based programs would strengthen the youth work field and create a sustainable system for training youth workers that would endure even after the BEST initiative and the funding from the Wallace Foundation ended.

Executive directors of numerous youth serving agencies around the region wrote letters supporting the development of the Certificate and expressing interest in having their employees enroll in the program. In 1999, PCCYFS, FNC and the College (CCP) received a joint grant from the William Penn Foundation to support the program for three years. This grant was critical to the success of the program. The grant funded a full-time faculty position at CCP to develop courses, teach courses and coordinate the program. The external financial support during the ramp-up phase meant that there was a full-time person inside the college who was dedicated solely to the Youth Work program. Without this financial support, a faculty member from another discipline would have had to grow the program while balancing other responsibilities, or a youth work professional would have been hired as an adjunct faculty to teach the courses. Building the program in the early days was very time intensive. Course proposals had to be developed and presented to committees, and the program had to be marketed within the College and to the youth work community. Having a full-time person dedicated to the Youth Work program was very beneficial and only possible because of the external funding source. Students began enrolling in January 2000, and the first students graduated in May 2002.

In 2000 when the Certificate was developed, CCP had a policy that all certificate programs had to be a minimum of 30 credits and had to contain a general education component including two semesters of English composition, one semester of mathematics and a one semester computer course. Thus the Academic Certificate was created first, and the nine-credit Proficiency Certificate was added later.

When the program first opened in 2000, the first students were youth workers recruited from youth serving agencies within the FNC and PCCYFS networks. Due to the grant, the first cohorts of students were able to take the courses tuition free, and these students gave valuable input that helped faculty shape the courses. Early students came from a wide range of youth serving settings including youth development, child welfare, behavioral health, and juvenile justice agencies. Because the settings from which the students came were so diverse, faculty responded by developing a curriculum that was applicable to a variety of settings. Rather than focusing on one setting such as after school programs or foster care, the faculty developed a curriculum that focused on skills and knowledge that would be valuable to youth workers across a wide range of settings.

Quickly, the program began attracting students from local youth agencies and around the college. The college has an active Human Services Associate Degree program with several hundred students enrolled. These students made a natural audience for the youth work courses, many of whom took the courses as electives and/or earned the Youth Work Certificate concurrently with the Human Services degree. As mentioned earlier, the certificates were designed with this audience in mind. Students interested in social and behavioral sciences and juvenile justice have also taken the youth work courses. A few education majors have taken the courses and expressed that the courses would be very helpful to them as future teachers. In fact, some questioned why more teachers are not taught about youth development and crisis intervention. However, education majors at the college have no general electives and thus the youth work courses do not count towards their associate degree, which discourages most education majors from taking youth work courses. Some education majors seem more interested in social and emotional development than in teaching academics; however, they may still choose to be classroom teachers because of the higher salary, benefits, status and job security that comes with being a classroom teacher as opposed to a youth worker.

Essential Skills and Knowledge

Development of the curriculum revolved around the essential questions of who is a youth worker and what does a youth worker need to know or be able to do in order to work effectively with youth. Answering these questions proved quite difficult. At the time the program was developed and even today, there is no universally agreed upon definition of who qualifies as a youth worker or what skills and knowledge are necessary to work effectively with youth. The faculty and the advisory committee, made up of experienced youth work professionals, developed the curriculum largely based on their experiences working with youth. Ultimately, the faculty chose to define the term "youth work" broadly to include people who work with youth in a variety of settings including out of school time and youth development programs, group homes, recreation centers, juvenile justice facilities, mental health programs, foster care agencies, libraries and others. This broad definition has been important to the success of the program. Students come from and go to many different types of programs. If the certificate programs had specialized only in OST programs or residential youth workers (as some suggested in the early days of the program), the audience may have been too narrow to attract students and be viable as a program. Further, it was the faculty's experience that many youth workers move between different settings, for example, working in a community center and later working in a residential program. An overly specialized program could be limiting for graduates with perhaps decades of work experience ahead of them. Therefore, an intentional decision was made to define youth worker broadly for the purposes of the program and to focus on the skills and knowledge that a youth worker would need in order to be successful across many settings. Case studies and vignettes used in activities and assignments are always drawn from a wide variety of youth serving settings.

The philosophy of the program is that youth workers must have a realistic and balanced view of young people. Regardless of where they work, youth workers must recognize young people's strengths and the ways in which young people can contribute to their communities (Benson, 2006). Even youth workers who are employed in treatment facilities and detention centers must see beyond labels and recognize that young people need to be treated with respect and offered opportunities to make meaningful contributions to their communities. Consistent with a positive youth development philosophy, the program teaches youth workers about ways to support the positive development of young people. For example, students learn:

- How to help young people develop competencies and assets.
- About giving young people voice and choice.
- How to engage family members and other caring adults and encourage them to think positively about young people's potential.
- How to create opportunities for young people to take on leadership roles and to serve others.
- The importance of peers and youth culture in a young person's development.

The program also prepares them for the challenges and problems that some youth experience such as depression, anger management and substance abuse. Although not trained as therapists, youth workers should be able to recognize warning signs and communicate their concerns to the youth and his or her family. For example, youth workers are taught ways to:

- Deescalate an agitated youth.
- Manage disruptive behavior without allowing it to derail the entire group.
- Recognize warning signs of abuse or neglect and report it to appropriate authorities.
- Recognize warning signs of common mental health disorders, communicate concerns to the youth and his or her family, and help connect the youth with appropriate support services.

Another critical component of the program is for students to become familiar with theories of adolescent development, and how the nature of adolescence has changed over time and varies across cultures. These theories are taught by experienced youth workers and with an eye towards how the knowledge or skill may be useful to youth workers. For example, an understanding of Erikson's theory of adolescent identity formation and the concepts of temporary identities and psychosocial moratorium may make a youth worker more likely to interpret behavior in the context of development, rather than solely reacting to the behavior. Youth work students also explore Albert Bandura's theory of social learning and how this applies to youth work. Activities and discussions explore how a youth program can create a social environment that promotes prosocial and discourages antisocial behavior. Students also discuss examples, such as street gangs, which provide their members with a sense of belonging, mastery and purpose and essentially use social reinforcement for antisocial goals.

Place Within the Institution

The certificate programs are housed within the Psychology, Education and Human Services (PEHS) department, but are most closely aligned with the Associate's degree in Human Services. This close relationship between the Youth Work Certificate and the Human Services Associate Degree has influenced the certificate in significant ways from its inception. For example, when the program was founded, the committee that hired faculty to develop and teach courses selected someone with a social work background (this writer). If the hiring committee had been drawn from the Education faculty they might have selected someone else and everything from the name of the program to the specific readings, activities and assignments would likely look different. The fact that the institution had a long standing, respected program in Human Services was very beneficial in that the Youth Work program was able to attract students from that program to take youth work courses and was also able to draw upon the credibility that the Human Services program had established among employers and the community. Conceptually, Education and Youth Work would seem like a natural fit; however, the Education program at CCP is very proscribed in order to fulfill the mandates of the state department of education and requirements at transfer institutions. There are no general electives in the Associate's degree in Education. Hence, the youth work courses cannot be counted towards the education degree and few education students take the youth work courses. Those education students who take the youth work courses generally report that they were valuable; in fact, some education students change their career plans and decide instead to become youth workers. There seems to be no practical way to have more education students take the youth work courses given the stringent requirements placed on teacher education programs by the state department of education.

Students

Between 2002 and 2010 over 65 students earned the 33-credit Academic Certificate and over 150 students completed the three youth work courses necessary for the nine-credit Proficiency Certificate. Hundreds more have taken one or more youth work courses (often as electives towards another degree program) but not earned a certificate. The Youth Work Certificate attracts a wide range of students. Although every student is unique most fit into one of the following five categories:

1. *College-aged students who are looking for their first career:* This group is young and therefore often has an easy time relating to the experiences of youth. They tend to dress like youth and listen to the same music. They often have experience working with youth in volunteer positions as coaches, youth group leaders or camp counselors. Internships and volunteer experiences are important for these students so that they learn about the field. Many of these students have less work and family responsibilities and thus can attend college full-time and proceed through the program more quickly. They also have many years ahead of them in the workforce so it makes economic and practical sense for them to acquire as much education as possible. Many of these students have already made the decision to attend college and are now trying to choose a major and a career. One risk with these students is that they are often still engaging in career exploration and they are more likely to change their major or change their career plans than some of the older and more experienced students.

2. *Career changers without prior college:* These students are often working in low wage jobs in fields such as retail or healthcare. They are usually looking for a more rewarding job and perhaps higher pay. The certificate appeals to them because it can be completed quickly and helps them gain entry-level positions. However, these students often have family and financial obligations, which means they have to take a smaller course load. Another challenge for this group is that to really advance they need a baccalaureate degree, which can take several years going part-time.

3. *Career changers with college degrees:* Some students have considerable college education and work experience in fields not related to youth work. This group has many advantages in that they have already completed general education courses and they only need courses in the major. The Academic Certificate combined with their bachelor's degree can open doors to full-time salaried positions. However, depending on their previous employment, a youth work position may pay less than their salary in their previous field. Although their primary motivation for changing careers is usually to obtain a more rewarding job, most people have financial obligations and cannot afford to take a significant salary cut.

4. *Non-degreed youth workers who wish to enhance their skills and/or advance:* These students possess a lot of practical experience working with youth, but their lack of a degree or certificate has limited their ability to advance. They often have family and financial responsibilities that require that they attend college part-time. The support they receive from their employers varies greatly. Some employers actively encourage their frontline youth workers

to seek more education, while other students have told sad anecdotes about co-workers and supervisors who disparage "book learning" and are skeptical of their co-workers' attempts to further their education as a waste of time.

5. *Degreed youth workers*: This group of students has both experience working with youth and a high level of formal education. They typically are very engaged in classes and produce high quality assignments. One challenge in reaching this group is that they may already be familiar with basic concepts in youth development and thus the instructor needs to work to keep them engaged and sufficiently challenged. They use the program to either enhance or refresh their skills or as a stop en route to a graduate program.

Different students come with different strengths and different challenges. Younger students have the advantage of being familiar with youth culture, being less likely to disparage youth, and often are able to attend college full-time and thus progress more quickly. Older students have the advantage of being able to contribute their wisdom and life experience to the classroom. From an instructor's perspective, the diversity of students in the program represents a great opportunity and a potential challenge. Among the advantages of the diversity is that it leads to a dynamism and energy in the classroom and provides an opportunity for students to learn from one another and to move beyond generational and racial stereotypes. However, the diversity of educational levels can present a challenge when selecting readings and designing activities. One method for handling this is to give students choices of assignments. For example, in one class the instructor designed a writing assignment that is rather structured for students with less experience and skill in academic writing. Students who felt comfortable were given more leeway and allowed to choose a topic of their interest on which to research and write.

Program Successes

Since its inception, the Youth Work program has been evaluated in many ways. Surveys of current students and former students conducted for a recent program audit showed students satisfaction with the program to be quite high. In a recent survey, seven of the ten former students specifically praised the quality of the faculty in the program. There were no negative comments about the program reported on the surveys. A healthy sense of connectedness exists within the program where students engage with faculty, with one another and with professionals in the youth work field. The program is small enough that students and faculty know one another and the instructors and program coordinator are able to offer support to students who are struggling.

Students reported that the program helped them professionally by improving their counseling skills, improving self-confidence and giving them a fuller view of youth development. Also, many students reported personal growth from having taken the youth work courses. Graduates commented that an understanding of youth development has improved their communication with their children, that they use the behavior management techniques they learned in class at home, and that they have more patience and understanding when dealing with their own children and youth in their neighborhood.

The program has maintained a close relationship with youth serving agencies and dozens of agencies have sent employees to the program, hired program graduates and/or accepted students for internship placements. In 2002, during the early years of the program, a staff member at PCCYFS conducted a phone survey of supervisors of the youth workers who were enrolled in the program. The supervisors' responses were overwhelmingly positive in describing how the program had helped their employees. They stated that their employees seemed more insightful and patient when working with youth. Although it is hard to draw a definitive causal line from a classroom experience to a youth worker's interactions with youth, one plausible explanation is that workers become better able to place the youth's behavior in the context of the youth's development rather than reacting emotionally to the youth. Anecdotally, the program coordinator has spoken to executive directors of youth serving agencies who have praised the program and described in detail how the program has helped their workers who attended.

Many graduates of the certificate program have gone on to attain associate degrees, baccalaureate degrees and even master degrees. Students reported on the survey that baccalaureate schools accepted the youth work credits they earned at CCP and they felt well prepared for the demands of the baccalaureate program. A survey of current students in the program showed that 79% planned to earn an associate degree and 74% planned to earn a baccalaureate degree. A survey of graduates showed that 80% of those who transferred to a baccalaureate program felt that the program had prepared them very well and 20% felt that the program had prepared them fairly well. No students checked that the program did not prepare them well.

Challenges

Recognition of Certificate by Employers

Despite efforts by some funders and intermediaries, most youth serving agencies in the Philadelphia region do not have a formal system for recognizing and rewarding educational credentials. It is difficult to estimate how much currency certificates have among employers. The certificate program at CCP, including the practicum, is clearly useful for people looking to enter the youth work field. The classes and internship allow the prospective youth worker to make contacts in the field, to learn about various career paths involving working with youth and to learn to speak the language of youth work. In short, it opens doors that would otherwise be shut. For those already in the youth work field, the material benefits vary. Some employers might provide a salary increase for earning the certificate, but this is probably not common. Despite some efforts, most youth serving agencies do not have a formal policy whereby they would reward the certificate with a raise. The certificate combined with evidence of leadership skills might allow a frontline youth worker to advance to a mid-level supervisory or administrative job. Significant advancement in the youth work field usually requires at least an Associate's degree and often a Bachelor's degree. For this reason many students use the certificate as a first step towards an Associate's or Bachelor's degree.

Teaching General Academic Skills

Community College of Philadelphia is an open access institution; however, new students are required to take a placement test in English and mathematics. Many students enter the Youth Work program with deficiencies in reading, writing and mathematics. Students can take the youth work courses and earn the Proficiency Certificate regardless of their math score although they need to complete college level math courses to earn the Academic Certificate or an Associate's Degree. In order to take youth work courses, they must place at the college level in reading and writing or pass developmental English courses. This represents a significant hurdle for many prospective students who might need a semester or a year of developmental courses prior to taking their first youth work course. This adds considerably to the cost and the time involved in earning a Certificate. Furthermore, it may discourage students who are eager to study the subject of Youth Work but less excited about the prospect of taking a remedial English composition course.

Getting Incumbent Youth Workers to go Back to School

The program has attracted enough students to remain viable for more than a decade. However, from a young person's perspective, the chances of encountering a youth worker who has formal college level preparation in youth work still remains relatively low. Getting youth workers to attend college has proven challenging. Unlike health care or teaching where there is a strict credentialing system, most frontline youth workers are able to enter the field without college. Thus, there is less incentive for them to attend college. One of the lessons learned is that it is easier to get college students interested in the field of youth work than it is to get youth workers to make the decision to go back to school. Psychologically, enrolling in a youth work course when one is already in college is a small step with little risk. If they like the course, they may pursue the certificate and a career in youth work, but if not, they can count the course as an elective towards another degree. However, for a youth worker to go back to school is a much larger step that involves navigating a large institution, completing complicated forms, and taking an anxiety-producing entrance exam.

Student Challenges Balancing School, Work and Family Responsibilities

A survey was recently conducted of students who took some youth work courses but left before earning the Academic Certificate. When asked their reason for leaving, 60% cited conflicts between class and work schedules, 40% mentioned family demands, 10% cited financial problems and 10% checked no longer interested in youth work field. Interestingly, academic problems and dissatisfaction with the program were both offered as choices on the anonymous survey, and none of the former students who completed the survey indicated either of these choices as the reason they left the program. Anecdotally, many students who leave the program report struggling to balance school with other responsibilities and some prospective students never enter the program for the same reason. If funds were available, it would be ideal if youth serving agencies could pay tuition and even pay youth workers for the time they are in class, similar to a professional development workshop. One agency many years ago did allow its employees to list their time spent in class at CCP on their time sheets using the reasoning that it counted as professional development similar to a workshop, but this is very rare. Most students have to find time to attend class outside of work hours.

While tuition is a barrier for some students, it may not be the biggest barrier. Recently a foundation offered scholarships to youth workers to attend CCP's Youth Work program or other college-based programs related to youth work. The number of applicants was very low suggesting that other barriers such as lacking the time to attend college, lacking confidence in their ability to be successful in college, or not seeing the value in attending college exist. Another hypothesis discussed but difficult to test is that youth workers do not envision themselves remaining in the youth work field for very long, or think they already possess the necessary skills and knowledge and thus do not see the point of professional development. A survey is currently underway of the youth worker workforce across Pennsylvania asking youth workers among other things what they see as their professional development needs and how long they plan to remain in the field.

Low Status of the Youth Work Profession

Some students are likely deterred from entering the program because youth work is often not recognized as a profession and youth workers are not recognized as professionals. As college students engage in career exploration, they may be seeking a career with more glamour and prestige.

Lessons Learned

In the decade that the certificate programs have been in existence, we have learned many lessons, which anyone who has a similar program or is thinking of creating a similar program should keep in mind.

1. Have funding for the start up phase if possible. Having a grant to cover the salary of a full-time youth program coordinator at CCP was critical in providing the resources necessary for the program to attract students and establish credibility in its early years.

2. Hire experienced youth workers to teach the courses. Everyone who teaches in the Youth Work program at CCP has experience working with youth. This has been a selling point for the program and has likely contributed to the high levels of satisfaction among the students.

3. Be resourceful in designing activities and assignments. Anyone planning to teach a college course in youth work or youth development should be prepared to be resourceful and creative. Professors in established disciplines such as biology or history have extensive resources available to them including textbooks, test banks, web sites and activities. The knowledge base in youth work is neither as established nor as widely accessible. Youth work professors need to read publications in the field, search web sites and other places for useful activities, assignments and readings. They should be prepared to borrow ideas from other disciplines such as education, social work and psychology which all have something to contribute to the conversation about how to help young people thrive and succeed.

4. Be prepared to serve students with a wide range of general education skills. Students looking to enter or advance within the youth work profession range from those with college degrees and years of professional experience to those who have never been to college before and those who have never worked in a youth program. Instructors in our program look for readings, assignments and activities that will be accessible to students with less formal education while also stimulating and thought provoking to those with more formal education and more experience working with youth.

5. Have a broad definition of youth worker and teach skills and knowledge that are useful in a variety of settings. Youth workers' career paths often include working with youth in multiple settings over many years. Rather than teaching specialized skills, it is more beneficial to teach skills that are applicable to working with youth across multiple settings.

6. Maintain a close relationship with youth serving agencies. Let local agencies have input into the program. Encourage agencies to send students to the program, hire graduates and serve as internship sites. Seek feedback from agencies as to the content of the courses and how graduates are doing on the job.

7. Use the classroom as a vehicle for student engagement. Experts on community colleges, such as the developers of the Community College Survey

of Student Engagement (CCSSE), point out that engaged students are more likely to persist and be successful and students who have a friend at college are more likely to remain in college. Further, they point out that in a commuter college, the most likely place that students will make friends and engage with others is in the classroom (McClenney, 2003). Therefore, the classroom can be used as a place for youth work students to engage with one another, with faculty and with professionals from the youth work field. This ability to meet other people who share the goal of helping young people is important in getting youth workers to identify themselves as professionals and identify with the youth work profession. Students need to learn content, but they also benefit from the engagement that occurs in a classroom, which can only occur if an interactive pedagogy is used. Formal lectures will not lead students to engage with one another, with faculty or with the profession. Youth Work classes typically include role playing, small group activities, discussions, guest speakers and field trips which all increase student engagement.

8. Have clear and viable transfer paths for students. At community colleges, ambitious and academically well-prepared students avoid and are advised to avoid terminal credentials. Having a clear transfer path to baccalaureate and graduate degrees is essential in making the program a viable option for students who plan to remain in the field.

Conclusion

Anyone looking to create a sustainable system for educating youth workers should consider community colleges a valuable partner in this endeavor. Community colleges have a long history of creating programs to meet community needs. Housing a youth work program within a higher education institution has many advantages for students including the ability to earn transferable credit, gain access to financial aid to pay for courses, and earn greater recognition and respect for the field of youth work. Community College of Philadelphia's Youth Work program has for the past decade helped youth workers and aspiring youth workers to grow personally and professionally and, ultimately, better serve the youth in their communities.

References

Benson, P. (2006). *All kids are our kids* (2nd ed.). San Francisco: Jossey-Bass.
McClenney, K. (2003, September). Increasing student engagement. Presentation at Community College of Philadelphia faculty professional development session. Philadelphia, PA.

7

A CHICAGO STORY

Challenge and Change

Michael Heathfield

The City of Chicago has a long history of investment in the youth work field including professional development and training initiatives, college and university courses, field building not-for-profits, and processes designed to improve program quality. Not all of these have successfully survived a changed funding environment and the ever-changing challenges provided by the local, state and federal political context. The Chicago Youth Agency Partnership, with its city-wide convening and networking capacity, folded in 2003; Aurora University closed its downtown group work degree completion program targeted at youth workers in 2000; and as of 2008, the Chicago Youth Program Standards have been abandoned. However, a community college program has sustained itself for most of the last decade and continues to successfully provide diverse youth workers with relevant professional education experiences from a distinct philosophical viewpoint that connects more solidly to the ideology associated with the UK system of qualification for professional youth workers. This chapter details the emergence and implementation of the Harold Washington College youth work program and utilizes student assessment data to highlight the patterns of reported practice changes that occur when diverse youth workers come to college to learn more about youth work.

English Influences

Over the past decade, there has been a strong English influence over youth work training and professional education in Chicago. This has been driven by key workers and educators qualified from within the English youth work system. The author, from an English college with an honors degree and post-graduate routes to qualification for youth workers, moved to Chicago in 2000 and began working for the Chicago Area Project (CAP), a venerable 75-year-old not-for-profit. In 2002, CAP with support from the city's then Department of Youth Services, created the Youth Development Practitioner Certification Program (YDPCP). This program crammed specific elements of an English system into one simple course. In 2003, the course moved to Harold Washington College (HWC) attached with 3-credit hours through re-incarnating an old social work course. A second 3-credit hour course was quickly added. Then the Illinois Community College Board approved a basic and advanced college certificate, and an AA/AAS degree in youth work in fall 2007. The Associate's degree provides a youth work concentration within the Social Work discipline and requires over 60 credit hours, predominantly comprised of general education requirements.

Serendipitously, two other English youth workers became lead trainers in the youth work training that then emerged from CAP. Program standards were created and used as an assessment and training tool, program quality awards were awarded, and CAP's training initiatives involved all of the major Chicago providers such as After School Matters, Chicago Park District, Boys and Girls Clubs, and hundreds of small not-for-profit program providers.

This chance meeting of three "qualified" youth workers from England exerted specific influences over professional development initiatives in Chicago, some of which mark distinctions from the broader field that has developed here in the United States. Rather than "afterschool," "youth work" has been the primary label used in training for the field in the UK: The purpose of youth work is to facilitate and support young people's growth by encouraging their personal and social development and enabling them to have a voice, influence and place in their communities and society (National Youth Agency, 2001). All training materials at HWC draw on this UK definition.

Other features of the recent youth work college courses in Chicago derive from the very strong history of community organization involvement in professional development and have provided an ideological match with some elements of the English professional endorsement process for qualifying youth workers. These aspects include:

- A view of professional education premised on empowerment processes, rather than transmission models.
- A teaching, learning and assessment approach encouraging deep learning, holistic understanding and the interweaving of professional and personal growth.
- A significant focus on the concept of voice and the development of reflective practice.
- Explicit valuing of social justice and equality as central to the learning process and the field of practice.

The U.S. Context

However, the recent Chicago story is perhaps best grounded in its own U.S. context where both transatlantic parallels and distinctiveness can be highlighted. The most significant parallel is that the long history of youth work in the U.S. contains within it a range of adult concerns about children and young people. As Beck (1992) argues, in a post modern society, risk and trust are central concerns. A consistent focus of this trust and risk paradigm has been the perceived behavior and attitudes of adolescents. What children and young people do when they are not in school and not under the direct supervision of their parents or legal guardians are adult concerns with considerable pedigree on both sides of the Atlantic. In the UK, Smith (2002) identifies Sunday schools as the first formal manifestation of these concerns in the final years of the eighteenth century. By the mid–nineteenth century more familiar youth organizations had developed such as, the Young Men's Christian Association and the Boys' and Girls' Brigades. These developments were somewhat similar and parallel in the United States with the rise of settlement houses and well-known community activists such as, Jane Addams (Diliberto, 1999). Many of the nationally recognized traditional youth organizations have their origins in this historical period too (Delgado, 2002). The Boys and Girls Clubs of America identify the civil war period as their historical starting point when a small group of women formed the first 'Boys Club' to provide positive alternatives for young men to the life of the street (Boys and Girls Clubs of America, 2008). Boys and Girls Clubs continue to exert considerable interest and impact on the youth work field as they make adaptations relevant to the demands of twenty-first-century children and young people (Hirsch, 2005; McLaughlin, Irby, & Langman, 1994). The Boys and Girls Clubs of Chicago have consistently supported the HWC youth work program by continuing to require new employees to take the initial two youth work courses. However, traditional clubs are undergoing adaptations in relation to various drivers of change.

Four Seminal Points in the U.S. Field

At the federal level, four seminal points in the recent development of U.S. youth work can be identified from the literature as drivers of change in the field of youth work. All four define the national context within which HWC's youth work program resides and indicate some of the contradictions and complexities of the domain of the youth worker. The first seminal point was the publication by the Carnegie Foundation of *A Matter of Time: Risk and Opportunity in the Nonschool Hours* (Task Force on Youth Development and Community Programs, 1992), which initiated renewed investment and interest in early adolescence and programmatic responses to perceived challenges in this developmental period. The location of "risk times" for children and young people, the notion of transition from childhood to adulthood, and the sense of need to engage children in positive activity outside the traditions of home and school, all added impetus for the necessity to develop systematic program responses to young people when not in school. This was not a new discourse about youth but it did carry a renewed weight that gave rise to more attention and resources directed at the nonschool hours. The central concepts of space, relationships, safety, and developmental progression articulated in this report still resonate today and its impact is commonly noted (Quinn, 2000).

A second seminal point was the creation of the Federal 21st Century Learning Centers program. In 1998 (as reported in Dawson, MacAllum, & Warner, 2003), the Federal Department of Education created the 21st Century Learning Centers program to support schools and community-based agencies in developing expanded learning opportunities for children and young people in the nonschool hours, especially in areas of high poverty. While clearly linked to improving academic performance, the goal is to provide a broad array of enrichment activities (Department of Education, 2010). Since 2005, this single federal investment has delivered close to three billion dollars to the afterschool field in one form or another. Despite this very strong academic focus for the intended outcomes of this initiative, it also was concerned with a range of activities with community-based support for families. There was an obvious intention to complement the work of schools when working in high poverty areas. This federal focus is one that some authors see as corrupting to the broad associational and recreational view of long-standing community-based youth work (Pittman, 2004). This critique is also frequently applied to large-scale government policy and practice initiatives in the UK, where fears of social control and the pathologizing of young people are frequently voiced (Smith, 2003). This interpretation sees the dominance of the "schooling" function of the state overriding more broadly framed community association and informal education concerns.

The third seminal point speaks specifically to workforce development and the status of those working in youth work programs. In 2000, the U.S. Department of Labor designated the occupational category of Youth Development Practitioner as apprenticeable and in 2001 provided some seed money from which apprenticeship programs were established around the country (Dawson et al., 2003). This was an initiative that sought to improve the impact of the youth work elements of the Workforce Investment Act (WIA) and expressly identified youth workers, youth services, and the significant role they play in helping young people transition to adulthood, making successful and sustained connections to the world of work. The Chicago college program took the clumsy label of "youth development practitioner" in acknowledgement of this federal identification. In reality, the program relied on the older and simpler label of youth worker. The Department of Labor was clear in its intention, as quoted in Dawson et al.:

While WIA is the driving force behind our movement to create a youth worker occupation and apprenticeship, we see broad applicability for working with young people regardless of the funding source. We are seeking to upgrade the field of youth work through accreditation, training opportunities, apprenticeship and certification.

(2003, p. 6)

The fourth and final seminal point for the U.S. youth work domain was the publication of the first-ever federal report on the purpose, nature and impact of youth development programs (Eccles & Gootman, 2002). Produced by the National Research Council and Institute of Medicine, this marked a significant attempt to synthesize the emerging research about the field and point the direction of future federal investment in youth development programs, especially those in community-based settings. The terminology clearly in use here was that of "positive youth development." In a challenging critique of the orthodox paradigm of risk with regard to young people, Males (1999) provides a plethora of statistical evidence to support the thesis that the "teenager" construction serves to misdirect attention from the behavior of adults in society. Thus the dominant paradigm in use for young people, especially teenagers, is a deficit-paradigm (Smith, 2003), in which risk and how to minimize it, drive public discourse, policy and practice with regard to young people. This is a common transatlantic trait. Youth development, and especially "positive youth development," can be identified as a professional reaction to the dominance of the risk paradigm (Dawson et al., 2003). Heathfield (2004b) refers to "feeding the beast" as the pervasive influence of the deficit paradigm, even with those working solidly from a youth work or positive youth development frame of reference. Much current work, newly labeled "after-school" or "out-of school time," can still resonate with adult concerns driven from within the deficit paradigm. The philosophy of the HWC youth work program is explicit about countering the power of the deficit paradigm of young people. As will be shown in reflective journals from workers in the program, this is a key impact of the college program.

As can be seen in these four recent and highly significant reports and federal actions, there is a shift in terminology and a range of ways in which the broad field of youth work is framed. These changes can be best understood by identifying the mix of purpose, history and funding imperatives that still influence the field of work today. Pittman (2004) is particularly perceptive when she notes how the afterschool lobby has come to dominate the agenda in the United States and push the youth work voice to the background. She reviews the key elements of the British model for youth work and indicates much could be gained from taking a similar systematic approach to the domain here. A challenge for the HWC program is to utilize global materials about youth work to ensure a youth work perspective dominates while not simply making transatlantic comparisons.

Competing and Complementary Philosophies

These recent shifts in terminology and foci are best organized through reference to their distinct, and sometimes competing, philosophical and practical backgrounds. Listen, Inc. (2003) provides one of the clearest demarcations and categorizations of the U.S. field. In their Youth Engagement Continuum, they identify four key structural responses to young people. The first response is intervention, which they link clearly with a youth services approach, frequently attached to prevention and treatment outcomes and a tendency to individualize and pathologize young people. There is much similarity here with traditional notions of youth services within the aforementioned deficit paradigm. The second response is development in which most youth development practice is located. Much that is identified in this category matches positive youth development settings identified in the groundbreaking federal report on youth work (Eccles & Gootman, 2002). The third response is collective empowerment in which reside the practices of both youth leadership and civic engagement. The key additional elements in these practice forms are the increasing historical and cultural awareness of young people alongside a developing critical analysis of power and identity. In Listen, Inc.'s model these aspects are added to the youth development approach and build upon it. The fourth and final response is systemic change in which the practice of youth organizing is firmly located. In this practice young people exert considerable power and control over their own organizations. In fact, their mantra is "Community Organizing + Youth Development = Youth Organizing." Torres (2006) uses a qualitative approach to identify small groups of young people, and their supportive organizations, which work within this uncommon activist framework. Both Listen, Inc. and Torres identify activist youth work in which a critical reflection on structural power, and its abuses, are central to the empowerment process that young people engage in alongside youth workers.

In large part, these categorizations also relate to the major reproductive functions of the state. Schooling, policing and welfaring each exert powerful forces on youth work. Smith (2003) identifies the middle ground youth work occupies between social work and teaching in the UK. The U.S. after-school field can easily be associated with the power of the educating function of the state, with many programs being unfairly evaluated simply on their impact on school performance and grades (Halpern, Spielberger, & Robb, 2001) rather than a more realistic and broader array of socially desirable outcomes (Durlak & Weissberg, 2007).

The HWC youth work program presents workers with these philosophical and practical challenges and asks them to articulate a strong voice about their professional role in the lives of the children and young people with whom they work. Finding a valid and grounded voice as a youth worker, within the sometimes complementary and sometimes competing field, is a primary function of the youth work courses at the college. The core courses that constitute the HWC youth work program amount to 12 credit hours. The initial two 3-credit-hour courses are catalogued as Principles of Youth and Group Work and Social Problems and Social Action. Since 2002, these two courses constitute the Youth Development Practitioner Certification Program in Chicago. The third and final course in the college youth work sequence is a practicum for which students gain 6-credit hours. The practicum standard throughout many applied science programs requires 20 hours of weekly field work over the span of a standard 16-week semester. In common with many community college programs, our Associate's degree adds the standard general education courses to deliver a degree award between 60 and 64 credits. In the two initial college-based courses, worker reflection on their evolving thinking and practice is addressed by using on-line assessment data.

Voices of Change: Using Assessment Data

The assessment of student learning is seen as part of a revolution in education, according to Suskie (2004), in which a new paradigm of learning-centered education is replacing the more traditional paradigm that was teaching-centered. This is a shift that is global in nature (Boud & Falchikov, 2007) and one that is set to continue as resources for education and accountability for the use of those scarce resources are unlikely to abate. In the 1990s, the author was involved in an action research project on youth work courses in the UK in which the purpose was to improve student learning in professional education courses for youth workers. The findings of this research were part of the improving student learning movement (Bloxham & Heathfield, 1994; Bloxham & Heathfield, 1996; Heathfield & Bloxham, 1995; Heathfield & Bloxham 1996; Heathfield 1999a, b). Suskie (2004) identifies the American assessment movement as "action research" in which assessment findings are used in a continuous loop of learning through which student learning outcomes can be improved and all elements in the assessment cycle can be adjusted. In this sense, these assessment data are best categorized as formative, since there is no end point in mind, no body of knowledge to be tested, simply a consistent and rigorous approach to quality improvements in student learning.

The two foundational courses in the youth work concentration at HWC use an innovative web-based journaling system called Journey Mapping, which provides a rich source of both quantitative and qualitative demographic, professional and assessment data about the program. Dr. Barry Kibel created Journey Mapping while working for the Pacific Institute for Research and Evaluation, one of the national leaders in prevention research. Kibel's (1999) reflective journaling system was created out of his interest in capturing the spirit, essence and less tangible aspects of transformative learning through the stories of those involved in training and education experiences. Journaling has many parallels with the more recent interest in the concept of "appreciative inquiry" involved in both individual and organizational change (Quinn, 2000).

Students are required to make four substantial reflective journal entries about their learning experience and the practical implications for their own youth work practice. These occur at monthly intervals during the semester. Attached to the narrative journal element is a self-assessment survey tool through which students rate their progress in the acquisition and use of fourteen specific skill sets. This self-assessment is also taken at four points during the progress of the course providing intriguing subjective and indirect evidence of student learning throughout the progress of each sixteen-week semester. It is possible to criticize these data as unrepresentative and anecdotal. Kibel acknowledges that this is warranted, but argues that the system comes from within a different epistemological viewpoint that tries to bridge what can be seen as an artificial divide between quantitative and qualitative research paradigms. These data are highly subjective and indirect measures of learning, but Kibel borrows a concept from the legal profession to suggest that when enough stories are gathered, they then provide a "preponderance of evidence" about the effectiveness of the course or learning experience. The concept of "voice" has great importance in youth work practice, and therefore it also plays a significant role in the professional education of youth workers. In this sense, these assessment data could also be considered authentic assessments (Bloxham & Boyd, 2007).

The development of reflective practice is a course objective and one not uncommon in many human service and professional domains (Schön, 1983; Seligson & Stahl, 2003). This journaling element also provides the written aspect of these two initial courses, which rest largely on authentic assessments. These reflective narrative data provide rich detail to both the student learning experience and reported impact on practice. Since the inception of these two key youth work courses in 2002, this system has recorded over 1,600 separate journal entries. The later part of this chapter concentrates on these practice reflections and utilizes selected student voices as indicative of common patterns of challenge and change that have remained remarkably consistent over the eight years that these initial two college YDPCP courses have been in existence. The worker voices presented here are taken from journal entries from the 2008 and 2009 initial youth work class offered at HWC and yet are indicative of persistent themes in student journals since the creation of the Youth Development Practitioner Certification Program in 2002 (see also Williamson, Chapter 8, this volume). They are evocative, thoughtful and, as can be seen, are non-orthogonal and thus interweave a range of learning outcomes.

At a front line practice level, students commonly report changes in three important areas: improved listening and communication; enhanced programming—more youth decision making; and increased understanding of strengths-based work. A fourth, broader theme also consistently emerges which speaks more to an emerging identity as a youth worker and recognition of the broader field of practice.

Improved Listening and Communication

Throughout the interactive nature of these initial courses students frequently practice a range of group work and listening skills while being challenged to re-assess any preconceived or prejudicial notions they may have about young people as a class. For example, the first class involves completing a Youth, Truth, Sex and Drugs questionnaire in which the factual answers catch and compete with many assumptions about the behaviors of young people in comparison to adults. In every class, students are asked to work together to solve problems, produce quick posters, discuss and present findings, opinions, and practical strategies. Students are frequently asked to teach fellow students and the instructor. All of this active learning involves the actual demonstration of skills, group facilitation and enhanced listening. Authentic assessments also emphasize the utilization and presentation of practice skills, including a first assignment, which is a taped conversation with a young person with whom they are not familiar. Field-based evidence plays a strong role both in the learning assessment and professional relevance profile for the initial youth work courses.

> My conversations with youth in our programs are much more informative... Now, I realize that it has changed the way I listen in all settings of my life.
>
> Prior to taking this course I had no educational experience or training working with youth. However, I had three years experience working as a high school academic coach and as a youth intern in an arts program. Nonetheless, I was comfortable with my communication and relationship skills. Yet as I began to take this course I began to see myself and my workplace in a new light. My perspective of the youth themselves did not change. I was simply more determined to aid them in their development.

Greater Youth Decision Making

It is common in these initial courses to encounter workers with a service orientation to their work with young people, not dissimilar to the stance identified earlier by Listen, Inc. (2003). A key area of professional growth in this respect is initiated by a strong recognition of the positive contributions many young people make to communities globally and how this can start in youth programs by building youth engagement beyond the service framework, where leadership and significant decision-making power is transferred to young people in programs. The following worker tells the story of this shift and a new approach for engaging young people who were initially problematized and outside a very traditional program being offered by her employing community organization.

> *I must say I was having a lot of difficulty grasping the concept of youth participation … the idea of them having a greater voice and inclusiveness in decision-making processes. In my reality, with the (organization), I found it barely possible … There was a discussion in a staff meeting about the young guys that stand around the housing complex with nothing to do and that we need to reach out to them … the teens were tougher to engage.*

This worker makes a common acknowledgement that older teens are often absent from traditional programs, especially if they follow the dominant after-school framework. In Chicago the lack of teen participation in youth programming has received serious attention and resources with the creation of After School Matters, a non-profit organization that offers high school teens engaging activities during nonschool hours. This city-sponsored initiative represents an unprecedented investment in creating programming specifically for teenagers using an apprenticeship model (Halpern, 2009). It is my belief that this worker's challenge is directly related to the dominance of "after-school" in much youth programming. Teens can frequently see afterschool programs as "more school" or "school-lite." The worker above struggled with the notion of youth engagement within the regimentation of a drill team but steps into the role of youth worker when she moves out of the building and begins to meet these young people "where they are at" in a number of ways.

> *… After mingling with the young residents and talking to them, they told me that the main reason they stand around was because the basketball court on the premises had no hoops at all and was unusable. That's when the light bulb turned on in my head!… I got busy, walked around the housing complex and recruited the teen boys to organize themselves and take action! That action being the process of lobbying the Chicago Bulls organization as well as the CHA, to sponsor the basketball court restoration. We've had several very productive meetings … The guys eagerly participate; they provide wonderful input and useful feedback. It has been a very exciting and fulfilling experience for me…*

Increased Understanding of Strengths-based Work

The HWC program consistently challenges deficit approaches to working with young people; many workers note this change in their understanding about youth work. For some, this is a new development; for others, it is a reaffirmation of values and practices they already had.

This program has made many changes in the way we conduct our youth program. The most important change I would say is starting from strengths.

This course has given me a better understanding of what it means to be an effective youth worker, how to initially assess individuals from a strengths-based model, the benefits of great group facilitation, and how funders assess quality programming.

Overall the course has taught me to persistently see youth as diverse, creative individuals, no matter what stereotypes or judgment society or adults put on them. This is a perspective I already held but through the course, I felt consistently challenged to retain that view no matter what other sources say about youth. As we work with youth, it is their own passion and creativity that must drive our programs not only the energy of the workers.

It is also clear from these data that a larger theme emerges, which is less easy to categorize at a skill or practice level. This reported learning impact has more to do with an emerging or reconfirmed identity as a youth worker and an awareness of membership of a larger field of practice in which professional education and recognition are important.

Emerging Identity and Role of Youth Work

Students frequently talk of growth in self and make links between their identities both inside and outside of the work environment. It is not unusual for workers to talk of growth that spans a range of domains. These journals frequently intertwine identity, purpose and reported practice skills.

Through the program, I have deepened my understanding of who I am as a worker and person. This immediately translated to improvements in my work with youth. I have also been able to pinpoint a critical area for improvement in my church-based program, namely staff development …

This entire course has helped me identify my role as a youth worker, as well as understand my own strengths and weaknesses as a youth worker. That role, as I see myself in it, is one of supporting and exposing youth but also one of asking questions to challenge students to grow their expectations of themselves and to see themselves as agents of change in their own life.

I gained a clearer view of the role of youth work in helping youth own their own power and voice in their communities through reflection and hearing the experiences of others.

I will continue to stand by the fact that the greatest change this program has brought for me is my view towards youth work. It is not an easy task that can be done by anyone. It requires a certain degree of patience, emotional maturity and strength of character in order to be able to do a task like this. It often seems so many people see this type of job as a back up job that one only does if they are not able to find work in other places. However, this job is difficult.

Challenges and Change

Since 2002, the HWC program's initial courses have been financially supported through a grant to Chicago Area Project from the city's youth services. This important community partnership provided recruitment, retention services, materials, additional tutors, and the Journey Mapping web assessment system. Most significantly, this grant subsidized the tuition fees for all students in the two initial youth work YDPCP courses, three of which were offered in each academic year. From this annual pool of around 70 students in the first two courses in the degree sequence, between 6 and 10 students would join the full youth work degree program. In 2009, the Federal Housing and Urban Development (HUD) informed the city that their Community Development Block Grant funds could no longer be used for citywide training initiatives. This primarily affected the additional supports that had worked successfully around the two initial HWC courses that constitute the Youth Development Practitioner Certification Program. This key funding ended seven years of support at the end of 2009. The students now pay the full tuition costs, and HWC has attempted to replace the roles and resources provided by Chicago Area Project. In the first semester without these additional supports and resources, spring 2010 recruitment remained even but required concentrated effort from faculty to turn expressions of interest into registered, tuition-paid students.

The youth work degree program at HWC was designed around the two initial courses providing a wide engagement of citywide workers, from which a much smaller group could be recruited to the full Associate's degree. The field in Chicago is much like many other areas of the United States with many workers already degreed (Yohalem, Pittman, & Moore, 2006). However, there have always been degreed workers who have chosen to take all the youth-work specific courses at HWC because these were the only college-based professional education experiences available to them. In this respect, for both degreed youth workers and those more typical of community college students, college counts. Professional education college courses offer a currency that provides wider systemic credibility for the specific worker and the field in general (Mahoney, Levine, & Hinga, 2010).

There is little doubt that the key to quality youth work lies in the quality of the staff that work in these programs (Yohalem, Pittman, & Edwards, 2010). In Chicago, this has meant professional education that is college-based and designed as an initial and shared communal learning experience across a very diverse workforce. Alongside the removal of HUD support through the city's youth services, a second and perhaps surprising challenge has arisen to the youth work program. Over the past few years, a newer city focus on program quality has emerged in which "point of service" is the key focal point of training rather than professional education. This is not a movement specific to Chicago, indeed it fits a clear managerial agenda that has developed nationally. It is premised on using a standardized tool to initially assess program quality followed by a palate of short training opportunities around specific identified issues and skills. At some point in the future, programs are then re-assessed using the same tool and process. The kinds of learning identified by the worker narratives in this chapter, I believe, come from a more sustained engagement with a learning environment and a consistent community of learners that is more typically found in college courses than in short training courses now being offered to workers to help improve program quality. The new quality agenda also means that workers are now being encouraged to take training which is disconnected from any other systems of recognition, thus leaving workers with nothing to show for their commitment and time in training specifically geared to improve their practice. This is nothing new but does not seem like progress in terms of building both a field of practice and the status of those professionally employed within the field. This disinvestment from professional education for youth workers in Chicago sits in stark contrast to the recent English qualification system in which degreed and experienced youth workers have been encouraged to return to college to upgrade their professional education to a master's level. Indeed, one of the key English youth work trainers mentioned at the outset of this chapter has returned to England and is pursuing her Masters in Youth Work at no cost to herself, something she could never have done here in the United States. The other worker is now a lead trainer for the program quality initiative in Chicago and beyond.

From September 2010, professionally qualified youth worker status in England requires a minimum of a Bachelor's degree from a program validated by the National Youth Agency. There are currently around 40 programs in universities and colleges of higher education offering these routes to qualification for youth workers. In Chicago, the disconnect between college-based youth worker education, the local and national imperative to increase graduation rates, and an instrumental and managerial focus on program quality rather than a broader workforce development agenda, presents a complex future for the HWC youth work program. The future challenge for Chicago (and indeed the field) will be to sustain this long-standing and successful college-based initial professional education experience for all those working in the field of youth work. This will have to be done through connecting the newly dominant program quality agenda, so that targeted training and professional education responses for workers, their host programs, and the youth work field in general are coherent, coordinated and impact can be assessed. Articulate, educated youth workers, like the voices represented here, deserve nothing less.

Acknowledgment

This chapter is dedicated to Renae Ogletree 1951–2010.

References

Beck, U. (1992). *Risk society: Towards a new modernity.* London: Sage.

Bloxham, S., & Boyd, P. (2007). *Developing effective assessment in higher education: A practical guide.* Berkshire, UK: Open University Press/McGraw-Hill Education.

Bloxham, S., & Heathfield, M. (1994). Marking changes: Innovation in the design and assessment of a postgraduate diploma in youth and community work. In G. Gibbs (Ed.), *Improving student learning — theory and practice* (pp. 171–199). Oxford, UK: The Oxford Centre for Staff Development.

Bloxham, S., & Heathfield, M. (1996). The unexpected outcomes of critical professional learning. In J. Tait & P. Knight (Eds.), *The management of independent learning* (pp. 47–56). London: Kogan Page/SEDA.

Boud, D., & Falchikov, N. (Eds). (2007). *Rethinking assessment in higher education: Learning for the longer term.* London: Routledge.

Boys and Girls Clubs of America. (2008). Who we are. Retrieved October 21, 2008, from http://www.bgca.org/whoweare/history.asp

Dawson, A. L., MacAllum, K., & Warner, N. (2003). *Establishing BEST youth development practitioner apprenticeship programs for youth workers.* Washington, DC: National Training Institute for Community Youth Work, Academy for Educational Development.

Delgado, M. (2002). *New frontiers for youth development in the twenty-first century.* New York: Columbia University Press.

Diliberto, G. (1999). *A useful woman: The early life of Jane Addams.* New York: A Lisa Drew Book/Scribner.

Durlak, J. A., & Weissberg, R. P. (2007). *The impact of after-school programs that promote personal and social skills.* Chicago, IL: Collaborative for Academic, Social, Emotional Learning.

Eccles, J., & Gootman, J. A. (2002) (Eds.). *Community programs to promote youth development.* National Research Council and Institute of Medicine, Committee on Community-Level Programs for Youth. Board on Children, Youth, and Families, Division of Behavioral and Social Sciences and Education. Washington, DC: National Academy Press.

Halpern, R. (2009). *The means to grow up.* New York: Routledge.

Halpern, R., Spielberger, J., & Robb, S. (2001). *Evaluation of the MOST (making the Most of Out-of-School Time) initiative: Final report.* Chicago, IL: Chapin Hall Center for Children at the University of Chicago.

Heathfield, M. (1999a). Group-based assessment: An evaluation of the use of assessed tasks as a method of fostering higher quality learning. In S. Brown & A. Glasner (Eds.), *Assessment matters in higher education* (pp. 132–145). Leicester, UK: Open University Press.

Heathfield, M. (1999b, March 26). How to assess student groupwork. *The Times Higher Education Supplement,* 40–41.

Heathfield, M. (2004a, June). Stumbling toward youth work clarity. *Youth Today,* 20. Washington, DC: American Youth Work Center.

Heathfield, M. (2004b, November). Feeding the beast. *Youth Today,* 16. Washington, DC: American Youth Work Center.

Heathfield, M., & Bloxham, S. (1995). Rejecting the theory/practice dichotomy in youth and community work training. *Youth and Policy, 50,* 35–48.

Heathfield, M., & Bloxham, S. (1996). From theory to reality: Research in practice and on action. In G. Gibbs (Ed.), *Improving student learning — using research to improve student learning* (pp. 107–115). Oxford, UK: The Oxford Centre for Staff Development.

Hirsch, B. J. (2005). *A place to call home: After-school programs for urban youth.* New York: Teachers College Press.

Kibel, B. M. (1999). *Success stories as hard data: An introduction to results mapping.* Prevention in Practice Library Series. New York: Kluwer Academic/Plenum Publishers.

Listen Inc. (2003). *An emerging model for working with youth.* Occasional Papers Series on Youth Organizing No. 1. Brooklyn, NY: Funders' Collaborative on Youth Organizing.

Mahoney, J. L., Levine, M. D., & Hinga, B. (2010). The development of after-school program educators through university-community partnerships. *Applied Developmental Science, 14,* 89–105.

Males, M. A. (1999) *Framing youth: Ten myths about the next generation.* Monroe, ME: Common Courage Press.

McLaughlin, M. W., Irby, M. A., & Langman, J. (1994). *Urban sanctuaries: Neighborhood organizations in the lives and futures of inner-city youth.* San Francisco: Jossey-Bass.

National Youth Agency. (2001). *The NYA guide to youth work in England.* Leicester, UK: Author. Retrieved June 10, 2010, from http://www.slideshare.net/martinthompson/nya-guide-to-youth-work

Pittman, K. (2004, September/October). S.O.S. for youth. *Youth Today.* Washington, DC: American Youth Work Center. Retrieved June 10, 2010, from http://forumfyi.org/node/536

Quinn, R. E. (2000). *Change the world: How ordinary people can achieve extraordinary results.* San Francisco: Jossey Bass.

Schön, D. A. (1983). *The reflective practitioner.* New York: Basic Books.

Seligson, M., & Stahl, P. (2003). *Bringing yourself to work: A guide to successful staff development in after-school programs.* Boston, MA: Teachers College Press.

Smith, M. K. (2002). Youth work: An introduction. The encyclopedia of informal education. Retrieved from http://www.infed.org/youthwork/b-yw.htm

Smith, M. K. (2003). From youth work to youth development. The new government framework for English youth services, Youth and Policy, 79. Retrieved from http://www.infed.org/archives/jeffs_and_smith/smith_youth_work_to_youth_development.htm

Suskie, L. (2004). *Assessing student learning: A common sense guide.* Bolton, MA: Anker.

Task Force on Youth Development and Community Programs. (1992). *A matter of time: Risk and opportunity in the nonschool hours.* New York: Carnegie Corporation.

Torres, M. (2006). *Youth activists in the age of postmodern globalization.* Chicago, IL: Chapin Hall Center for Children at the University of Chicago.

U.S. Department of Education. (2010). *Guide to U.S. Department of Education programs.* Washington, DC: Office of Communications and Outreach. Retrieved August 19, 2010, from http://www.ed.gov/programs/gtep/gtep.pdf

Yohalem, N., Pittman, K., & Moore, D. (2006). *Growing the next generation of youth work professionals: Workforce opportunities and challenges.* Houston, TX: Cornerstones for Kids. Retrieved from http://www.nextgencoalition.org/files/NextGen-OppsAndChallenges.pdf

Yohalem, N., Pittman, K., & Edwards, S. (2010). *Strengthening the youth development/after-school workforce.* Washington, DC: Forum for Youth Investment.

8

THE JOURNEY TO BECOMING A YOUTH WORKER

Camille Williamson

Throughout my education and career, I have held an interest in the same population: youth and young adults. As a young person growing up on the south side of Chicago, I became interested in youth development and social services for youth at an early age first as a participant and then as a worker. When I was a teenager, I was a participant in youth organizing initiatives at Southwest Youth Collaborative (SWYC) and served as a youth outreach worker at the Adolescent Young Adult Clinic located at John H. Stroger Hospital of Cook County. I provided peer education in clinics, my high school, and on Chicago's public transit trains to inform youth about safer sex practices, STDs and HIV/AIDS. I was an outspoken young person, unsatisfied with the world, and wanted to be a part of its advancement. Nurtured by my parents and a few teachers, my greatest influence for youth work came from a fellow youth worker at the Department of Adolescent Medicine at Stroger Hospital, who was responsible for adolescent outreach and their connection to medical services within the department. This colleague had a unique way of talking with youth that was not authoritarian, but rather exploratory and always respectful. She took an interest in my thoughts, feelings, dreams, and fears. She was always genuine and remained committed to youth empowerment. While other adults in my life were telling me what to do, she asked what did *I* think I should do. I did not consider her a peer, but definitely an adult that I trusted would listen to me and challenge me to think. In fact, the entire adolescent medical team made an incredible impact on my life as they provided the resources and guidance for me and other youth to begin our own youth-led AIDS outreach group. It was an empowering experience to be a co-founder of Chicagoland Youth Against

AIDS established at the Department of Adolescent Medicine. Surrounded by professionals that had expertise in healthcare and youth work, I realized that youth work wasn't just about programs for youth; it is also inclusive of a skill set necessary for all professionals that work with youth. These early experiences spawned my interest in youth work.

Entry into College

At that time in my life I was preparing to attend college. I held a major interest in adolescent therapy but knew I didn't want to deliver traditional clinical services. Hence began my journey into higher education in the fields of child development, psychology, and sociology. I appreciated the knowledge I absorbed at the University of Illinois at Urbana-Champaign; however, most of what I learned was theory-based without any way to apply this knowledge to a population of youth. During that time I gained a lot of volunteer experience with youth in the Juvenile Detention Center of Champaign, Illinois and during an internship at the Sonia Shankman Orthogenic School at the University of Chicago. In both of these professional experiences, I met several youth that not only had mental health diagnoses but also life experiences of abuse, inequities, and ageism. Most of the youth I met did not feel a sense of empowerment and most of them did not know who they wanted to become. They did not talk about adults in their lives that gave them a safe space for self-discovery and transition into adulthood. Of course, there were some youth who had severe mental health issues that required an extensive level of care, but several higher-functioning youth still looked upon their lives with such despair. This reminded me of my dissatisfaction with the world when I was younger. My salvation was the nurturing environment to explore myself without the judgments of unassailable adults.

Near the end of my college career, I shifted my academic interests to social work when I realized that my goal of being a therapist would not allow me to focus on youth development with an emphasis of social justice. I then decided that I would pursue a graduate degree in clinical social work at the University of Chicago School of Social Service Administration (SSA). This educational opportunity was very fulfilling as I gained extensive knowledge and practical experience in program development, management, clinical skills, and advocacy. However, none of my courses focused on youth work specifically with regard to learning how to provide youth a place to develop a leadership role in addressing their own concerns and meeting their own developmental milestones. Some of my graduate-level coursework overlapped with my undergraduate experience, but I experienced the same gap in youth work learning objectives in the social work program.

Entry into Field

Upon graduation from SSA I became, and still currently serve as, the director of a TRIO Talent Search program at SWYC, a federally funded program designed to expose and assist college ready students to enter post-secondary programs of study. I work with students in four public schools on the southwest side of Chicago exposing them to college access and career development. My education and professional experience leading up to this particular position was valuable as I use it all to deliver effective youth programming. As I reflect upon my career path, it's certain that my early experience with caring adults made me want to get the education to be an effective and influential youth worker. I draw upon my own experiences as a way to guide my connection with youth by being an adult that listens with the intent to understand, involve, and support them.

When I became a director of a new program at SWYC, I sought more professional development to provide comprehensive programming to students. I learned of the Advanced Youth Development Youth Worker Certification program at Harold Washington Community College after I took the basic 7-day Advanced Youth Development training with Chicago Area Project. I thought, "Wow, why wasn't there a youth worker learning track in my undergraduate and graduate institutions?" Quite naturally, I leapt at the opportunity to learn more skills that would enhance my toolkit. My post-secondary education is rooted in theory and clinical work with teenagers and young adults, but not necessarily community development with this population. Of course, theorists such as Erikson and Piaget were great foundations for learning about children and this knowledge base is crucial to understanding human development and behavior in children and adolescents. However, in addition to this understanding, all youth workers need a toolkit in their practice of engagement, programs, and empowerment of youth.

Back to School

The Youth Worker Certification Program is comprised of four Youth Practitioner courses that utilize a few methods to help students gain and sharpen their skills, which include small group activities, individual assignments, and journey mapping (see Heathfield, Chapter 7, this volume for a fuller description). The Level 1 course focuses on working with youth as individuals and in groups. At the time, I had already gained extensive experience working with youth as individuals, but not in groups. Thus, the small group activities helped me to learn how to work in a collaborative manner with other youth workers (including other professionals that work with youth). For example, one of our class activities was to build a tower using only tape, construction paper, and paper clips. The goal was to compete with other teams to build the tallest tower without it toppling over. The group had to coalesce around a common goal and access each other's talents to bring it to fruition. I am a natural leader, and often as natural leaders emerge they can attract and hold everyone's attention. However, leaders don't have all the answers. This was my first lesson in that I realized that while leaders are smart and knowledgeable, they need to be able to recognize other peoples' strengths and talents. I was challenged to work more productively with adults and to sharpen my listening ability. These skills are important for consensus building with colleagues and the development of comprehensive youth programs. Needless to say, although our tower did not topple over, my groups' tower was not the tallest; but I learned that collaborating with partners such as teachers, doctors, and other social workers is paramount for positive youth development.

In addition to small group exercises during class, there was a space for students to challenge themselves on an individual basis and have the creativity to do so. I got this opportunity with the second homework assignment when we were asked to complete a project with a group of youth at our respective agencies. This assignment gave me the space to practice working with youth in a group in which they decided what they wanted to create with each other. I chose to work on a restorative justice project with three students in my program that committed serious infractions on an overnight college tour. These young men decided to drink alcohol in their hotel room. Of course, alcohol and the consumption of alcoholic beverages was not allowed on our field trips. According to the code of conduct for Chicago Public Schools, the penalty for this behavior is expulsion. These three young males were all seniors in high school. I worked with the principal of the high school to ensure that they would not be expelled, but instead complete a project that showed that they understood how dangerous their actions were and how they could set a better example for other peers. After some discussion, they decided that the best way to show their peers how to make better decisions was to provide them with information. During their school suspension, these students met at my office to complete their restorative justice project. They created a Power Point presentation and brochure about alcohol consumption on college campuses. They focused on national statistics of students incurring alcohol poisoning, alcohol related car collisions, and do's and don'ts when drinking. I was proud that they were able to provide their classmates with the peer education to make better decisions about this particular issue. This was my second learned lesson in that given the opportunity to learn and be creative, and the support to learn through mistakes, youth are able to gain their own resources to educate and support their peers. Some of their resources include adults that they trust and respect. This rapport is established among adults and youth when youth are able to resolve an issue together without a top–down approach.

The main principles of youth work practice are to develop a working relationship with youth where they are able to access their leadership ability and commit them to common goals with their peers. The aforementioned activities helped me to understand that as a youth worker my number one goal is to help young people find their own path in the safest way possible. This requires me to approach youth with high standards as well as the space and encouragement to explore and develop their talents while acquiring the skills to be successful adults. I certainly did not have any experiences such as this in undergraduate or graduate school and I don't think I would have learned it intentionally had I not taken the Youth Practitioner courses. These assignments forced me to confront notions of adultism within myself and challenged me to be more trusting of the journey rather than controlling the entire experience of working with young people.

My learning continued with other courses that addressed community development and intentionally recognizing and involving youth in community organizing and advancement. Coursework in Asset-Based Community Development taught me how to work with youth and adults to accomplish a common goal that's a focal point of all stakeholders within a community. At the time of this course, I was already a proponent of community organizing with youth at the pinnacle of this progression. However, I was challenged to think about how youth work and community development inclusive of adults can be implemented into my program design and implementation. As a director of a Talent Search program, I have some standard grant benchmarks to meet each year, which are to have a certain percentage of students graduate, complete the FAFSA, and apply and enroll into a post-secondary institution. Although these grant requirements do not include educating youth and parents about community issues and encouraging them to become involved in community development, I began to see that this concept was a necessity in my program design in order to provide parents with the supports to help their children. Therefore, I made some changes to my program delivery, which included parent chaperones on the annual spring break tour to provide mentorship to students, individual consultations with parents regarding the college process so that they can also get the support to apply and enroll in college, and an annual spring break community project.

These programmatic changes occurred as a result of reflection and analysis of program intentionality. Journey mapping was a learning tool employed in the program that allowed me to reflect upon my learning by answering the same questions on a monthly basis. The questions that were most helpful in my reflections were, "What is working well for you in the course and how has your learning improved your work?" Although the questions were always the same, my answers changed. My reflections became more developed and salient to my current position. This level of reflection took me further than any other journal entries that were required for undergraduate or graduate courses as they forced me to reflect upon class, work, and how to practice youth work throughout the rest of my career. To that end, this was my fourth learned lesson: youth workers need the space to reflect individually and with colleagues to determine best practices and career paths. Therefore, academia, trainings, and conferences are all necessary for the professional development of all youth workers.

This reflective experience is much more developed in the seminar course and report writing course as students are able to reflect with each other during class discussion and the instructor through individual assignments. Report writing allowed me to evaluate the functionality of my program from youths' perspectives. I learned through their eyes what needed to change to make the Talent Search program more conducive to their needs. Thus, more programmatic changes occurred to provide youth with more individualized time for career and college research. This was also a very important lesson, as many adults don't ask youth what they need to invest in their own future. However, it is crucial to ask youth this question because they are the leaders of our future society, so they must be challenged to think about how to advance themselves, their community, and the world.

Consequently, a seminar course complemented the aforementioned learning lesson. This course was a collective journey with a small group of classmates in which we all reflected upon the challenges of our respective workplaces and discussed the resources that we didn't have to do our best work with our youth and families. One of the most common themes about each classmate's experience was that it was very rare for our organizations to ask us what we needed to do a better job for more comprehensive positive youth development. This was pivotal for me as it made me realize the extreme vulnerability that our youth encompass because not only is it rare for adults to ask them what they need and want, it is also rare for agencies to ask youth workers what they need to be better practitioners and advocates for youth. It was at this time that I realized my career preferences were changing based upon what I was learning in class and about my professional goals. This particular experience made me realize that I needed to start involving myself in more policy work that affects youth and parents. Moreover, I was able to see how I needed to use my acquired experience and education to broaden my career goals with specific objectives.

Overall, the Youth Worker Certification Program gave me a much broader way to think about youth development that matched my emphasis in social justice for young people and a number of different ways to practice it through empowering them. As I think back on my learning experience in the program, I see that I was not only learning how to work with young people as individuals or groups but especially as an important part of the community in which they reside as well as the global community of young people. I gained more practical tools for my work with youth. Specifically, I learned how to assist in the development of young people by challenging them to prepare for their future the best way they see fit. As a youth worker it is my job to provide them with resources, social and emotional support, a safe space to make mistakes, and most importantly, advocacy.

Professionalized Youth Work

There are a number of ways that professionals can obtain knowledge to work with young people. The subjects are expansive in terms of variety. Psychology, social work, and education, just to name a few, certainly have aspects of child and youth development; however, the focal point of these subjects is not inclusive of equipping future practitioners with a large toolkit for effective youth work. The aforementioned statement is not to negate the importance and relevance of theory as it applies to the overall goal of learning, but only to show that elements of "youth work" are not always acknowledged and infused within these career tracks. Furthermore, it is becoming increasingly apparent that any professional that interacts with youth could benefit from the basic skill set of a youth worker, as it will ultimately enhance effectiveness and outcomes. For example, I often have to work with teachers and school administrators. However, there are glaring differences in our approaches to working with youth. Several of the teachers at my schools utilize a lecture style approach to teaching, and I often observe students bored and uninterested during class. My approach to working with youth is reflective of the 5 C's of positive youth development developed by Catalano, Berglund, Ryan, Lonczak, and Hawkins (1999): *Competence, Confidence, Connections, Character,* and *Caring.* Competence refers to increasing critical thinking skills, socialization, and academic and professional goal setting. Confidence is reflective of encouraging positive emotional development in youth by focusing on self-esteem and identity development. Connections addresses positive interpersonal relationships with youth and adults. Character is focused on making good personal decisions regarding healthy behaviors, developing personal standards, and a barometer for right and wrong. Finally, caring, is very important in terms of community development as it pertains to empathy which is a sustainability measure for community improvements.

These pillars help me to take an intentional approach to how I engage with youth and their families and ensure that my programming is reflective of these goals. For example, this year the students chose to visit schools in St. Louis, Missouri and the theme for the 2010 SWYC Talent Search spring break college tour was diversity. My staff and partners at our high school scheduled a series of activities that were reflective of the five Cs. We began the tour with the students completing their first journal entry by defining diversity to allow them to reflect at the beginning of our journey. During the tour, I took the students to "Race," an exhibit at the Missouri Museum of Natural History through which they learned about health and education disparities based upon race and class, historical implications of race, and events in United States history that were geared towards equal rights regarding race, such as the Civil Rights Movement. I also took the students to see the movie *Skin,* a true story of two white African parents who gave birth to a black child during the era of apartheid in South

Africa. Finally, the community project for this tour was a day of volunteering at a group home for various differently-abled adults. Throughout the tour we had several dialogues with the students on an individual basis and in groups about diversity to reflect upon their experiences. The students kept a daily journal during the tour and reflected upon these experiences. After reading these entries, it was clear that students had gained a different appreciation and definition of what diversity means. They began to learn how to look beyond race, interact with other people outside their group of friends, and empathize with others. This was a very rewarding experience for me as youth worker as I was able to watch students learn, reflect, and gain a broader worldview. This opportunity of learning is important for human development.

Additionally, comprehensive positive youth development must be infused in our human systems, such as education and child welfare, which consistently fail our youth. Of course, there are other elements (racism, classism, and sexism) that impede the advancement rates of youth, especially youth of color, impoverished youth, and socially vulnerable youth. Although these are problems that require time and collective effort to resolve, youth workers can start now in how they design and implement services and programs. Moreover, youth workers can become involved in the process for how these human systems engage and serve our youth. Specifically, youth workers must be a part of how policy and reform take place for systems such as juvenile justice and education systems to name a few. Chicago has very serious problems with both these systems, which negatively impact our children's future. Currently, the Cook County Juvenile Detention Center is under major scrutiny for the abusive treatment of youth within this holding system. There have been reports of physical abuse from guards and cases of severe neglect such as not allowing youth to bathe and change their underwear. An article in the *Chicago Sun Times* noted that this facility has been under "gross mismanagement" for years (Sweeney, Pallasch, & Patterson, 2005). These conditions were so horrible that public outcry from several youth agencies and community members including SWYC began the Audy Home Campaign, which is a grassroots organizing initiative to improve conditions at this facility, monitor its function, and furthermore re-direct funding streams to programming and services for youth. This is a prominent example of how reform of a public system is a necessity and moreover must be inclusive of youth. As a result of the Audy Home Campaign, a group of youth from SWYC participated in talks and monitoring conditions at the detention center reflecting that change is slow, yet progressive when youth are at the apex of reform. And the need for reform does not end and begin with one public system. After all, systems such as healthcare, criminal justice, and education are inextricably intertwined. Many youth that find themselves in the juvenile detention center are those that have been failed by the education system. Public education reform is not a new topic, as there have been several phases of restructuring. The first phase of public school curriculum during the first half of the twentieth century consisted mainly of tracking students based upon perceived scholastic ability. This led to scholastic achievement being a predictor of vocational ability and course placements for students in high school. Then mid-century, a shift occurred to choice curriculum in which students could begin to choose their classes. This, of course, co-occurring during the Civil Rights Movement was indicative of a need for social change reflective of the student's future plans. This time period also reflects the establishment of TRIO programs, which are specifically aimed and assisting low-income, first generation students to attend college. Although students who enroll in TRIO programs consistently apply and enroll in college, the change in the public education system did not vastly improve the equity in education and academic achievement among students of color and low socio-economic status. I believe this can be attributed to racism as a factor in school system administration and poor secondary preparation of students during elementary school. Since the 1990s, the current shift is college preparation for all students. And the process to transitioning to post-secondary education has not been standardized by the school system. Currently, there is no clear indication that this curriculum change is also the only answer for education reform. Consequently, there was no decrease in the national high school drop-out rate from 1975–1995 (Lee & Ready, 2009). Furthermore, ninth grade students who present with lower scholastic achievement were more likely to fail core college prep courses and not attend college in 2004 than in 1994. Also, more absenteeism occurred in 2004 than in 1994 with students with higher scholastic achievement (Lee & Ready, 2009). So the question is: What is happening in public schools and how does the current system need to be reformed to improve education outcomes for students?

I argue that education reform should not be a top-down process, but rather one that includes an assessment of students' needs from students to determine how they can best learn and prepare themselves for their future. Most of the students in my program are amazed that my staff and I have an interest in what they think and feel about their future. Many of them discuss how no one has ever asked them what careers interest them the most or what personal fears they have about facing their future. Positive youth development affects positive achievements in education. Hence, there is a need to use such an approach in educating our future leaders of the world. School curriculum should be inclusive of youths' wants, needs, perspectives, and creative expression. The drive for this change is already occurring at places like What Kids Can Do (WKCD) in Rhode Island, an organization geared towards improving college readiness in high school students. The founders of WKCD, Barbara Cervone and Kathleen Cushman, are working with youth to ensure that their voices are being heard regarding college preparedness and the transition to post-secondary education. In 2001, Barbara Cervone, who was the national director of the Annenberg Challenge Grant program, left this position to establish WKCD. At the time of her departure, Annenberg was the nation's largest private investor in public school reform. Currently, WKCD is using various forms of media including 12 books published by their own non-for-profit publishing extension (Next Generation Press) to send a message to educators, policy makers, parents, and other students about some of the barriers and challenges to enrolling and completing college and other post secondary programs of study. Students of WKCD have used their voices to empower themselves and their peers. Similarly to the Audy Home Campaign, it is their voices that are the force needed to thrust education reform.

Conclusion

Youth workers need more academic and professional development. I am excited about the impetus to make youth work more professional. Historically, I think youth work has been looked down upon as a lowly job with little or no need for extensive education and training. I think this is a classist and ageist ideology as it pertains to what is considered a profession and how the education and training is disseminated to produce highly skilled youth workers that focus on the empowerment of youth. Youth workers do not earn high-paying salaries and are not always seen as vital members of the professional community. The problem with this is that it prevents all practitioners of youth work from the benefits of learning through experience sharing, support from colleagues, and building better programs and services for youth with youth. Specifically, youth workers have a great impact on the lives of young people. They consistently fill in the gaps ensuring that youth are not ignored, abused, and/or extinguished and provide safe spaces for positive development and long-standing advocacy. However, youth workers alone cannot comprehensively make essential improvements in the lives of young people. Instead, all practitioners of youth work need to be a part of motivating, educating, and empowering our young people. Who are the practitioners? Doctors, lawyers, teachers, out-of-school time (OST) staff, and even police officers are all practitioners in a way. We all have a job to do, and it requires a commitment to form partnerships across these professions, as it is necessary for the advancement of our young people. As a society that is ever evolving, we need to invest more in the lives of our youth as they are the key to our survival and advancement as humans. Youth are not to be constantly controlled, but should be regarded as respected individuals that are stakeholders in their future.

The world does not belong to us; it is on loan from our children. What return will be gained in the investment if we to do not invest in their optimal well-being? Thus, youth work needs its own place in academia as a major of study, but also as an integral part of the career fields that focus on youth and young adults. These professions include education, pediatric medicine, child welfare workers, and civil servants. We need intentional youth work learning experiences that equip us all with the professional skills and knowledge to be effective practitioners. Youth work skills can and should be a part of our multi-disciplinary approach to empowering our young people. I look forward to the expansion of youth work in our academia through courses, internships, and even global exchanges to further develop our skills. My experience in the Youth Worker Certification Program at Harold Washington Community College will forever be a valuable one as I have gained a toolkit, a support system of colleagues and academicians, and a new approach to positive youth development.

References

Catalano R. F., Berglund, M. L., Ryan J. A. M., Lonczak, H. S., & Hawkins, J. D. (1999). *Positive youth development in the United States: Research findings on evaluations of positive youth development programs*. Seattle: University of Washington, School of Social Work, Social Development Research Group.

Lee, V., & Ready, D. D. (2009). U.S. high school curriculum: Three phases of contemporary research and reform. *The Future of Children, 19*, 135–156.

Sweeney, A., Pallasch, A. M., & Patterson, S. (2005, August 18). Juvenile Center staff face scrutiny: Criminal background checks set as abuse complaints continue. *Chicago Sun Times*.

9

ON BECOMING AN ACADEMIC PROFESSION

Dana Fusco

Much of the 1990s was dedicated to understanding the impact of youth programs on a host of developmental outcomes (Dryfoos, 1999; Kahne et al., 2001; Posner & Vandell, 1994; Vandell & Ramanan, 1991). Most salient among these findings was that staff quality was the most consistent factor contributing to program effectiveness (Anderson-Butcher, Cash, Saltzburg, Midle, & Pace, 2004; Little, Wimer, & Weiss, 2008; McLaughlin, Irby, & Langman, 1994; Metz, Bandy, & Burkhauser, 2009; Noam & Fiore, 2004; Phelan, 2005). Every framework of program quality that has since emerged has addressed the need for well-trained and qualified staff (see Palmer, Anderson, & Sabatelli, 2009 for a review). How staff quality is defined, how one goes about developing it, and how it links to developmental outcomes for clients has been the subject of much discussion in professional education across allied health and human service fields (e.g., see Guskey, 1995, for a similar discussion in education; Benner, Sutphen, Leonard, & Day, 2010, for nursing; and Freedberg, 2009, for social work).

Some would argue that knowing one's work develops from years of experience, years of trying and testing approaches, years of negotiating with and advocating for one's clients, and from occasionally attending professional development workshops. There is a stick-with-it disposition for those who describe youth work as their calling. Much like the apprentice-turned-master, "sticking-with-it" yields a deep and layered understanding of practice translating into positive outcomes for children and youth. However, the percentage of youth workers who stick-with-it long enough to develop mastery is slim. Turnover is a challenge for many youth-serving agencies due to the part-time nature of the work, lack of career trajectories, and low wages. Because turnover is disruptive to providing and sustaining the kinds of services that are likely to make an impact in the lives of children and youth, agencies often seek ways of providing incentives to keep talented staff longer. However, restrictive budgets make the availability of even non-financial perks a challenge. Attracting, retaining and developing quality staff may ultimately require more than what most individual organizations can successfully manage on their own.

With the unequivocal recognition that staff retention and quality are key ingredients for effective youth programming, the past decade has shifted its attention to the development of the workforce (Cornerstone for Kids, 2006; Dennehy, Gannett, & Robbins, 2006; Foundations Inc., 2010; Fusco, 2003). Degrees and credit-bearing coursework are emerging as part of a broader educational strategy for addressing staff quality. Within the past decade, institutions such as Acadia University, Bank Street College, Community College of Philadelphia, Cornell Extension, Penn State, Rutgers University, Harvard, Kent State, Pitt University, City University of New York, Charter Oaks College, Harold Washington College, University of California Irvine, Beloit College, and others have joined those who paved the way as early as the 1970s, such as University of Minnesota and University of Wisconsin-Milwaukee, in the development of training and degree programs to support youth work professionals.

However, this trend has not been without its challenges. In the United States, most educational programs for youth workers remain on the periphery of academic departments. As such, they receive wavering institutional support, struggle to maintain enrollment numbers, and are vulnerable to shifts in funding patterns. Further, few professors in academia are familiar with youth work or worse, use their personal experiences with "youth" to sufficiently dismiss youth work as necessary of a scholarly enterprise. As such, scholars in the area of youth work struggle through tenure and promotion decisions, particularly in four-year research colleges where the "publish or perish" culture is most prominent (Astroth, 2003). Add to this that youth work education (henceforth, YWE) has a fragmented presence in higher education, and its future seems bleak. Programs that have been successful, i.e., have become a mainstay in the institution have found at least one inside advocate, usually a faculty member, who serves as the program's voice. Advocates help ensure that colleagues understand the depth and breadth of youth work, and see the value in what students in the program are learning. Community support for such programs is often strong, which keeps some programs running even with lower than desired enrollments. However, as recent personal communications has revealed, even inside advocates are concerned about the future of the field. And, the concern is international. YWE is much further along in places like Australia, Canada, England and other parts of the United Kingdom. Yet, there is much debate both within academia and within the government about how far advanced education for youth workers should go; the discussion being largely a matter of financing such a project.

I remain optimistic, but realize that sometimes it entails accepting that progress can be two steps forward and one step back. It's a matter of convincing people inside and outside the university why university based programs matter. We need a stock of 'ready to go' arguments and evidence to give to those wanting to develop new or sustain a program.

(J. Bessant, Australia, personal communication, July 15, 2010)

If YWE is to have a future in higher education, we must understand that the challenges in our midst will not be resolved with a fresh coat of paint. We need a brick-and-mortar approach. In this chapter, the author posits that many of the challenges faced by youth work educators in higher education are in part the result of youth work lacking a disciplinary structure. While YWE is informed by a growing body of knowledge, that knowledge is not formalized in a coherent structure. As such, youth work has not reached the status of an academic profession. In fact, the language itself is cause for confusion. Is the discipline called youth work, youth development, social education, afterschool education, out-of-school time, informal education, youth studies, nonformal learning, community education, community development, or something else? If those most closely engaged in the field do not agree on the language and content, then it will be difficult for the discipline to grow deep roots within higher education. Here the author explores what it might mean for YWE to become legitimized as an academic profession that is squarely situated in higher education. The premise of the argument draws from the theoretical and empirical disciplines: the sociology of education and the sociology of knowledge, to help frame an understanding of how academic disciplines and professions emerge and become legitimized within higher education. The author borrows from the history of other disciplines and professions to draw parallels. The purpose of the analysis is to help shape next steps in YWE, and the body of knowledge that drives it, by understanding the institutional context in which knowledge is most likely to be created and recapitulated.

On Becoming an Academic Discipline and Profession

An academic profession is one that has exclusive powers to recruit and train new members; has exclusive powers to judge who is qualified; is responsible for regulating the quality of professional work; and is grounded in a complex body of knowledge or discipline (Light, 1974). While there are several frameworks for classifying disciplines, most agree that consensus is critical. A discipline has an agreed-upon body of knowledge from which faculty draw and at least one professional association, which helps define and articulate that body of knowledge to the broader public (see Figure 9.1).

One of the principle aims of higher education is to support the emergence of new discoveries in the disciplines, to give birth to new knowledge. Typically

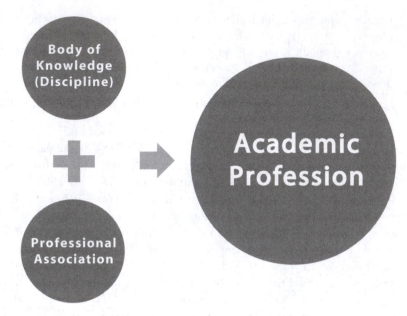

FIGURE 9.1 Elements of an academic profession.

disciplines, once created, are rarely dissolved. However, knowledge structures within universities do shift and become reorganized. A sociological analysis of the structure of knowledge in higher education conducted by Gumport and Snydman (2002) revealed four types of reorganization: (1) *knowledge differentiation*, departments or degree programs are split because knowledge becomes too specialized; (2) *knowledge promotion*, a department becomes a school or division, or a school becomes a college, elevating the status of the discipline; (3) *knowledge evolution*, a department or program changes its name to represent new thinking in the area; and (4) *knowledge consolidation*, departments or programs merge. The lack of reorganization, conversely, can reveal *knowledge stability*; this is typically seen in long-standing disciplines such as Chemistry, Music, English, and the Social Sciences. In their analysis, Gumport and Snydman (2002) found that the professional and applied areas show less knowledge stability (more reorganization) than other academic areas.

Youth work education has itself been subject to such reorganization. For instance, in 2005, Beloit College renamed its Department of Education, the Department of Education and Youth Studies, to reflect the emergence of three new academic tracks: Children and Schools, Adolescents and Schools, and Youth and Society. More typical is that new programs are simply added to an existing department's (school's or college's) offerings with no reorganization to the structure of the academic department, school or college. This approach suggests that the institution while supportive of the addition does not see the need for a different kind of academic representation. This is unfortunate because an additive approach does not have the same kind of visibility as comes with reorganization. However, it is also understandable. Reorganization in knowledge structure implies what I will call, *disciplinary power*; that is, the discipline has evolved to a point where it has both qualitative heft (specialized knowledge with a broad liberal education base) and quantitative heft (enrollment, FTEs, funding, resources). It is fair to say that YWE has not yet achieved such heft. To understand why, it is important to view knowledge development from the perspective of academia. The sections that follow will discuss how knowledge comes into being and why professional associations are necessary advocates in keeping a discipline strong.

The Emergence of Knowledge

Understanding how a body of knowledge comes into being is surprisingly complex. It requires attention to what counts as knowledge, how knowledge becomes validated, what modes of inquiry count for producing knowledge, what methods of communication are dominant in transmitting knowledge, and how knowledge becomes legitimized as worthy of inclusion into the discipline of study. Different disciplines have varied approaches to knowledge production and dissemination. In the traditional sense, most academic knowledge begins by identifying its object of study (light, ADHD, 18th-century literature, a bowl of fruit) and then setting out to explore some problem associated with understanding that object. Does light travel at different rates of speed in air versus water? Can ADHD be environmentally induced? Did women use literature in the 18th century as a subversive mechanism for expressing their political views? What medium can express the texture of a peach?

In addition to whatever content is included as the object(s) of study, disciplines have agreed upon methods or paradigms for approaching the study of that content. A paradigm gives researchers a way of looking at the world, an agreed-upon mode of inquiry, such that the community of researchers working collectively on an issue or set of issues has a roadmap, or shared understanding of the problem. From a scientific pragmatic viewpoint, without the map, research is disjointed, lacking a unified way to develop a substantial body of knowledge from which generalizations can be made. In the absence of a paradigm all facts seem equally relevant (Kuhn, 1996). Thomas Kuhn (1996) in his classic work on the structure of scientific revolutions posits that the development of a mature science occurs through the natural progression of transitioning from one paradigm to another. From this standpoint, the applied sciences are pre-paradigmatic: having more varied and less agreed upon orientations for studying any problem.

Paradigms help researchers build upon each other's work, to collectively study the "problem." As Biglan (1973) points out, there is lower social connectedness in applied and social science research than in pure and natural science research. Lower social connectedness in the social sciences is both the cause and the result of what Kuhn (1996) dubs a pre-paradigm. If viewed through a sociocultural lens, the formation of knowledge can be seen as an apprenticeship of thinking (Rogoff, 1990) where through dialogue and inter-action concepts are formed, deepened, and legitimized within a community of "scholars." A paradigm, then, is nothing more than the rules of that culture/ community that are embodied in the values and beliefs of the discipline and enacted in narrative, tools, and customs. If there are only loose social connec-tions, apprenticeship of thinking will be limited; thoughts are not extended and deepened in social milieu and the discipline (or that which is "thinkable") cannot fully mature.

A study of the sociology of knowledge provides additional insights into the evolution of thinking and the development of knowledge across disciplines. Early scientific discoveries might have been shared in personal communications that took months to travel across seas. Today, social connectedness is enhanced through technological innovations that allow for eased and quick communi-cations around the globe. Professional associations aid in sharing and com-munication through listservs, journals, conferences and the like. Interestingly, the low social connectedness within the pre-paradigmatic discipline of youth work might have served as an advantage allowing for the cross-germination of ideas across disciplines. In fact, the richness of ideas that results from cross-disciplinary dialogue may ultimately lead to the phasing out of separate disci-plines in the future (Edwards, 1996; Klein, 1999). It is quite possible that the applied sciences will never replicate the monolithic reliance on "paradigm" as did the natural sciences, which themselves are reaching across boundaries, i.e., the emergence of biochemistry and geophysics. That said, it is important to articulate our object(s) of study as well as the paradigm(s) through which we see it. By reviewing the knowledge claims that have received attention (and those that have not), that have been replicated (and have not), and by generating new problem sets for future research, we can map a more inclusive disciplinary structure that will provide a foundation for deepening the body of knowledge from which YWE can draw in the future.

Defining the Body(ies) of Knowledge

Professions rest on a body of knowledge. That body of knowledge emerges slowly and over time; sometimes coming directly from practitioners, sometimes from pure researchers, sometimes from applied researchers and other times in the partnership between practitioners and researchers. Today, many YWE pro-grams as a pull from various existing disciplines such as, psychology and educa-tion, and use that knowledge in the training and education of youth workers. This means that the existing body of knowledge from which we currently draw is not inclusive because it has not come from the unique experiences of youth workers in the broad and diverse contexts in which they may work.

Youth workers are employed and/or volunteer in a wide range of settings including afterschool programs, community-based youth programs, camps, foster care, group homes, schools, residential care, recreation centers, juvenile justice, employment centers, parks, museums, and so on. Not to mention the many additional settings where one finds people working with youth—churches, the army, hospitals, clinics, etc. A preliminary analysis of the state of the academic discipline of YWE must begin with a clear discernment of youth work, by defining its essence rather than focusing on its setting. As Bernard Davies (2005) articulated, "What distinguishes youth work from other related and often overlapping practices is its methods: how it seeks to express those values, and particularly its *process*" (p. 4). Davies set out to define a Manifesto "which by unpacking such slogans, spells out the practice's essential features, and then from these, without claiming superiority, identifies those which set it apart from other practices" (2005, p. 7). Davies' Manifesto does not define the practice, or set of activities in which young people are engaged but the configuration of space that young people and youth workers co-construct. This space is consistently recognized in much of the United Kingdom as "youth work." In the United States, we are urged to articulate what has come to be "youth work" here and then to more critically examine that space as contested, problematized, and unfinished.

Jerome Beker articulated a commonality, an essence, when he said, "What we have in common most basically is a developmental or mental health orientation to our work combined with the fact that we encounter the youngsters with whom we work in the life space, 'en milieu,' rather than in a formal psychotherapy or classroom setting" (2001, p. 357). There is a growing body of knowledge that articulates how to work "en milieu" (Bellefeuille & Ricks, 2008), create effective afterschool programs (Hirsch, 2005; Mahoney, Larson, & Eccles, 2005), promote positive youth development (McLaughlin, Irby & Langman, 1994; National Research Council and Institute of Medicine, 2002), and create participatory environments where young people have responsibilities and challenging experiences, actively participate in problem solving and decision making, and are treated with high expectations and respect (Zeldin, 1995; Zeldin, Kimball, & Price, 1995). This work in the United States is supported by a global knowledge base abroad (e.g., see Batsleer, 2008, for a discussion on informal learning in the United Kingdom; Jeffs & Smith, 2010, for youth work practice in the United Kingdom; Eisikovits, 1997, for a study of child and youth care in Israel; White, 2009, for a volume on youth work from Australia; and Capece, Schneider-Munoz, & Politz, 2007, for an edited volume, *Afterschool Around the Globe*). Unfortunately, to date there is little social connectedness among these bodies of research that cut across domains and thereby helps us define our core, our essence. Not surprisingly then there is also little connectedness among these bodies of knowledge within academia. Where in academia would a student learn about adolescent development, how to create a positive developmental environment, how to work in the life space, how to build community, how to engage youth in co-constructed, participatory and empowering methodologies? The content here is scattered across disciplines. Even academic programs in youth work, youth development or youth studies, often have either an orientation towards afterschool education *or* community youth development programs *or* youth care, etc. Rather than an inclusive discipline of youth work that draws upon the multiplicity of perspectives, there exist separate domains of practice with compartmentalized areas of study. While the argument could be made that these domains require isomorphic skill sets and specialized knowledge, it seems to me that there is also a character and flavor of youth work that could be defined as the guiding principles of the field. It is much easier to create concentrations later, much harder, though necessary, to find consensus earlier.

The National Research Council and Institute of Medicine (2002) posits that youth work is that which enhances the acquisition of personal and social assets, which leads to positive adolescent development, well-being and future success. They name eight features of positive developmental environments: Physical and psychological safety; appropriate structure; supportive relationships; opportunities to belong; positive social norms; support for efficacy and mattering; opportunities for skill building; and integration of family, school, and community efforts. Their review includes programs that are community-based including youth clubs, afterschool programs, youth development programs or other programs occurring during out-of-school time. It does not include other domains of youth work such as residential or "street" programs that do not have the same demarcation of time, as out-of-school time. In residential or streets programs, youth workers are engaged with youth 24/7. Are these domains of youth work similar enough to be included under one umbrella or is the content sufficiently different to warrant separate disciplines? Are they different merely because of where and when they occur or by what they aim to accomplish and hence the body of knowledge needed to understand and enact those aims? To date, there is no consensus on these questions.

A pragmatic argument for including the various domains of youth work practice and corresponding understandings under one disciplinary umbrella is that it would provide the field with quantitative heft (see Figure 9.2). Dale Curry, Associate Professor at Kent State, argues:

> If child and youth work defines itself as a profession by its body of knowledge, skills and values as most established professions have done (medicine, social work) rather than by the age of child/youth one works with, or setting (community based or out of home care) or by population (mental health, child welfare), then child and youth work is the largest human

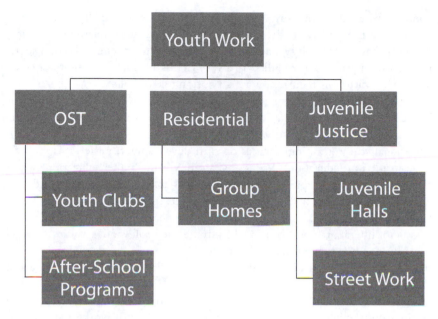

FIGURE 9.2 One domain or many?

service field/profession (larger than all others combined). The largest human service profession translates into potential jobs for students/seats in the classroom/tuition for universities.

(D. Curry, personal communication, July 18, 2010)

In addition to sheer quantity, there is a qualitative undertaking in establishing one umbrella of understanding. The disciplinary power of YWE might be gained through a common professional education design that includes a core curriculum (a common understanding of working with youth as a youth worker) with concentrations of specialized knowledge that build from domain-specificity such as, afterschool education, child and youth care, recreation and leisure studies, community education, youth ministry, or civic engagement. Mapping the knowledge base and analyzing that which cuts across youth work domains and that which is unique would help establish such a disciplinary structure. The design of one structure for YWE would provide students with the most flexible options in terms of employment opening their capacity to transition across domains or settings. Currently, it is not uncommon for a youth worker to study in education in preparation for work in an afterschool program, move into a program of social work in order to work at night in a group home, and then find himself in a family studies program as he pursues a director's position in a residential program. This is unfortunate not only because of the loss of resources (time and money) for students but because of the content missed along the way. A disciplinary structure would allow the field to define itself more consistently. For instance, the content of relational practice, strengths-based psychology, and principles of community education and social justice would provide three pillars to a very rich start. Such portability of credits across institutions is currently not an option for students.

In addition to the reasons for creating a unified disciplinary structure for YWE, there are also risks in not doing so. The current fragmentation of content makes the field of youth work vulnerable to being considered vocational. Vocational study (training) focuses on skill development, rather than knowledge formation (education). Vocational study within higher education, while serving a central function for the university, sits apart from the main academic affairs of the institution since it is not grounded in liberal arts (such as literature, philosophy, history, mathematics, and science). Somewhere seated in the middle of liberal arts and vocational study lie the professional studies. Professions such as nursing, education, accounting, and social work require a broad base from general education in addition to specialized content knowledge and skills (see Figure 9.3).

Conversations with academics throughout the country, including the author's own experience developing a program for youth workers at a senior college, have consistently demonstrated that there exists a tension in how youth work is viewed in academia. Disciplines outside of the canon (liberal arts and sciences) are marginalized from the academic mainstream. Interestingly, scholars of youth work who have become well-published and respected in the field, work within the converged space of youth work and one of the liberal arts; most typically psychology or sociology. Like most professions, youth work may become legitimized through its association with the liberal arts. The history of teacher education provides an interesting parallel. For instance, what were called "normal schools," developed for teacher "training" did not become

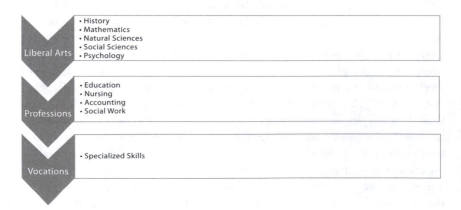

FIGURE 9.3 Higher education structure of knowledge.

"teacher colleges" until the late 1800s when enough scholars were attracted to the study of teaching. Often these scholars came from traditions in the liberal arts: e.g., Edward Lee Thorndike received his Ph.D. in Psychology and pioneered the field of Educational Psychology during his career at Columbia University, Teacher's College. Thus, teacher training was legitimized as having a valid body of knowledge through the work of Thorndike and others. Bringing a scientific paradigm to the study of teaching shifted the way the field was viewed from vocational to a legitimized professional study. A similar transition occurred in nursing (Yam, 2004). Not coincidentally, female workers also dominated these early vocations and the entry of men (as scholars, not practitioners) assisted in their legitimization within academia. Today, it is professional associations that give disciplines legitimacy (though the tensions remain palpable).

Professional Associations

Organizationally, educational institutions can be thought of as structures of knowledge. They decide what knowledge is worth knowing and at what level one should know it (i.e., K–12, postsecondary, associates, bachelors, graduate). As such disciplines become formalized through the hiring of faculty, the allocation of instructional materials and resources, the communication of the program to the outside world, and the awarding of degrees. Equally, academic institutions can de-legitimize bodies of knowledge by simply not offering them. They can, by virtue of inaction, deem a discipline not worthy of study. Thus, new disciplines in particular need advocates. When professional associations are formed, higher education is more likely to accept the emerging knowledge as a new academic profession (though some higher education institutions, particularly research universities, are known for being on the cusp of emerging knowledge and the generation of new areas of study). They embrace experimental areas sooner.

Normal schools (teacher training institutions) were established to create norms in teaching practices. The American Association of Colleges for Teacher Education (AACTE) emerged shortly thereafter. AACTE gave teacher education a national presence and one that was now in the public eye. Looking at the professional associations that are vetting the body of knowledge within youth work will uncover which knowledge claims are receiving support (and which are not). For instance, the National Afterschool Association is doing for afterschool education what AACTE has done for teacher education. The International Child and Youth Care Association is doing the same in the area of child and youth care. Associations bring validation to a field its body of knowledge, and assocated practice. They also, albeit sometimes unintentionally, take the spotlight away from parallel but less mature, paradigms. Much of this is tied to the organizing capacity of the association and how much support it receives not only in terms of major support but also through individual memberships. Joining an association then is a statement of endorsement of a discipline and a community of practice.

Members of professional associations create and review each other's work, and communicateaccepted "discoveries" through publications (online or written) as well as through conference presentations. For instance, the Association for Child & Youth Care Practice (ACYCP) created competencies for child and youth work practitioners. The competency framework was published through the Association's own journal, the *Journal of Child and Youth Care Work* in 2002. That framework was used to create the first ever credential in the United States through the North American Certification Project (see Chapter 3 of this volume).

Defining our body of knowledge and forming professional associations to help articulate it is the next natural step for the field but not the last. In order for any discipline to be self-perpetuating, it must help create the next generation of thinkers and scholars (see Figure 9.4). An academic profession presupposes an apprenticeship into the discipline through teaching and scholarship. Typi-

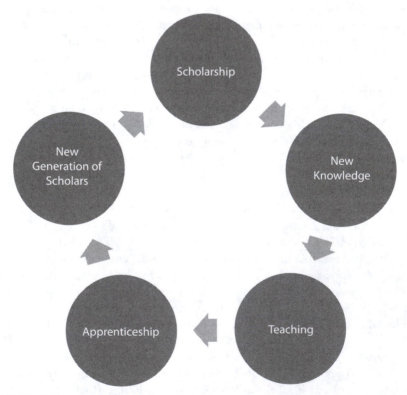

FIGURE 9.4 Cycle for generating new knowledge.

cally, this is the work of academia. Of course, traditional definitions of science and the scientific paradigm, including who can engage in it, have been challenged by postmodern writers who have argued that human behavior cannot be objectified as sole truth since in fact, there are many "truths" or ways of viewing and understanding the world (Gergen, 1991). In this postmodern spirit, newer paradigms such as, action research, have created a tradition that value the knowledge generated by practitioners "researching in action." These alternative paradigms embrace a more inclusive arrangement or partnership between practitioners and researchers and blur the lines between these distinctions such that disciplinary knowledge emerges from practice (as oposed to traditional arrangements of theory feeding practice).

The discovery of new knowledge in a discipline is essential to advancing the discipline and the field. Advancing youth work as a discipline, then, means paying attention to new issues that emerge in working with young people. Those who understand the issues must be a part of educating the next generation of professionals. Apprenticeship into the discipline would include a study of the history of youth and youth work. It is the study of paradigms that "prepares the student for membership in the particular scientific community with which he will later practice" (Kuhn, 1996, p. 11). The study of paradigms is essentially a study of the history of that science (or object of study). It includes learning who was engaged in research, their problem of study, their findings, and how their inquiries were situated within the broader community of research in that area. In higher education, it is faculty who recapitulate the discipline through such study. However, there is currently one doctoral program in youth work in the United States. It is perhaps a timely concern to be addressed in advancing the field.

Conclusion

In order for youth work education to become a mainstay in higher education, several things need to be considered. First, a representative and inclusive body of knowledge that makes up youth work should be defined, even if only as a preliminary step in charting some new conversations. At some point, consensus must be reached on the discipline of youth work and whether that discipline transcends domains of practice. Here I urge us to create disciplinary power by building a knowledge structure that includes that which is foundational (general across specific contexts of youth work practice) and that which is specialized (specific to the context). Mapping such knowledge would help the field have quantitative and qualitative heft and would support student learning. It is time to end the reliance on antiquated theories that view human development as a recapitulation or unfolding of a biological genesis tested solely in "backyards" rather than "communities." An inclusive knowledge base emerging from the places where youth (all youth) and youth workers are is critical to the future formation of the discipline and our continued understanding of youth and youth development. Forming a professional association will aid with this task and help represent the discipline as espoused by its members (practitioners, scholars, and scholar-practitioners). These are necessary steps for helping youth work education become legitimized as an academic profession and practice science.

The arguments posed here emerge from the sociological studies of education and knowledge. They are situated within the context of higher education and as such do not deal with the realities of the field on the ground. As is currently under negotiation in England and other parts of the United Kingdom, requiring postsecondary degrees for youth work has implications for the funding of youth programs. Going to scale with youth work education needs an economic study to determine in dollar amounts what the implications might be for the cost of the quality programs. In the United Kingdom, all students of youth work by 2010 were required to hold a B.A. with honors (or three years of full time study or the part time equivalent (Jeffs & Spence, 2007/2008). As those costs trickle down into program costs, it is not clear whether in the United States, the government, and the public would be willing to pay the higher premium. Alternative models might need consideration. In Israel, for example, only a small percentage of staff who work any given shift must be credentialed; they also have additional responsibility of staff supervision. Giving the field of youth work legitimacy through the university system, however, might drive home the point that there is a valued and necessary body of knowledge, a discipline, that is required of the youth work professional. We will need the arguments and the advocates for making this a reality, and it is the author's belief that the time is upon us to create the academic discipline and the academic profession for ensuring the future of youth work education and more importantly, for ensuring that all young people have access to quality youth work.

References

Anderson-Butcher, D., Cash, S. J., Saltzburg, S., Midle, T., & Pace, D. (2004). Institutions of youth development: The significance of supportive staff-youth relationships. *Journal of Human Behavior in the Social Environment, 9*, 83–99.

Astroth, K. A. (2003). Doorway, doormat, or doghouse? The challenges of facing 4-H youth development scholarship in land-grant universities. Commentary, *Journal of Extension, 41*, http://www.joe.org/joe/2003december/comm1.shtml

Batsleer, J. (2008). *Informal learning in youth work.* London: Sage.

Beker, J. (2001). Toward the unification of the child care field as a profession. *Child & Youth Care Forum, 30*, 355–362. Reprinted with permission from the *Journal of the Association for the Care of Children in Hospitals*, 1976.

Bellefeuille, G., & Ricks, F. (2008). *Standing on the precipice: Inquiry into the creative potential of child and youth care practice.* Edmonton, Alberta, Canada: MacEwan Press.

Benner, P., Sutphen, M., Leonard, V., & Day, L. (2010). *Educating nurses: A call for radical transformation.* San Francisco, CA: Jossey-Bass.

Biglan, A. (1973). The characteristics of subject matter in different academic areas. *Journal of Applied Psychology, 58*, 195–203.

Capece, J. H., Schneider-Munoz, A., & Politz, B. (Eds.). (2007). Afterschool around the globe: Policy, practices, and youth voice. *New Directions for Youth Development, 116.* New York: Wiley.

Cornerstone for Kids. (2006*). Growing the next generation of youth professionals: Workforce opportunities and challenges.* The Human Service Workforce Initiative: Houston, TX: Cornerstone for Kids.

Dennehy, J., Gannett, E., & Robbins, R. (2006). *Setting the stage for a youth development associate credential: A national review of professional credentials for the out-of-school time workforce.* Houston, TX: Cornerstone for Kids.

Dryfoos, J. G. (1999). The role of the school in children's out-of-school time. *The Future of Children, 9,* 117–134. Los Altos, CA: The David and Lucille Packard Foundation.

Edwards, A. (1996). *Interdisciplinary undergraduate programs: A directory* (2nd ed.). Acton, MA: Copley.

Eisikovits, R. A. (1997). *The anthropology of child and youth care work.* New York: The Hawthorne Press.

Foundations, Inc. (2010). *Out-of-school time: Leveraging higher education for quality.* Morristown, NJ: Author.

Freedberg, S. (2009). *Relational theory for social work practice: A feminist perspective.* New York: Routledge.

Fusco, D. (2003). *A landscape study of youth workers in out-of-school time.* Unpublished manuscript, College of the City University of New York, CUNY Workforce Development Initiative.

Gergen, K. J. (1991). *The saturated self: Dilemmas of identity in contemporary life.* New York: Basic Books.

Gumport, P. J., & Snydman, S. K. (2002). The formal organization of knowledge: An analysis of academic structure. *The Journal of Higher Education, 73,* 375–408.

Guskey, T. R. (1995). Professional development in education: In search of the optimal mix. In T. R. Guskey & M. Huberman (Eds.), *Professional development in education: New paradigms & practices* (pp. 114–132). New York: Teachers College Press.

Hirsch, B. J. (2005). *A place to call home: After-school programs for urban youth.* Washington, DC: American Psychological Association and New York: Teachers College Press.

Jeffs, T., & Smith, M. (2010). *Youth work practice.* Hampshire, UK: Palgrave Macmillan.

Jeffs, T., & Spence, J. (2007/2008). Farewell to all that? The uncertain future of youth and community work education. *Youth & Policy, 97/98,* 135–166.

Kahne, J., Nagaoka, J., Brown, A., O'Brien, J., Quinn, T., & Thiede, K. (2001, June). Assessing after-school programs as contexts for youth development. *Youth & Society, 32,* 421–446.

Klein, J. T. (1999). *Mapping interdisciplinary studies.* Washington, DC: Association of American Colleges and Universities.

Kuhn, T S. (1996). *The structure of scientific revolutions* (3rd ed.). Chicago: University of Chicago Press.

Light Jr., D. (1974). Introduction: The structure of the academic professions. *Sociology of Education, 47,* 2–28.

Little, P. M. D., Wimer, C., & Weiss, H. B. (2008). *After school programs in the 21st century: Their potential and what it takes to achieve it.* Cambridge, MA: Harvard Family Research Project.

McLaughlin, M. W., Irby, M. A., & Langman, J. (1994). *Urban sanctuaries: Neighborhood organizations in the lives and futures of inner-city youth.* San Francisco, CA: Jossey-Bass.

National Research Council and Institute of Medicine. (2002). Community programs to promote youth development. In J. Eccles & J. A. Gootman (Eds.), *Board on Children, Youth, and Families, Division of Behavioral and Social Sciences and Education.* Washington, DC: National Academy Press.

Noam, G. G., & Fiore, N. (2004, November). Relationships across multiple settings: An overview. *New Directions for Youth Development, 103,* 9–16.

Palmer, K. L., Anderson, S. A., & Sabatelli, R. M. (2009). How is the afterschool field defining program quality? *Afterschool Matters, 8,* 9–15.

Phelan, J. (2005). Child and youth care education: The creation of articulate practitioners. *Child & Youth Care Forum, 34*, 347–355.

Posner, J. K., & Vandell, D. L. (1994). Low-income children's after-school care: Are there beneficial effects of after-school programs? *Child Development, 65*, 440–456.

Rogoff, B. (1990). *Apprenticeship in thinking: Cognitive development in social context*. New York: Oxford University Press.

Vandell, D. L., & Ramanan, J. (1991). Children of the national longitudinal survey of youth: choices in after-school care and child development. *Developmental Psychology, 27*, 637–643.

White, R. (Ed.). (2009). *Concepts and methods of youth work*. Hobart: Australia Clearinghouse for Youth Studies.

Yam, B. (2004). From vocation to profession: The quest for professionalization of nursing. *British Journal of Nursing, 13*, 978–982.

Zeldin, S. (1995). *Opportunities and supports for youth development: Lessons from research implications for community leaders and scholars*. Washington, DC: Academy for Educational Development, Center for Youth Development and Policy Research.

Zeldin, S., Kimball, M., & Price, L. (1995). *What are the day-to-day experiences that promote youth development? An annotated bibliography of research on adolescents and their families*. Washington, DC: Academy for Educational Development, Center for Youth Development and Policy Research.

10

PREPARING THE NEXT GENERATION OF PROFESSORIATE IN YOUTH STUDIES

Mapping the Contested Spaces

Ross VeLure Roholt and Michael Baizerman

The topic of preparing the next generation of professoriate is crucial for the fields of youth studies and youth work because the best or even the most likely ways of preparing the next generation of faculty is not self-evident. Youth studies and youth work, along with work with youth in the community, are all contested spaces, rife with territorial conflicts and challenges over credentialing and other zoning issues; the university and the community are sites of tension and outright conflict and there is tension too in their relationships. The subtitle of this chapter suggests what we will do here: map the contested spaces of these two fields—youth studies and youth work, make distinctions, present categories, themes and issues and frame questions—all as ways to open this important topic for continuing analysis, reflection and conversations about our two fields and their possible and likely futures.

We begin with a very brief overview of the preparation of professoriate, primarily in the United States, over the last 200 years. This history allows us to briefly understand the current tension over preparing youth workers, and by extension, the preparation of youth studies faculty. Then we make distinctions, first within youth studies and youth work and then between these. Next, we use our University of Minnesota curricula distinctions to show academic and professional zoning in the current university. A final section presents five orienting questions for the field as we consider the future mapping of faculty in youth studies and youth work. All of these sections show the contested spaces which must be recognized so as to address adequately the topic of the future professoriate in youth studies (and youth work). Together these explorations and questions are basic to understanding our perspective(s) on the topic; some of these we note and discuss in the final section. We recognize that we are using a Weberian ideal-type strategy to show, disclose and discuss this topic. Such a strategy uses a selection of "certain aspects of behavior or institutions," or occupational roles, we add, which are "observable in the real world" but which are "exaggerated ... to form a coherent intellectual construction" to help understand a larger theory and the world at large (Gerth & Mills, 1946, p. 59). This means that it will be easy to critique our essay on grounds of being too abstract and theoretical and, hence, not (im) practical. To consider or to engage on these terms is to enter the conversation in a contested space, as we suggest next.

Preparing Faculty: A Brief History

Two hundred years ago, those who taught practitioners in the crafts of weaving and pottery were master craftspeople, mentors, and, if they worked at institutes and schools, teachers. Those who wanted to learn the crafts apprenticed themselves to masters; those who went to formal school were students. These structures of formal learning were very old, with antecedents in communities world-wide, across crafts and beyond, to include spiritual practice and healing, raising children, and learning to be skilled in sports and in the theatre, for example. Formal schools and formal education were (and are) only one structure of learning, the one most often called *education*.

Over the last two hundred years and into the present, much that was considered learning out of school in informal and non-formal learning spaces moved into formal learning settings, i.e., schools, institutes, colleges and universities. This was true for medicine, teaching, clergy, and a vast array of other occupations. In related sociopolitical and economic processes, many occupations became professions under law and in everyday speech. Criteria for professions included extended formal education in core knowledge, attitudes, values, and skills of the occupation/profession. This learning was increasingly delivered in formal educational settings.

When the profession involved applied work, as in medicine, social work, and teaching, for example, field training was also included. The ancient Greek distinctions between what we now call philosophy and theory, on the one side, and practice, on the other side, were bureaucratized, with distinctions between "knowledge about" and "knowledge how to" fitting the deeper Greek distinctions between and among the abstract and the concrete, the general and the particular. For many reasons, the abstract/general knowledge about was valorized as higher in thought and social status than concrete/particular knowledge and skill, the level of practical skill. Theory came to be treated as impractical by many engaged in practical work: these are contested spaces. Bringing these two sets into relation in school was the responsibility of a particular type of faculty, e.g., field supervisor, field instructor, while in everyday work in a profession this was the practitioner's responsibility, if not skill; "integration" of theory and practice was to be done by the worker, the site of skilled to expert practice and beyond (to phronesis, wisdom, to Aristotle) (Dreyfus & Dreyfus, 2004).

Where youth studies and youth work are to be learned in the future is related directly to who will teach and who will study these subjects, where, how and when. It is not inherent in the subject that the teacher and learner must be educated in formal school settings, i.e., that the teachers be college/university faculty and the professoriate be college/university employees. That it is so now, is a choice; where and what the arrangements will be also is a choice. Indeed, are institutions of higher learning the best site and are faculty the best people to prepare teachers and other masters in youth studies and youth work? This question remains contested in youth studies and youth work with disagreement over whether universities or community-based youth agencies should provide entry level training for youth workers (Astroth, Garza, & Taylor, 2004). Both groups have reasonable positions, although a combination may prove to be richer, as has been done in other fields (e.g., social work and teaching), with students expected to complete coursework on theory and practice and intensive fieldwork with appropriate field supervision by an experienced practitioner. We go deeper into this topic by examining next the distinction between youth studies and youth work.

Youth Studies and Youth Work: Some Distinctions

Youth studies and youth work are multiple contested sites, within and across the two. Youth studies can refer to disciplines and professions, to the set of such studies across disciplines and professions, to the study of the practice called youth work (in its many types and forms), and, as in the United Kingdom, to a category of books on young people. It is not a self-evident category. Neither is youth work, which can refer to work with youth/young person(s) and to a family of semi-to-full professions, to an occupational category, and to a job title. Even though all are contested, each can be a site of teaching and learning. When used to refer to university programs and study, youth studies focuses on codified knowledge (Eraut, 2000), e.g., knowledge about youth, young people and the young person. For example, in the program at the University of Minnesota, the curriculum is organized around five major questions and the multiple contested responses: Who are young people? Why are we interested? What should we do? What should I do? How should work with youth be done? Youth work as a site of teaching and learning concentrates on direct practice understanding and skill, often referred to as knowledge how to. Schematically, there are at least five formal relations between youth studies and youth work (see Figure 10.1):

1. Independent. This relationship can be found in the distinction above, with youth studies being the site for learning about youth and young people and youth work being the site for learning how to work with youth and young

people. Each has its own territory and does not seek to align closely with the other.

2. Closely aligned, with one having prominence. In the United States this arrangement can be found in discussions about improving youth work, or what many call synonymously, youth development work. This places the theory of youth development as prominent and youth work practice as flowing directly from this theoretical knowledge (knowledge about) (Edginton, Kowalski, & Randall, 2005). In other places, e.g., the UK, the relationship is reversed.

3. Partially overlapping. The two can be seen as being distinct but also sharing some important and central aspects.

4. One includes the other. In this way of understanding the relationship between the two, one is seen as being a smaller part of the other, e.g., one part of a larger whole.

5. The two are the same. They can also be understood as equal and the same. They are simply different ways of talking about the same thing. One has its origins in practice while the other in formal education, with both focus-

1. Independent

2. Closely aligned, with one having prominence

3. Partially overlapping

4. One includes the other

5. The two are the same

FIGURE 10.1 Five formal relationships between youth studies and youth work.

ing on deepening our understanding of young people, as well as becoming more skillful working with and on behalf of young people (policy, program management, evaluation, preparing faculty, etc.). This is the perspective we take in the Youth Studies program in the School of Social Work, College of Education and Human Development, at the University of Minnesota.

In colleges and universities, the valued direction in the relations between youth studies and youth work is from youth studies to youth work—from theory and principle and data to practice in everyday life. Ideally, theory/principles/data should guide practice. Therefore practice is the application in everyday life of theory/principle/data. In Europe until recently, the preferred model in institutes for learning to do youth work (i.e., practice) was philosophy to practice and philosophy to theory to practice. In the United States, possibly with the exception of existential youth work, guidance and counseling, the philosophical underpinned but did not explicitly drive practice. Instead, for reasons having to do with dominant philosophies, ideologies and practices in the natural sciences as adapted in the social/sociobehavioral sciences, practice in the United States came to be seen as applied science (all of this is ideal-type, of course, with many (most) youth work practitioners working from and in the concrete/particular).

Youth work, however, is not a simple category, but is rather a Wittengenstinian "family of resemblances" (Manser, 1967), one which crosses multiple academic disciplines and semi-to-full professions. There are multiple communities of practice (Wenger, 1998) within the category of youth work. Further, there is direct youth work, hands-on work, and indirect youth work, planning, policy making, managing, supervising, and evaluating.

University of Minnesota Youth Studies Program: Academic and Professional Zoning

Each community of practice has its own, yet often phenotypically-similar notions of what are its core knowledge, values and skills, and what expertise/competence is. These multiple paradigms, models, and theories within youth work can be contested spaces between the craft orientations (Eisikovits & Beker, 2001) of, say, child and youth care and street work on the practice level, and psychology, sociology, and child development on the theoretical level. Much of this becomes clear if we begin with some distinctions we use to frame the Youth Studies curriculum at the University of Minnesota. One of the five central questions of the Youth Studies curriculum is, *who are youth?* Depending on the community of practice and academic field, the following answers are all possible:

- Young person, the individual person of this age who is at a particular stage of development, e.g., adolescent, or a unique individual living in the world (e.g., Nakkula & Toshalis, 2006; Way, 1998).
- Young people, the sociological category of a population or generation with similarities among people of this age along with difference based on race, gender, class, sexual orientation, etc. (e.g., Qvortrup, Bardy, Sgritta, 1994; Wyness, 2006).
- "Youth," with the quotation marks refers to the representation of young people in the media as lazy, risky, and dangerous, including super predator, promiscuous, and addicted (Males, 1999; Skelton & Valentine, 1998; Sternheimer, 2006).
- Youth, without the question marks, is the cultural understanding of people of a particular age best captured in the question: what does it mean, to whom, to be a particular age (e.g., 15) around here, now? What are the cultural expectations and possibilities for people of certain ages (Gelder & Thornton, 1997; Lesko, 2001)?
- Youthhood, the way culture, society, and generation come together to structure how one grows up, e.g., the pathways that are made easily accessible and those that are made more difficult to obtain (Cote & Allahar, 1994; Flynn & Brotherton, 2008; Moss & Petrie, 2002).

The definition of young person most closely aligned with one's disciplinary perspective and gaze is the one most often taken-for-granted and taken without critical questioning as true. The preparation of youth studies and youth work faculty in a particular discipline, e.g., psychology, sociology, anthropology, political science, shapes the response to the simple question, who are youth? This not only informs how young people are understood and how their actions are interpreted but also what model of work with youth is justified (see Table 10.1). This is one way "knowledge about" comes to be connected to "knowledge how to."

Again, what is self-evident is that the field of youth work and the communities of practice within the field is broad, diverse, and often not reducible to a common core of known principles, values or skills, not necessarily (or reasonably) integrated (or integratable) and frequently contested as to truth–status, professions and control over students. None of this is either surprising or necessarily troublesome or bad. Rather, we name it as another element to notice and understand as we search for understanding about preparing the next professoriate in youth studies and youth work. Consider and reflect on the material presented. Think of it as spatialized, as spaces of learning and teaching, with ideas and paradigms as spaces too. Think too of theory and skill as spaces rather than as levels, for example. In this metaphoric language, the topic we are addressing can be thought of as a geographic question, a focus on the where the site of work is to be done. The who (teachers/students) of the work, the what/curricula and how of the work, the pedagogy, are each geographies too: who will do

TABLE 10.1 Connecting Knowledge About with Knowledge How To

Youth Studies Disciplinary Gaze	Who are Youth?	Youth Work Focus	Youth Work Example
Development Psychology Philosophy	Youth Person	Direct work	Prevention of unhealthy behaviors and promotion of healthy activity
Sociology	Young Person	Indirect work	Policy work and advocacy on racial make-up of juvenile justice system
Journalism Cultural Studies Media Studies	"Youth"	Indirect and direct work	Public service announcements Critical media work with young people
Anthropology Cultural Studies (New) sociology	Youth	Indirect and direct	Involving young people in peace building and community building efforts
Political Science Economics Adolescent Development	Youthhood	Indirect	Creating new spaces and opportunities for young people in communities.

the work is spread across, say, where it will be done and how it will be done is intimately connected to where and what will be done and who will do it. This spatializing of the topics allows the issues we are discussing to be geographies of learning and teaching, and this opens possibilities immensely: No longer must the learning site be a material place only; it can be a virtual place. Thus, obviously, there are now different insides/insiders and outsides/outsiders than when there were only brick walls and rhetorical walls and disciplinary walls, etc., between and among learning sites, learners and curricula. Thus, one person can teach at once, youth work to the whole United States, indeed the world.

Now remember that youth work as practiced in the United States in a vast array of settings using numerous paradigms of practice and conceptions of youth (e.g., developmental, psychological, constructivist) is typically organization/agency-based work. If we move from the material to the virtual university, and if we are moving from the Modern to the Late Modern to Post–Modern university, then we must consider too how the site of practice, the agency, changes in each of these three formations, e.g., from formal bureaucratic-type to rhizomic in shape and practice. Similarly, conceptions of youth change as we move across these formations. So too, do scholarly paradigms and faculty practice. In the move from modernity through late modernity to post-modernity, the future is surely not necessarily an extension of the past, and its past, while the present (some argue), is created out of the future-as-envisioned rather than caused by the past. In short, since the future is unpredictable and uncertain, preparing future faculty in youth studies and youth work will also have to take into consideration the possibility that the core elements of beliefs, knowledge, practice, and organizations may be radically different in purpose, legitimacy, form and practice (function).

All of this and much more can be brought into reflection on the preparation of professors for youth studies and youth work. If our point is clear and taken, the topic is most complex because of the multiple, contested elements which constitute the knowledge, skills, values and beliefs of the practice, work with young people (direct youth work) and one their behalf (indirect youth work); and because we are in a time period of great uncertainty. One way to engage these reticula of change is to accept the following questions as an address which calls the field of youth studies and youth work to respond, and by so doing comes to define the future of the fields, making it easier (hopefully) to engage the issue of preparing the next generation of professoriate.

Five Questions to Frame the Debate

Youth studies and youth work are likely to continue to be contested spaces. The training of future professors in youth studies and youth work remains unclear and without an obvious, single, organizational, and scholarly location within the university, as currently organized in the United States. While other countries have created programs of study in both Youth Studies (Australia) and Community and Youth Work (United Kingdom), in the United States both of these programmatic arrangements are likely to encounter competition and resistance from other disciplines and professional training programs, such as social work, psychology, youth development, and human services. In the United States, no single group or discipline is inherently a more reasonable site, and what may matter most is how these next several questions are answered and by whom.

Who Determines the Players in Designing the Preparation Programs for Future Youth Studies and Youth Work Professoriate?

This question makes explicit how current and future faculty training programs are and will be in part a political process. Deciding who will be at the table, who has the qualifications to participate in creating future training programs in youth studies and/or youth work shapes much of what will be decided and how. Will multiple disciplinary backgrounds have equal representation? Will practice fields have a space reserved in the decision-making group (which ones)? This is a critical first question because how it is answered will pre-form what is "appropriate" knowledge and what is taken to be "quality" practice for youth studies and youth work, thereby focusing, directing, and limiting the preparation of future faculty. There is much clarity and agreement on these issues within specific professions, there is far less across several professions, therefore here too are contested spaces.

There are many approaches to understanding young people. In the United States, the emphasis has been on young people as adolescent, the individualized understanding of young people as going through a natural process of growing up. Youth development is the dominant frame for understanding young people in the United States in both scholarship and practice (Silbereisen & Lerner, 2007). Obviously, this is not the only way to understand young people or to frame practice with young people, nor to frame youth studies and youth work used for decades elsewhere around the world. Models of youth, of youth studies, and of youth work are core elements in curriculum in the two fields.

What Is the Curriculum for Youth Studies/Youth Work Faculty (e.g., What Can We Expect Them to Know and Know How To Do)?

The curriculum for preparing future youth studies/youth work faculty is deeply contested and often divided, as noted. Unlike other semi-to-full professional preparation fields, youth studies and youth work are filled with more questions than agreements on core issues. There is strong advocacy for explicit and specific frameworks to ground scholarship and practice and these often are met with equally robust advocacy for alternative frameworks. For example, after exploring the issues for youth studies and youth work in this chapter, it comes as no surprise that youth development has hundreds of definitions (Delgado, 2002) and has several competing conceptualizations (e.g., positive youth development, community youth development, social justice youth development).

This is indeed a problem for those who want clear conceptual and operational definitions of youth development and youth work. By extension, it also creates problems for those who want to support the fields by preparing the future professoriate. The choices are a single disciplinary frame or a multidisciplinary frame. Each poses particular challenges. The first limits the possible ways of understanding young people, and the work, while the second is difficult to organize, manage, and fund in the current and likely future in fiscally scarce university settings.

Curriculum discloses contested spaces around the research preparation of future faculty. Current dominant perspectives on science as such are neo-positivist social science, interpretive science (hermeneutics), and the human sciences. Each includes an epistemological stance and appropriate methodologies. Each has obvious and profound consequences for defining what are youth studies and youth work scholarships. How can research support and aid the improvement, development and innovation of practice with and on the behalf of young people is the crucial practical question in a moment when practice is based on "empirical data."

In contrast to these dominant perspectives is practical science, as adapted by Strasser (1985), following Aristotle. Practical science is to Strasser (1985) "... a science which is conceived in order to make possible, to improve, and to correct a definite kind of extra-scientific praxis" (p. 59). This science does not debate what methods might be more useful (e.g., qualitative vs. quantitative), but instead turns youth studies and youth work scholars and practitioners towards exploring and learning how they can improve, enhance, and deepen their and others work with young people. Debates on these and related issues are crucial for defining a field and for it gaining legitimacy in the university. Thus it directly affects the preparation of future faculty.

Do We Still Need Youth as a Field-forming Category?

There are many difficulties that emerge when personhood and human development are framed as stage processes based on age/time. In this conception, age becomes primary and reified—it is the reason for one's actions and behaviors (Wyn & White, 1997). It can be troubling when this frame becomes dominant and is also seen as natural rather than as one portrait (Deutsch, 1992) of the person, distinct from among many, one that may or may not be agreed to by the person himself. Regardless of agreement, this theoretical base and derivative portrait provide rationales for both the study of persons of this age and for quality work with them. It emphasizes certain intended outcomes and ignores others. A portrait also separates out young people as distinct and different; they are "othered" (Dimitriadis, 2008), which carries theoretical and real consequences for them and the field.

Who Determines What Is Faculty?

Given the overall contested space of youth studies and youth work, who is faculty is somewhat unclear. What is commonly understood as a basic qualification is the attainment of one or more advanced degrees of higher education. This fits the historical movement in faculty preparation towards a focus on theoretical and university-type knowledge, "knowledge about." This type of knowledge has been privileged over others, e.g., knowledge how to do. Thus future faculty must, it is assumed, master this type of knowledge. In effect this has limited the possible composition of current and future youth studies and youth work faculty by excluding those without such credentials. If the minimum requirement or essential qualification for faculty is attainment of a graduate degree, what type of knowledge and groups of people necessary to teach youth studies and youth work are excluded? Where are the spaces and pathways for competent and expert practitioners to assume faculty status and role? What are the consequences for the field and for preparation of faculty for exclusion on these grounds?

This question brings up a secondary question: What role will young people have in preparing future faculty in youth studies and youth work? Choosing these qualifications over any and all others also prevents young people themselves from being seen as contributing to the overall teaching and preparation of youth scholars and youth workers. They are seen as service recipients and not resources and co-contributors to the overall preparation and curriculum, even though they may be qualified to contribute to both. It is already clear that young people can contribute to community change efforts (e.g., Checkoway et al., 2003), and it is equally plausible that they are competent and capable to contribute to the preparation of future faculty. It is in the ethos of youth work (and youth studies) that young people can fulfill some faculty roles in preparing the future youth studies/youth work professoriate. Yet, few university-based programs invite young people to help prepare youth workers or faculty of youth workers. Why? In part because they, like expert practitioners, do not bring what many think is the appropriate form of knowledge for faculty preparation.

Is a Separate Youth Studies/Youth Work Faculty Necessary?

What do we gain by segregating and possibly isolating the preparation of future youth studies and youth work faculty by keeping them away from other disciplinary and experiential perspectives? There is an assumption that certain types of content and preparatory experiences will produce youth studies faculty of a high quality, while also providing needed leadership for an emerging practice and field. This seems to be pushing against current thinking in higher education that calls for more interdisciplinary spaces where scholars and practitioners can join together around a common theme for innovative teaching, learning, and research. What is the driving force behind clarifying and creating formal and distinct pathways for youth studies and youth work faculty?

This exclusionary approach might result in faculty who are fully youth studies and youth work. Yet, in its accomplishment, the field may lose what makes U.S. youth studies and youth work distinct—its multidisciplinary scholarly base, one grounded in multiple and diverse perspectives. Multidisciplinary has been troublesome to those who want greater clarity and a unique body of knowledge so as to begin to build a stronger professional field, one with clear boundaries between it and the outside worlds of social work, education, adolescent development, and so on. Yet, the exclusion of outsiders and the inclusion of a single discipline do not always produce stronger practice, better practitioners or better and more relevant research. When organized formally, faculty begin to share ways of knowing, begin to develop a professional and scholarly gaze. This gaze both illuminates and obscures the topic of study, while those ideas that are taken-for-granted as true remain salient and are given considerable attention in teaching and scholarship, and those that are obscured are quickly forgotten or marginalized and not included in teaching or scholarship. This limits the subject by limiting its field of vision and frames of practice (Cohen, 1997).

This raises questions not only for the preparation of future youth studies/ youth work faculty, but also whether having designated faculty leads to more effective preparation of youth workers and in turn to significant improvement in young people's overall everyday experience. The logical chain is in practice too hard (and expensive) to disentangle and prove. But it remains the goal of the preparation of faculty.

Conclusions

Preparing future youth studies/youth work faculty is difficult because everything in the higher education world is changing at an increasingly rapid rate. Structures and missions that have been guaranteed for centuries are eroding, and it is not clear what will take their place or the form of the future university. Within this uncertainty, developing preparation programs for faculty in defined fields will be challenging, while in an undefined field like youth studies and youth work, which is most often described as contested and diverse, it will be even more difficult. As long as youth as an idea and population and work with them directly and indirectly are all contested, it is reasonable to expect that the questions of who to prepare, how, when, by whom they are to be prepared will remain contested as well. Responses, if not answers, must be worked out locally, not universally. It is also uncertain whether semi-professions will have clear roads to professional status since the ground rules for achieving professional status are changing and the roads are increasingly muddy and bumpy. Added to this is the good possibility that it is not at all clear that young people, certainly in the West and North, will continue to be valorized and focused on, given their shrinking demography. This is in contrast to the South and East, where youth populations are rapidly expanding to a relatively high percentage of the total population. It is likely there where the future of youth studies and youth work will be most active and consequential (and be less tied to individual youth persons than to populations of youth).

In these areas, universities may not be the leaders in developing the practice and theory as they are too few, too poor, and costs are high. Hence, training for those who work with youth is more likely to be closer to community with more emphasis on practice than on research and with faculty being local (craft) masters. In the end, we may be entering the debate on the preparation of the new professoriate at the moment when the question has traction in the United States, yet, ironically, when the center of gravity is moving elsewhere—out of the United States, out of universities and away from graduate-degree prepared faculty. The future of the preparation of faculty is unclear, and neither simple to imagine or to construct.

References

Astroth, K., Garza, P., & Taylor, B. (2004). Getting down to business: Defining competencies for entry-level youth workers. *New Directions for Youth Development, 104,* 25–37.

Checkoway, B., Richards-Schuster, K., Abdullah, S., Aragon, M., Facio, E., Figueroa, L., Reddy, E., et al. (2003). Young people as competent citizens. *Community Development Journal, 38,* 298–309.

Cohen, P. (1997). *Rethinking the youth question: Education, labour and cultural studies.* Hampshire, UK: Macmillan.

Cote, J., & Allahar, A. (1994). *Generation on hold: Coming of age in the late twentieth century.* New York: New York University Press.

Delgado, M. (2002). *New frontiers for youth development in the twenty-first century: Revitalizing and broadening youth development.* New York: Columbia University Press.

Deutsch, E. (1992). *Creative being: The crafting of person and world.* Honolulu: University of Hawaii Press.

Dimitriadis, G. (2008). *Studying urban youth culture.* New York: Peter Lang.

Dreyfus, H., & Dreyfus, S. (2004). The ethical implications of the five-stage skill-acquisition model. *Bulletin of Science, Technology and Society, 24,* 251–264.

Eisikovits, Z., & Beker, J. (2001). Beyond professionalism: The child and youth care worker as craftsman. *Child and Youth Care Forum, 30,* 415–434.

Edginton, C., Kowalski, C., & Randall, S. (2005). *Youth work: Emerging perspectives in youth development.* Champagne, IL: Sagamore.

Eraut, M. (2000). Non-formal learning and tacit knowledge in professional work. *British Journal of Educational Psychology, 70,* 113–136.

Flynn, M., & Brotherton, D. (Eds.). (2008). *Globalizing the streets: Cross-cultural perspectives on youth, social control, and empowerment.* New York: Columbia University Press.

Gelder, K., & Thornton, S. (Eds.). (1997). *The subcultures reader.* London: Routledge.

Gerth, H., & Mills, C. (Eds.). (1946). *From Max Weber: Essays in sociology.* New York: Oxford University Press.

Lesko, N. (2001). *Act your age! A cultural construction of adolescence.* New York: Routledge Farmer.

Males, M. (1999). *Framing youth: Ten myths about the next generation.* Monroe, ME: Common Courage Press.

Manser, A. (1967). Games and family resemblances. *Philosophy, 42,* 210–225.

Moss, P., & Petrie, P. (2002). *From children's services to children's spaces: Public policy, children and childhood.* New York: Routledge Farmer.

Nakkula, M., & Toshalis, E. (2006). *Understanding youth: Adolescent development for educators.* Cambridge, MA: Harvard Education Press.

Qvortrup, J., Bardy, M., & Sgritta, G. (1994). *Childhood matters: Social theory, practice, and politics.* Aldershot, UK: Avebury.

Silbereisen, R., & Lerner, R. (Eds.). (2007). *Approaches to positive youth development.* Thousand Oaks, CA: Sage.

Skelton, T., & Valentine, G. (1998). *Cool places: Geographies of youth culture.* New York: Routledge.

Strasser, S. (1985). *Understanding and explanation: Basic ideas concerning the humanity of the human sciences.* Pittsburg, PA: Duquesne University Press.

Sternheimer, K. (2006). *Kids these days: Facts and fiction about today's youth.* Lanham, MD: Rowman and Littlefield.

Way, N. (1998). *Everyday courage: The lives and stories of urban teenagers.* New York: New York University Press.

Wenger, E. (1998). *Communities of practice: Learning, meaning, and identity.* Cambridge, UK: Cambridge University Press.

Wyn, J., & White, R. (1997). *Rethinking youth.* Thousand Oaks, CA: Sage.

Wyness, M. (2006). *Childhood and Society: An Introduction to the sociology of childhood.* New York: Palgrave Macmillan.

11

YOUTH DEVELOPMENT NETWORK

A Site for the Professional Development of Youth Workers

Jacqueline Davis-Manigaulte

Youth development workers are lifelong learners who gain additional insight into how to successfully work with youth and with their colleagues through a variety of formal, informal and incidental learning experiences. Understanding the impact of youth workers' varied learning experiences is critical to creating effective professional development opportunities for youth workers and for the development of the field. This chapter focuses on the dissertation study of The Youth Development Network (YDN) that engaged youth workers in a series of meetings and related activities over a period of six years resulting in numerous rich and varied opportunities for growth and professional development for the participants. The purpose of the study was to determine what key learning and actions resulted from participation in the network (Davis-Manigaulte, 2008). This information may help shape future professional development efforts for youth workers—particularly in relation to how they learn from each other, serve as expert practitioners and inform their field of work. Following is an overview of the research project, sample profiles of project participants, key findings and implications of the study.

Research Overview

The Youth Development Network was philanthropically funded in 1994 to build the capability of 14 community-based organizations in New York City to understand and use a positive youth development approach in their work. YDN solicited participating member agencies through a competitive process. Its intent was as follows:

The Network strives to become a coalition committed to a shared view of positive youth outcome goals; the design and use of unobtrusive tools for measuring programs' performance; principles of effective organizational structures and good program practices based upon knowledge of "real life" situations and founded in theoretical writings and research findings; and increasing access to effective models of staff development for youth and adult staff within youth development organizations.

(Davis-Manigaulte, 2008, p. 6)

YDN provided funds to participating agencies to build two cohorts of youth development workers (approximately 40 per cohort; 2–3 years of engagement per cohort). Cohort members participated in training and other activities sponsored by a cross-agency network and were expected to bring what they learned back to their agencies. The first cohort consisted of eight agencies, and the second included six new agencies. (Several agencies were represented in both cohorts and some participated in only one.) The number of staff per agency ranged from three to eight. Network members:

- Received training based on a nationally recognized curriculum, Advancing Youth Development.
- Worked with others in the network on committees that addressed topics such as best practices, marketing and dissemination, school-based programming, youth development credentialing, technology, evaluation, and organizational support.
- Participated in bimonthly meetings and forums on specific topics with expert researchers in the field.
- Conducted peer assessments of each participating agency.

Network member accomplishments involved cross-agency collaboration to come to agreement about how to better help youth and build capabilities within and beyond network members for youth development. Accomplishments included (Davis-Manigaulte, 2008, pp. 6–7):

- Identification of best practices that were promulgated and used in participating agencies.
- Identification of outcomes for which participating agencies agreed to be held accountable.
- Identification of core competencies for youth workers and effective staff development methodologies to transmit these competencies.
- Development of an effective dissemination strategy for promoting positive youth development principles.
- Resources such as "a series of flipbooks" on topics such as: "Best Practices," "Youth Outcomes" and "Core Competencies for Youth Development Workers;" as well as reports on various youth development related topics such as multiculturalism and primary care providers.

Research Methods

The 2008 study was a qualitative investigation of how the YDN functioned. The researcher was intrigued with the value of this approach, both in terms of development of individual capabilities, and also in how a network of this kind could foster and spread collective learning within and across agencies. The research questions were: (1) What and how did youth development staff members learn about themselves and their practice through their YDN experience? (2) In what ways did the youth development staff members' practice reportedly change as a result of participation in the YDN? (3) What factors facilitated and/ or impeded the learning and practice of staff participants (Davis-Manigaulte, 2008, p. 8). The researcher was a participant observer in some YDN activities. Also, YDN members completed a survey describing a significant network-related learning experience. Twenty-two of 39 surveys were completed for a response rate of 56%. Four frontline workers and five management staff were then interviewed in-depth about the changes in practice that resulted from the experience. In addition, the primary supervisor and a peer colleague of each interviewee were asked to complete a short feedback form and provide examples of changes observed in the YDN member they knew. The researcher also reviewed documents and talked informally to many people in the context of her observation and attendance at network sessions such as Saturday courses, youth development forums, large group and committee meetings.

An inductive, semi-grounded theory strategy was used to code and analyze the data. The researcher was also guided in other ways by the literature. Initially, the researcher intended to base the analysis on a team learning framework developed by Kasl, Marsick, and Dechant (1997) that sheds light on team learning processes, outcomes, and conditions for group and organizational learning. During data analysis, however, the researcher found that Wenger's (1998) community of practice framework was a better fit for explaining the data. Network members emphasized the way they, and their participating agencies, gained an appreciation for youth development as a professional identity and developed their confidence and capabilities; they also developed tools and resources related to their work. These are key characteristics of communities of practice (Wenger, 1998).

The researcher first presented survey results, which provided an overall picture of "network makeup and operation" (and was most helpful in preparing for the interviews). Afterwards, holistic profiles were developed for each of the nine interviewees, followed by cross-case analysis. Even though the sample was relatively small, the researcher looked for differences in findings by role (i.e., frontline vs. management) and by level (i.e., middle level management vs. program directors). However, many managers had earlier been frontline workers and could, therefore, take both perspectives. Over the period of the study, interviewees also changed positions and sometimes agencies. However, for this study, interviews were focused on the individuals' experiences during participation in the YDN itself rather than experiences acquired or views held because of subsequent new positions. The study also included analysis of the ways that network experiences of individuals were leveraged to support learning within and across agencies and factors that facilitated and/or impeded learning and its application.

Three Network Member Profiles

Following are profiles of three YDN members, one from each staffing level, who participated in semi-structured interviews. The profiles provide insight about the study participants and the network experience. They are based on information included in the research case narratives. They include an initial quote from the interviewees that reflects how they felt the program influenced them, demographic and professional background information, and key examples of what was learned, how learning occurred, and application of learning.

Anthony's Profile

> *I had the opportunity to rub shoulders with some of the smartest people I have ever met—being exposed to new ideas and thoughts regarding our field and my involvement in several committees was an education for me, and I know I am a better manager as a result.*

Anthony is a male in the "45 years and above" age group. At the time of the interview, he was a Program Coordinator at a youth development program in Queens, New York, and had been in that position for three years and with the agency for nine. Anthony described his position as middle management. He had some college education. While volunteering, he was offered a part-time position and then became a full-time staff member. As a Program Coordinator, Anthony is responsible for the agency's Beacon After-school Program, including staff recruitment, training, and supervision, as well as program planning, implementation, and documentation. He participated in the YDN for approximately three years, serving as the primary representative from his agency, which was involved in the second cohort (1998–2001). He was an active participant in the dissemination committee, which focused on sharing the message of positive youth development as well as resources to support workers' implementation of the related concepts.

The key change in himself that Anthony cited was his increased confidence in sharing his ideas with his colleagues, who he initially felt were more knowledgeable than he was about the field of youth development because his previous work experience was in an entirely different field. Anthony also pointed out several times during the interview that his experience with the program provided a framework for many of the things he had been doing instinctively as a youth worker. The learning for him appeared to be knowing the formal youth development concepts related to his actions and being more intentional in his efforts to incorporate those practices into his work with youth and colleagues.

Anthony's learning was influenced by a variety of experiences. His initial experiences occurred in the YDN meetings and committee sessions, where he listened and observed a great deal and reflected on points raised during the discussions. He reiterated that the dialogue and exchange of information that occurred during the meetings was one of the influential aspects of his experience. He also identified committee work as a vehicle through which he learned, particularly in the dissemination committee through which he helped train other youth workers in the youth development principles. In addition, he cited the site assessment of another youth agency conducted by a team of youth workers and youth from his agency as a network experience that strongly impacted his learning.

There are several ways that Anthony applied what he learned through his network experiences to his practice at his worksite. He incorporated the positive youth development principles that he learned and taught other youth workers through his work with the dissemination committee into the orientation program he conducted for new staff at his agency. In addition, during staff development and program planning, he used the site assessment experience as a common frame of reference for the staff to create a shared understanding of the environment that the agency was striving to achieve. Finally, he incorporated what he learned about positive youth development into his work with youth, individually and in group settings, in a more intentional way.

Celinda's Profile

> *The Networks project really helped all of us to name what it was that we do—and to understand that. And to begin to talk about structures, practice, principles and all of those things that really … allow us to bond as people in the work…. no matter how different our programs; that's the commonality.*

Celinda is a female in the "45 years and above" age group. At the time of the interview, she had been in the position of Division Director for a major youth development and social service organization in Brooklyn for five years and at the agency for 18 years. Celinda described her position as upper management. She is a college graduate and has done postgraduate work. She was highly involved in several network committees, including the outcomes, assessment, and evaluation committees. Celinda's commitment and passion for her work were most evident. She agreed to an interview (held in the evening) although her workdays were very full. At that time she was co-director of a new community-based high school with an after–school component and a wide variety of services and supports for the youth and their families. It was an extensive collaboration with the city's education department, as well as many other agencies and organizations. Celinda cited her realization of the importance of youth work as a profession as one of her key learning outcomes. She reflected,

> *In some ways, I think that before Networks, I felt like we weren't respected and nobody really gave a damn or whatever. And after Networks, there was a sense of ownership and just a sense of professionalism. It's a different kind of ownership about what we do. Really feeling like [we influence] a lot of young people.*

In addition to a stronger sense of identity, Celinda discussed her clearer understanding and respect for youth and their potential to benefit the community.

> *You know that any child that has an opportunity to contribute in ways that they feel are meaningful, they're going to do well. They're learning to be focused, they're learning that they can set goals, they're learning they have power, that they can control some things, that they can make choices.... So this is, I think, a lot of what's come out of the network.*

Also, Celinda's enhanced understanding of youth work, and respect for youth, led to an increased awareness and willingness to advocate for youth development programs. Celinda identified the discussions in the committee meetings as a major way that learning occurred for her.

> *Well, I think that, for me, when I started participating in the Networks, it was very powerful for me. Because [sitting] roundtable with other people who were doing the work and listening to people's perspectives about what youth work is, the different ways that work happens, different designs for programs, people's passion and conviction about what the priorities are, what young people need. And that's an education.*

In addition to participating in group discussions, Celinda also learned by reading material she received from the network, which she felt was very informative and affirming in regard to her understanding and connection to youth development work. She commented, "... I couldn't read enough. I have two binders that I put together from Networks articles that we received. And I've read practically all of them. And saw myself in the articles from the network—I could relate." Celinda shared that she redesigned a counselor log to include the information needed to reflect the needs of the program and outcomes the group wished to address:

> *Well, I think that documentation was one of the things. We talked about the competency areas. And I'm sitting there, we do outreach, we do outreach.... And I'm going back and, again, because this was the pet peeve that I had for years feeling like how can we [best do] that? And I remember redesigning the counselor*

log. And feeling like this is what I want. I think without, you know, the label that negative [so-and-so] youth. But understanding the person....

She wanted to be sure that staff understood what they were doing, how it addressed critical needs, and how best to document the agency's services and outcomes.

Gayle's Profile

I wanted to be there. I liked going to the source. I liked going into what I call the cubicles, the think tank and thinking and processing it, debating and challenging and bully consensus, and the reflecting back. I liked all of that.

Gayle is a female in the "45 and above" age group. At the time of the interview, she was the Executive Director at a youth development program in Manhattan. She had been in that position for 12 years and with the agency for 12 years as well. Gayle described her position as upper management. She has a postgraduate degree. Gayle was invited to join the first cohort of the YDN by one of the staff members responsible for the creation of the program. She did not join then because she did not feel that she had staff to cover the program operations in her absence at that time. She explained that:

I'd been here a couple of years but not long enough to say I was ready to commit myself to giving up my time to do something that would want a lot of time. I didn't want to start something that I didn't think I could fully participate in and complete. So the second phase I was invited in along with my other colleagues and I felt that now I had a better grasp of what needed to be done, I had built a more solid infrastructure with staffing and I could spend more time looking at some of these larger issues—and seeing what the implications could be with our own programs, so I joined the second round.

Strengthening of her professional network appeared to be a valuable outcome for Gayle. She described the value of professional networking with one of her YDN colleagues: "I have this issue I just want to walk it through with you, and get your feedback on, and I knew that his feedback was the best he had to offer, and he did some thinking on it and vice versa. So we'll have these deep conversations about staffing, managing staff and what's working, not working."

The committees were the primary vehicle for learning for Gayle. She participated in several, including the organizational structure, dissemination, and evaluation committees—she was more active in some than others; however, she felt that she wanted to get a "broader picture" of the thinking and issues related to youth development programming. In her involvement with one committee she stated, "I think that the whole process in that committee was significant to me ... seeing these other powerhouses, and the thinking process. I can still just visualize all the meetings in that room."

As the Executive Director of her agency, Gayle was able to take action to ensure that the youth development approach was incorporated into the agency's mission and supported through the agency budget. Her program was already operating in this way; however, the network experience seemed to reinforce her efforts. She recalled,

> *Bringing the language into my own [agency] documents and to my own practice. That was it, in terms of organization. I was able to take all the organizational stuff, because I can read it, talk it, and then apply it into this organization—making sure that we use the concepts in our mission. I was able to change the mission and was able to include it, but I have done that before. And I just validated the one that I had done, because it was values between academic and social outcomes of the kids here.*

Research Findings

Key findings of the YDN study help to reveal how the creation of this network enabled members to learn. Some of this learning was natural and organic. But learning also happened because of the mix of activities designed into the community, for example:

- Opportunities to work together through committees on frameworks, guidelines and tools;
- Site visits using assessment tools created by network members;
- Socialization with youth development leaders and experts through symposia and other gatherings; and
- Readings, manuals, and other materials that were distributed and discussed.

The findings from the study show that deep learning occurred related to seeing oneself and the field as "professional," and growing one's competencies to be an effective practitioner in the field. Strategies for learning included training, but what stood out were informal and incidental learning approaches that were catalyzed by the collaborative generation and sharing of new ideas. The network created interaction opportunities. Information and new ideas were then brought back and applied in home agencies through training of others, meetings and symposia, and other mechanisms such as subsequent interaction with youth and colleagues.

What Was Learned—Individual and Collective Professional Identity

An overwhelming finding from the study—which caused the researcher to move toward a community of practice framework for making sense of the results—was the unanimous agreement that the network experience developed

TABLE 11.1 Sample Learning Outcomes — Professional Identity as Youth Workers (Adapted from Davis-Manigaulte, 2008, pp. 93-94)

Celinda	"For me, being there [in networks], I felt like, 'Oh, finally! Finally! There are other people out there who really feel like this is important.'... having had that experience made me — you know when something becomes crystal clear? When your belief, when the experiences that you've had and what you've come to trust in and know that that's the right thing to do, crystallizes? It was all so crystal clear."
Nia	"I think the network helped me understand that I work in a field. That it is something viable, this is your career. Being a youth worker is equated with that. It provides that sense of the professional that I don't know if I would have thought about it prior to [the network]."
Celinda	"It was a big deal. You know, here you've got—you're naming these things. We carved out a field. Youth work. And I felt like, I'm part of this? I [told] my mother and ... my entire family. I could not stop talking about it."
Simone	"Being in that network, hearing from other practitioners, opens up your mind more broadly, to see beyond just your agency. Think about youth development really as something that we want to effect citywide or even nationwide.... It's been a process for me to think about it more globally, rather than just within our agency.... Really thinking more about the field and what we are doing to affect the field."
Anthony	One of the things that really stays with me is just being in a room full of people and all these different backgrounds, but so many of them have so much to offer in terms of experience and messages flying around and understanding that this is almost like a movement.... Here there's so many people that I've met that are in the same field and helping you to understand the broadness of the field."

an individual and collective "sense of identity and professionalism as youth development workers" (Davis-Manigaulte, 2008, p. 92). The data in Table 11.1 illustrate this forging of a common professional youth worker identity.

Related to this finding was a deep understanding of the positive youth development approach that underlay the creation of the network and heightened awareness of, and capability in, the core competencies that the network articulated. Core competencies described in the interviews were based on YDN's framework and related to:

• Program development based on knowledge of the underlying positive youth development framework—and of adolescent developmental stages—with a view to fostering youth empowerment [within the context of one's own agency and organizational policies and procedures].
• Assessment through reflection on one's practice and performance.

- Communication to maintain a relationship of trust with young people and to convey information in the spirit intended.
- Community and family engagement based on understanding and respect for culture, community, and family structure.
- Implementation via skilled group work, and ability to motivate and engage youth as well as respond well to their needs and interests.
- Advocacy/networking with schools and external systems based on knowledge of youth rights and the social context of youth.
- Intervention, including ability to deal with conflicts and knowledge of intervention strategies (adapted from Davis-Manigaulte, 2008, p. 96).

There was unanimous agreement about the value of engaging with, and applying, various core competencies framed by the positive youth development approach. Moreover, analysis showed that the three top competencies mentioned pertained to critical thinking via appreciation for, and understanding of, different perspectives; understanding youth and their developmental needs; and the ability to engage in self-assessment and self-learning (Davis-Manigaulte, 2008, pp. 172–175).

How People Learned—Collective Reflection In, On, and Through Action

Participants in the YDN identified various formal and informal learning strategies that helped them develop insights and capabilities. Chief among these were reflection, committee work, and site assessment that fostered individual growth but that often did so through collective, social learning in, on, and through action. There appeared to be a "continuum [in the nature] of reflection among youth workers" based on level of responsibility. Interviewees who were in charge of programs spoke more often about how "reflection related to program improvement strategies and issues such as overall goals and accountability of youth development workers" (Davis-Manigaulte, 2008, p.178). By contrast, frontline workers often described ways that the YDN helped them to reflect on their interaction with youth and colleagues, and to think about their own development. For example, John described how reflecting on his own development shaped his current work:

> I reflect back on my youth. Looking at what some of the young people do here and how they interact with each other, how they interact with you. I look back and see I made some hasty decisions.... I thought that I knew it all and everything. But I also see the great potential that they have and I also see how I had a great potential, but how it could be easily lost if you don't do this, whatever that may be.

> (Davis-Manigaulte, 2008, p. 108)

Likewise, Alexa remembered

> A lot of my generation was on drugs or drinking and they were like only 14/15 [years of age]. I remember smoking just because it was something to do, or something that I could fit in with. And then to take Best Practices and understand that, well, that's because you [youth] are looking for somewhere to link.... I know what it was like for me, and I don't want you [youth] to go through it.
>
> (Davis-Manigaulte, 2008, p. 125)

No matter their level of responsibility, many interviewees learned a great deal by participating in committees and task forces. They learned much through "dialogue with 'powerful individuals' within the youth development field" and "shared the inclination to initially listen and observe before expressing their thoughts.... [They] valued the opportunity to see the sharing and negotiation process implemented as they addressed various aspects and issues related to their youth development work agenda" (Davis-Manigaulte, 2008, pp. 177–178). Frontline workers felt appreciated and acknowledged for contributions they made and learned still more by observing their senior role models in action.

Site assessments were appreciated as vehicles for gaining diverse perspectives, getting valuable feedback, assessing their programs against the field, and engaging in dialogue with knowledgeable others whom interviewees might call upon in the future. Anthony, for example, appreciated his role in doing assessments at other sites: "unless you go out and see what other people are doing, you don't get new ideas and you don't get different perspectives. And then you don't know" (Davis-Manigaulte, 2008, p. 110). Jessica, conversely, gained a lot from feedback from other youth workers who visited her site for an assessment: "the team was comprised of line staff at other agencies at Networks. They organized interviews with the Executive Director, with myself, with line staff, with [youth], with everyone to get feedback from everyone.... they were outlining some strengths and weaknesses" (Davis-Manigaulte, 2008, p.127). Jessica and her colleagues then took this feedback into account in reviewing and changing their programs.

In this study factors that facilitated learning included: (1) Setting and operations—the environment in which meetings and events occurred were welcoming, included snacks and supports (such as compilation of notes from meetings) to help move work forward; (2) Training opportunities and perks—such as traveling to statewide and national conferences that agencies could not usually afford to send staff; and (3) YDN staff—were engaging, warm and encouraging of participants during network activities and follow-up (Davis-Manigaulte, 2008, p. 184). The last category was also identified as critical for helping participants apply the learning in their own agencies. In addition, organizational support and supervisory support were also found to be important for both learning and application of learning in agencies. However, a factor that hindered learning for some was a feeling of intimidation based on hierarchy that interfered with the ability of many to participate freely in collective reflection and discussion (particularly during many of the initial sessions). Network directors "were aware of the issue … and worked closely with the groups to minimize the impact of this impediment" (Davis-Manigaulte, 2008, p. 192).

Conclusion

The researcher concluded that, despite some differences, in several ways, this youth development network functioned like the communities of practice described by Wenger (1998) in that professional identity, commitment, engagement and learning developed through the collaborative community ties that were fostered through its various activities. The YDN met the definition of communities of practice (Wenger, McDermott, & Synder, 2002), i.e., "groups of people who share a concern, a set of problems, or a passion about a topic, and who deepened their knowledge and expertise in this area by interacting on an ongoing basis." Evidence cited by the researcher (Davis-Manigaulte, 2008, pp. 190–191) for this conclusion included the following:

- Intense group discussions that members engaged in to learn of each other's practices as they attempted to define and adopt standards of practice and effective strategies for obtaining positive outcomes for youth that helped them make meaning of their practice.
- Intentional strategies to encourage buy-in and ownership, e.g., committees, meeting and symposia discussion groups, site assessments, etc.
- Artifacts created by network members to capture and share their learning with others, e.g., flip books, practices, tools, common language and symbols.

While the YDN had several features of a community of practice, there are also ways in which the group did not function as a community of practice, most notably because it was a structured group that was organized by a lead agency that provided the foundation for how the network would operate. It pulled together agency members from several different agencies, as opposed to a group of colleagues from the same agency that evolved internally to address a common issue or need. Given the limited number of staff at some agencies, it would have been somewhat challenging to produce a community of practice within a youth development agency with the type of unique, rich dialogue exchange described by the YDN participants. Thus the group's ability to function as the expert practitioners that created the many artifacts and references that resulted from the network experience would have been limited.

The YDN modeled an approach for authentically capturing and documenting the expertise of youth work practitioners to inform the field. The YDN staff was respectful of the wealth of knowledge that existed within the program and worked closely with the youth workers to facilitate a process that generated final products representative of the participants' shared knowledge. Researchers and evaluators are also seeking the involvement of practitioners as experts. As Keen (2009) discusses in describing attempts to obtain authentic evaluation data for Australian community based programs, "the CSOs (community sector organizations) speak of both internal and external research and development in the context of evaluation. Internal evaluation is likely to be conducted with researchers and practitioners as a process evaluation to improve practice and assist in organizational learning and the capacity of researchers and practitioners (as experts in their area)" (p. 6). When practitioners function in this capacity there are potential benefits for the individuals, as well as the programs and the given field of practice.

In summary, the Youth Development Network created an environment that allowed youth workers to create a body of knowledge with practitioners as experts, based on their ongoing dialogue about their shared experiences in the field and consensus reached through their ongoing work in communities and symposia and conference discussion groups. This setting provided meaningful venues in which to address and identify best practices and effective strategies for addressing common issues related to conducting high quality youth programs. The artifacts and the multitude of stories shared throughout the study are indicative of the long-term impact of the network, which is currently in the community of practice stage of development that Wenger describes as "memorable" in that "the community is no longer central, but people still remember it as a significant part of their identities" (Wenger, 1998, p. 3). Youth workers valued the YDN learning approaches, and they seemed to be meaningful for workers at various levels—from frontline workers to program directors. In this dynamic field where youth workers continue to function as tutors, counselors, group leaders, data managers, fund developers, evaluators, marketers, and many other roles, there is always more to learn. Group learning networks/communities of practice are a valuable option for learning and creation of a professional network with practitioner experts can continue to provide for growth and support for the field and its members.

References

Davis-Manigaulte, J. (2008). *An interpretive case study of a youth development network: How learning informs agency practice.* Unpublished Ed.D. dissertation. Teachers College, Columbia University, New York.

Kasl, E., Marsick, V. J., & Dechant, K. (1997). Teams as learners. *The Journal of Applied Behavioral Science, 33*, 227–246.

Keen, S. (2009, November). A study of Sydney-based community organizations. Research, evaluation and innovation. CSI Issues Paper No. 8. Retrieved October 30, 2010, from http://www.csi.edu.au/uploads/31642/ufiles/CSI-Issues-Paper-No.8%20.pdf.

Wenger, E. (1998). *Communities of practice: Learning, meaning, and identity.* Cambridge, UK: Cambridge University Press.

Wenger, E., McDermott, R., & Synder, W. (2002). *Cultivating communities of practice: A guide to managing knowledge.* Cambridge, MA: Harvard Business School Press.

SECTION III

Contexts of Youth Work

12

YOUTH WORK PRACTICE IN ENGLAND

Helen Jones

The first professionally qualified youth workers in England completed their studies during the 1940s. At the time, the concept of the full-time paid youth worker was relatively recent, having come into being during the 1920s. From the mid-nineteenth century onwards, youth work had been undertaken largely by philanthropic volunteers. This chapter focuses on the training and development of today's paid workers over six decades later, and looks at some of the current controversies in the field. Although many people who work with young people refer to themselves as "youth workers," in England the term also applies to a profession with specific characteristics and principles. I will go on to suggest that our predecessors developed values, knowledge and techniques, which are in danger of being overlooked and even forgotten by today's youth workers.

Youth Worker Training and Education in England

As early as 1937, the National Council of Girls' Clubs (the organization which brought together the voluntary girls' clubs and mixed clubs of the nation) was running 18-month courses, which involved both club-based practical experience and theoretical study of "all aspects of club work." Many participants were university graduates who could look forward to "a good career" at a time when there was a shortage of people to become full-time paid club leaders (Yorkshire Association of Girls' Clubs, 1937). Subsequent courses combined club work and the social sciences with practical experience. The vision was that of the professional who brought together underpinning knowledge with relevant skills and attitudes; a recognized qualification that supported this vision followed in 1945.

It is interesting that qualifications mainly grew out of women's work with girls while at the same time the men of the NABC (National Association of Boys' Clubs) were skeptical about the value of training (Bradford, 2007). For them, youth leadership, to use the contemporaneous term, was an innate (and essentially masculine) skill.

Today youth work in England is in another process of transition: it is becoming a graduate profession. Everybody entering the profession must have a university honors degree (the equivalent of the bachelor's degree in the United States) and a youth work qualification. People without university level qualifications can become "youth support workers." For this status, lower level qualifications are required. England's National Youth Agency (NYA) sets out the curriculum and validates qualifications at both stages. From September 2010, students who intend to be professional youth workers must embark on qualifications which are at honors degree level or higher, gradually creating a profession which is on par with school teaching and social work. This will achieve an aspiration evident in the McNair Report, published in 1944 by the Board of Education, which saw youth leadership and school teaching as inter-linked albeit clearly separate professions for which training of a comparable duration was appropriate.

With the onset of these new professional requirements came renewed interest in youth work education. In 2008 a double edition of the scholarly journal *Youth and Policy* was devoted to the subject of youth work training. It focused on discussions concerning aspects of university-level courses. Interestingly, the authors did not focus on curricular matters, concerning which there appears to be a fair level of consensus, but on the identity of students entering courses, the teaching of values and ethics, the position of youth work in academic institutions and the vexed question of whether competency-based programs generate competent workers. Universities offering youth work courses which carry professional validation by the NYA face considerable practical and bureaucratic challenges. The curriculum is outlined by the NYA and grounded in the National Occupational Standards (NOS) for youth work. National Occupational Standards are a description of "the skills, knowledge and understanding needed to undertake a particular task or job to a nationally recognized level of competence" and are compiled with extensive consultation with the field by Lifelong Learning UK (LLUK, 2008). NOS tends to focus on the practical rather than theoretical aspects: 50 contributing actions range from enable young people to work effectively in groups, and plan, prepare and facilitate work with young people to challenge oppressive behavior in young people (LLUK, 2008). Employers are at the heart of the NYA validation processes. Tony Jeffs and Jean Spence comment that employers' control of the process has "devalued theory and focused almost exclusively upon skills, thereby curtailing the capacity of workers to build theory in practice and establish professional sovereignty" (2008, p. 154). They see a tension between the employers' and

NYA's focus on practical skills and the universities' desire to focus on theoretical knowledge and understanding.

Nonetheless the way in which the curriculum, as outlined by the NYA, is delivered over the three year full-time honors degree is decided by each university. For university validation, courses also need to ensure they adhere to the national Quality Assurance Agency's (QAA) Benchmarks. The QAA exists to ensure that universities in the UK maintain academic standards and that there is comparability across institutions. Benchmarks are intended to show what a student completing a qualification in a subject area should have achieved and to ensure comparability between subject areas and different universities' qualifications. Thus each new youth work degree faces two validation procedures and has to meet standards set by different national bodies.

Despite the challenges of validation, as indicated previously, the curriculum itself is generally uncontroversial. It brings together elements of social science: social policy, sociology and psychology. The history of youth work is often located within the study of the development of the welfare state. Students learn about working with groups and individuals, leadership, techniques to use with challenging groups and working with conflict. They study elements of advocacy, advice and guidance and counseling. Generally towards the end of their courses, students study management since many will take on significant managerial and supervisory responsibilities at an early point in their careers. Degree courses also usually include research methodologies and the completion of a dissertation. In addition, each student has to complete over 800 hours of work placement with relevant agencies during their three-year program, and to achieve a "pass" each year. During placements they receive supervision from the agency. Universities emphasize the development of reflexivity or reflection on practice during the time spent engaging in practice. Often using structured approaches based on the reflective learning cycle identified by Kolb (1984), students are required to reflect systematically on their learning and learn to relate theory to practice and to ground their practice in theory. For example, students at the University of Huddersfield have to complete regular recordings concerning their practice under the headings: description, understanding, generalizing and implications for future action. These curricular matters are largely uncontested.

Challenges to Youth Work Education

The position of youth and community work in the academy is not entirely comfortable. Caught between faculties of education and social science, humanities and health, academic staff can find it hard to produce the world class research sought by universities due to their subject's interdisciplinary nature and the scarcity of journals. However, as discussed below, the recent closure of courses has been rooted in issues of retention rather than the cross–departmental nature of the courses. Universities express concern with poor rates of retention on their professional youth work courses. This has been cited as a contributory factor in the closure of some reputable honors degree programs. The issue is the result of a complex interplay of elements: youth and community work courses include both academic and practice-based aspects and thus require great commitment.

In 1944 the McNair Committee noted the "zest" required by youth workers and concluded that, "it is not unreasonable to put the average working life of the youth leader at about 15 or 20 years" (Board of Education, 1944). This duration was, they acknowledged, lower than that which would be expected of a school teacher. It also had implications for recruitment. The committee concluded that, "It is time for men and women to give up youth leadership when it becomes apparent that they have lost touch with the outlook of young people or that their tolerance has worn thin" (Board of Education, 1944). Today, local authority employers have reported difficulties concerning the recruitment and retention of youth workers. The time and money invested in workforce development is only worthwhile if sufficient staff remain in post, but the profession experiences a high rate of turnover. McNair's understanding and acceptance appear unrealistic in the real world of the twenty-first century where employers are not able, on financial grounds, to support high turnover.

Sue Robertson notes that the University of Chichester found that many youth work students are the first in their families to go to university (Robertson, 2008). This is also true at the University of Huddersfield and anecdotal evidence suggests this is usually the case elsewhere. Such students are often unfamiliar with the culture and demands of studying at university and require additional academic and pastoral support. Some are critical of the level of pastoral support which now characterizes universities in general and which is deemed particularly necessary in courses such as youth work. For them, students are "cosseted" and supportive techniques characteristic of youth work are being used on the students themselves. Rather than modeling good practice, this can be interpreted as promoting dependence when autonomous, resilient and resourceful students and future workers are needed. Jeffs and Spence conclude, "By treating students as delicate and immature, unready for the rigors of the world, they both enable those unsuited to practice to qualify, and fail to bring to maturity those who would rise to the challenge and enter practice as confident and enthusiastic professionals" (2008, p. 156).

Another issue of increasing concern is the age of students embarking on full-time courses in youth work. Whereas age limits once ensured entrants were in their twenties, many are now teenagers themselves. Sue Robertson (2008) observes that the mean age for youth work students was 29.2 years in 1999 but 24.6 in 2003. The downward trend continues. Yet, some agencies are reluctant to accept students who are scarcely older than their members or clients on work placement. Together with age, a further area giving cause for concern is the increased feminization of the workforce. Robertson laments the situation stating that youth work needs both male and female workers, in particular "those men who will challenge sexual oppression and the 'macho' attitudes of many young men, but also female workers with a feminist perspective" (2008, p. 95). Although much youth work has its nineteenth-century origins in women working with girls, during much of the twentieth-century youth work tended to mean male workers focusing on boys while girls watched from the sidelines and women workers were few in number. The situation was gradually rectified during the 1980s and 1990s when men and women entered the field in comparable numbers but there is now some alarm in terms of the lack of men choosing to become youth workers. Just as the population of youth includes similar numbers of both young men and young women, as Robertson (2008) suggests a similar balance should pertain in the workforce, but the profession is currently in danger of emulating school teaching and other work with young people and children in becoming associated with only one sex. While university courses in youth work, which once were largely comprised of mature men are nowadays dominated by young women, many courses recruit encouraging numbers of students from ethnic minority groups. Figures for students with disabilities are similarly buoyant, although the proportion affected by dyslexia, rather than other forms of disability, is high (Robertson, 2008). Employers have raised concerns about the impact of the high proportion of entrants to the profession requiring support in the production of written material including reports and funding bids.

As indicated above there is a tendency for youth work courses to attract high numbers of non-traditional students, whose initial recruitment helps institutions to achieve their goals in terms of widening access, but who have many demands on their time and may not have realistic expectations concerning university study. Many have had previous negative experiences of education and require particular support and guidance in order to succeed. Some discover that the profession is not what they expected and transfer to alternative routes. Yet again, wisdom is to be found in the McNair Report: "Even under the best conditions, some mistakes in initial selection are unavoidable and the first term or two of the training course should be regarded as probationary" (Board of Education, 1944). Unfortunately, British universities are not in a position to be so sanguine concerning retention. The expectation is that the "right" students will be accepted and they will finish their courses on schedule, three years after enrolling.

Youth Work as a Profession

For more than six decades, youth work in England has been referred to as a profession rather than an occupation, but this status has been questioned on a number of grounds. First, it is a field which involves many unpaid, unqualified volunteers whose contributions are central to the work of many organizations including both major voluntary organizations like Scouts and Guides and smaller local groups. Second, it can be argued that youth work lacks some of the characteristics or traits, which are signifiers of a true profession. These include a statement of ethics, a professional association, and, as Banks stated, "a system of qualification and controlled entry, state licensing of practitioners and a specialist or esoteric body of knowledge" (Banks, 1999, p. 5). Youth work has the first of these: the NYA adopted its statement "Ethical Conduct in Youth Work" in 2000 following extensive consultation. It covers the nature and purpose of youth work and its underpinning principles including four particularly significant areas:

- Voluntarism: the young people engage with the worker through their own choice;
- Association: the centrality of working with groups;
- Informality: workers act with integrity and are friendly, forming adult-to-adult relationships with young people; and
- Education: youth workers are informal educators, seeing opportunities to engage in education in all sorts of situations (NYA, 2000).

However, the professional association, controlled entry and state licensing are lacking. Anybody who achieves the professional qualification cannot be stripped of their status as a professional regardless of their misdemeanors. While they might fail to secure employment on various grounds, they remain professionally qualified youth workers.

Although the profession lacks a system of state licensing, there are extensive checks to ensure that qualifications retain currency and quality and to make certain that students graduating with youth work degrees at different universities enter employment with comparable knowledge, skills and values. As discussed previously, the validation of a youth work course is a complex procedure. The NYA undertakes annual monitoring and evaluation and revalidates all courses on a five-year basis. It could be suggested that, in combination, the QAA outcomes and NYA criteria form the "specialist or esoteric body of knowledge" (Banks, 1999, p. 5) and ensure it forms the central dimension of professional training and education.

Nonetheless, while youth work may have some of the characteristics of a profession, its intrinsic informality is potentially its greatest downfall. Many workers espouse informal dress in order to reduce barriers in their engagement with young people but this can be perceived as "unprofessional." Workers who are with young people outside school hours, during evenings and weekends, inevitably are not at work during normal office hours. Youth work still has to shake off its association with games of table tennis and pool. It also faces critics who question why some young people are apparently rewarded for bad behavior by being involved in activities by youth workers while those who have behaved well are not invited. It could be posited that the development of a recognized profession with articulate leaders could serve to challenge such misconceptions and explain the rationale.

Principles of Practice

The existence of a qualification in youth work together with National Occupational Standards and stated ethics might suggest a unanimity concerning the definition of the term, "youth work." However, this is not the case, and attempts to posit a simple definition for the term lead to contested territory. Even the age span to which the term "youth" may be applied is not agreed upon unanimously and has changed over time. In England, most work currently focuses on 13- to 19-year-olds with some junior work undertaken with younger age groups. Many workers have identified a particular need to engage with 11- to 13-year-olds who seem to fall between the remits held by play workers, who focus on younger children, and youth workers, who focus on teenagers. The needs of 11- to 13-year-olds are addressed in countries including Wales. Young people with special needs, aged up to 25, fall within the definition of "youth." Other current discussions on how youth work is defined focus particularly on the two concepts of voluntary engagement or "voluntarism" and "association," both of which were cited by the NYA as central tenets (NYA, 2000).

Voluntarism or voluntary engagement was originally identified overtly as one of youth work's core values during the 1930s when there were debates about whether participation in "youth service" should be a matter of compulsion. Apparently Winston Churchill favored compulsory youth service during the 1930s (Bradford, 2007), and it was introduced in comparable activities for young people elsewhere in Europe (particularly in Germany's Hitler Youth). Nowadays controversy is centered on the role of youth workers within contexts where young people do not choose to be such as prisons, youth detention centers and even high schools. Youth workers in such contexts argue that there is scope to work with young people who have chosen to participate and to form relationships with them which enshrine the value of voluntarism. This is true despite the compulsion inherent in the location and the apparent contradiction intrinsic to the idea of engaging in informal education within a structured, custodial setting. For example, a YMCA project brought a youth worker together with young men detained in a youth detention center for a course concerning parenthood. Participants were not forced to sign up for the sessions but committed voluntarily to forming a group ensuring voluntarism remained a crucial facet of the engagement (Qureshi, 2009). In some high schools, youth workers are employed to work with young people whose behavior has led to their exclusion from classes or to provide forms of pastoral and extra-curricular support. Projects for young people who have been excluded from school frequently employ qualified youth workers who may even assist with aspects of teaching.

Association, arguably, has been undermined somewhat by government policies which have shifted the focus from relationships where the group is the basis
of youth work practice to engagement with individual young people. England's youth workers traditionally concentrated on groups (or gangs), and saw
the position of young people in the context of both their chosen companions
and also with wider society as fundamental. As the Youth Advisory Council,
appointed by the Minister of Education, declared in 1945, "The collective discipline of the whole group grows from the individual self-discipline of each
member. And each member in seeking the good of the group will find gain as
an individual." For many, the decreasing value applied to association is neither
exclusive to youth work nor recent but rather began under Conservative governments between 1979 and 1997 led by Margaret Thatcher and her successor
John Major. Thatcher's oft-quoted assertion (made to the popular *Women's Own*
magazine on 31 October 1987), "There is no such thing as society. There are
individual men and women, and there are families," not only acknowledged,
but also welcomed, the shift away from an appreciation of the significance of
groups for young people in particular. The resultant approach tends to regard a
group as a collection of individuals, each with their own independent rationale
for involvement and with a limited group vision rather than as an association
of inter-dependency. The group is seen as a good place for an individual young
person to develop while the value of the group or community, as an end in its
own right is lost.

It is worth noting here that a major strand of work, which has existed
throughout the period, is referred to as "youth and community work." Like
youth work, this has education (as opposed to welfare) at its core. Many academics and practitioners argue that the term encapsulates a more appropriate
approach both ideologically and practically as it places young people not only
in groups but also in the context of the wider communities in which they live:
youth and community development workers engage with a wider constituency,
sometimes focusing on adults and sometimes doing inter-generational work.
Where young people are in essentially "adult" situations, such as parenthood,
it could be argued that community work techniques when employed by youth
workers are more relevant to them. The majority of universities actually offer
"youth and community work" or "youth and community development" courses
rather than "youth work," resulting in ongoing tensions with the NYA. This
also creates tensions with community work bodies whose role in the establishment of such courses tends to be minor in comparison with the NYA, possibly
because there are no formalized professional terms and conditions for community work. Youth workers continue to see themselves as informal or social educators but how to measure the educational impact of their work in more formal
terms has become another contentious area. "Informal education" once meant
that workers took young people's interests and concerns as their starting point
and worked with them to design programs. From the 1970s onwards, workers

cited Paulo Freire as an inspiration and talked of "conscientization," fostering structural analysis and a questioning approach. Youth workers would seek to identify structural reasons for an issue such as youth unemployment, but nowadays they are more likely to devise individualized training-based solutions: the pathologizing of young people blames the individuals for their inability to find employment or education.

The introduction of curricula has left workers with less flexibility and almost certainly serves to suppress the development of radicalism in both workers and young people. Numerous forms of accreditation have been introduced, from various certificates intended to encourage aspects of literacy and numeracy to the long-established Duke of Edinburgh Award, which involves physical activity as well as skills and volunteering. While members of uniformed voluntary groups have long sported badges achieved for a wide range of activities, statutory youth workers increasingly are required to assess and accredit young people's activities using a wide range of more formal frameworks. These often focus on "transferable skills." Advocates of accreditation point out that the informal approach taken by youth workers supports young people who have failed to achieve in formal education settings (school, in particular) in securing alternative forms of accreditation in a society where credentials are vital for securing almost all forms of paid employment. Young people who do not thrive in classroom environments can succeed in alternative settings which should be assessed and rewarded. In 2009 a group of youth workers circulated an open letter which generated the In Defense of Youth Work campaign. The letter condemned "the insidious way in which delivering accredited outcomes ... has formalized and thus undermined the importance of relationships in the work" (Taylor, 2009). Critics suggest that young people are often scarcely aware that they are engaged in accredited activities and neither comprehend the concept of transferable skills nor are able to identify them. Whether potential employers understand or value the resultant certificates is also a moot point.

The Impact of Government Policy on Youth Work Values

Alongside the birth of officially recognized training courses, the 1940s saw the increase of state involvement in youth work and the advent of a system which still pertains: local authorities remain responsible for a large proportion of publicly funded work with young people in England. Inevitably political parties establish policies which they believe to be in the country's best interests and changes of government, as well as changes in locally elected councils, have an impact on the precise nature and funding of the work. Periodic moral panics concerning young people's activities and aspects of youth culture have led to the state reacting through changes to policy. In 1960, the Albemarle Report issued by the Ministry of Education followed the arrival of the first modern youth culture in the form of "teddy boys" as well as race riots in a number of cities.

Teddy boys were working-class young men from the 1950s who had distinctive haircuts, dress, and who listened to American rock-and-roll music. Fifty years later, policies designed to prepare young people for adulthood through participation in employment, education or training and initiatives intended to address youth offending, have also seen the state reacting to perceived challenges.

The series of policies introduced by the Labour governments led first by Tony Blair and then by Gordon Brown during the period 1997–2010 enshrined the shift away from association and towards an understanding of young people as problems and victims. Many were designed with the well-meant intention of tackling "social exclusion," the term used to sum up what can happen when people or areas have a combination of problems, such as unemployment, discrimination, poor skills, low incomes, poor housing, high crime and family breakdown. However in practice, policies outlined in reports including *Bridging the Gap* (Social Exclusion Unit, 1999), *Every Child Matters* (Department for Education and Skills, DfES, 2003) and *Youth Matters* (DfES, 2005) generated a shift towards targeted work where individual young people were pathologized as "troubled or troublesome." Funding was re-directed away from universal work, leaving some workers feeling that cherished aspects of their profession were being undermined.

Bridging the Gap introduced the Connexions program, which aimed to take a holistic approach to every teenager's transition at 16 years of age from compulsory schooling to further study, training or employment. A significant creation in the Labour government's early days in the late 1990s, its tagline was "The best start in life for every young person." Ostensibly a universal service, it was intended that every individual young person would be linked with a Personal Adviser, providing tailored support, mentoring, advice and guidance on everything from education, employment and housing to relationships and health to support them in making a smooth transition to further education or employment (Department for Education and Employment, DfEE, 2000). The coordination of services was intended to reduce duplication and to create "joined-up services." Personal data about individuals were to be shared between youth workers, school teachers, social workers, health service staff and other services so that young people were no longer obliged to repeat the same information to numerous different professionals. The service would be staffed by people trained in the Connexions Personal Adviser, initially drawn from the ranks of youth workers, careers guidance staff and a range of other people working with the age group who studied a hastily devised "diploma." However, Connexions rapidly failed to become a universal service: governmental preoccupation with anyone considered to be at risk of becoming NEET (the recently coined acronym for young people Not in Education, Employment or Training) resulted in an almost exclusively targeted service. Young people who were not "at risk" found that careers guidance services were no longer available to respond to their needs. Critics also raised concerns about the surveillance inherent in the practice of joined-up thinking and by 2007 Mark Smith, a provocative writer and commentator on youth work for several decades, was describing Connexions as a "dismally failed" service, although its brand-name had achieved recognition amongst young people.

The series of policies with a direct impact on youth work has led to workers feeling that they are facing constant change, with regard both to their practice and organizational structures. The fact that policies concerning aspects of education require years rather than months to generate measurable impacts has not been recognized by policy makers, so modifications have been introduced with frequency, leaving many workers disillusioned. Indeed, Tony Jeffs and Mark Smith (2010) have summed up the policy context as "volatile and often incoherent." In addition, the concerns around youth offending have generated legislation which has an impact on young people such as the implementation of the 1998 Crime and Disorder Act which introduced ASBOs (Anti-Social Behavior Orders). ASBOs outline behaviors in which the named individual is forbidden from engaging and contravention of the terms results in further sanctions including potential incarceration. For many young people, ASBOs are geographic and prohibit them from entering particular streets or areas. Dispersal orders prevent groups of young people from assembling in specific areas and give the police powers to disperse them. While youth workers are not involved in the implementation of these, they are often working with young people whose freedom of movement is restricted and who may have been identified for targeted interventions. In consequence, some see youth workers evolving into "soft police," undertaking "detached work" (work with young people where they choose to gather such as streets and parks) at the behest of elected councilors and the police and obliged to ensure that their focus is on locating and "encouraging" the participation of specific individuals.

To an increasing extent, youth workers work alongside other professionals. Indeed, the desirability of creating a coherent approach to working with children and young people and working in cross-professional teams has achieved dominance. Policies have been developed to generate this, including the 2004 Children Act which introduced the *Every Child Matters* program. This focused on five identified outcomes, namely: be healthy, stay safe, enjoy and achieve, make a positive contribution and achieve economic well-being. These applied to teenagers as well as children and have met with almost universal acceptance: debates tend to concern the practicalities of policy implementation rather than critiques of its ideological basis. Hoyle, however, has explored *Every Child Matters'* hegemonic dimension and the extent to which its superficially commonsense outcomes serve to shift attention away from England's deep structural inequalities (Hoyle, 2008). Youth workers may focus on reducing the rates of sexually transmitted diseases and teenage pregnancy through sex education, or educating young people concerning the risks of drugs and alcohol, yet research shows that the risks of all of these are linked to disadvantage. The five outcomes are embedded within a particular contemporary Western ideological framework and, in common with much of England's social policy, reflect "white, middle class, patriarchal, heterosexual, Christian, able-bodied ideals" (Hoyle, 2008) although these are not overtly expressed. Indeed, as Hoyle points out, spirituality is absent from the document. Nonetheless, *Every Child Matters* led directly to the attempts to streamline services to children and young people by locating the different professionals involved in multi-disciplinary teams or "Integrated Services."

Bringing teams of professionals together highlighted the extent to which those with different professional trainings used the same terms in different ways, making true communication problematic. In addition, they identified different priorities in the same situations and placed them in orders of significance which did not correspond: for example, a youth worker, a midwife, a school teacher and a social worker would not share a perception concerning the relative importance of the different issues generated by a pregnant 15-year-old. Moreover, there is a tendency for each to believe that their assessment is "correct" and inherently superior, generating an attitude which pervades their encounters with other professionals. Outsiders have identified "professional silos" as undermining the quality of service experienced by clients. For this reason, a common core of knowledge and skills for professionals working with children and young people has been identified. It is suggested that all people intending to work with children and young people should start their courses by learning this shared language. Some universities offer a common first year of study for students intending to enter a range of interpersonal professions but this may have shortcomings. The danger associated with sharing elements of training is the dilution of the key elements of each separate profession: the creation of people who work with young people using aspects of different professions rather than youth workers. Those seeking to protect youth work in a pure form rehearse an argument expressed by McNair in 1944: "We do not think that training for youth leadership should be attempted within the course designed for training teachers or other kinds of social workers although during their training youth leaders, teachers and social workers will necessarily take some account of each other's field of service" (Board of Education, 1944).

While there is controversy concerning the value of sharing initial training, advanced, master's level courses are being delivered by universities in the light of the demands generated by the inception of Integrated Services. Local authority supervisors are increasingly managing people from different professional backgrounds and few deny the value of bringing youth workers, social workers, early years (i.e., pre-school) workers, school support staff, youth offending workers and others from the panoply of professionals who work with children and young people together to study. The opportunity to progress to managing multi-disciplinary teams may serve to enhance retention of senior staff by presenting new and interesting challenges.

The Future of Youth Work in England

Many would argue that youth workers should be proud of the professionalization of their sector. After many years' struggle, workers are finally on a par with other professionals and their skills, values and knowledge are appropriately accredited, celebrated and rewarded. In addition to working in the traditional posts in youth centers and community centers, running activities such as youth clubs and school holiday programs, they are sought by youth offending and drugs agencies, they work in schools and health contexts and play a significant part in local authorities' multi-disciplinary teams. Their skill in forming adult-to-adult relationships with young people results in their being sought to engage with young people whom other agencies have failed to reach. Becoming a graduate profession will ensure workers with more sophisticated understandings of the practice and context of the work and will result in parity in esteem across the different professions.

Others are unconvinced by the changes, sometimes tending to look back to a golden age when workers had scope to exercise autonomy and spontaneity and were not constrained by administrative requirements. Mark Smith has written excoriatingly about the direction which state-sponsored youth work is taking in England. In 2007 he suggested that it "is better described as a conservative version of the north American tradition of youth development rather than youth work." He declared, "Things have gone from bad to worse." He cited a series of points to support his thesis including the increase of managerialism and bureaucratization in the public sector and the shift from universal services to the targeting of young people deemed "problematic." Yet Smith was more optimistic about programs undertaken by workers employed by many Christian churches, whose youth workers apparently outnumber those employed by the state, and whose funding often comes from sources not subject to the state-generated restrictions. He also commended the growth and extension of Muslim youth work, and the work of grassroots community organizations. While some voluntary groups receive state funding, others rely on sources of funding which allow greater freedom and may be able to respond flexibly to situations. For example, youth workers from a voluntary organization may be permitted to engage with young people whose consumption of alcohol and illicit drugs would require statutory employees to withdraw.

According to Smith, youth workers in England should "do what is right rather than what is correct" and challenge the risk-averse process-focus which increasingly characterizes the public sector (Smith, 2007). The preoccupation with record-keeping and data collection served to create a surveillance of young people which undermined youth workers' ability to "offer a place of sanctuary" and, as Hoyle pointed out, young people's rights to privacy under Article 8 of the European Convention on Human Rights is being contravened (Hoyle, 2008). It has been suggested that workers have even been distracted from

engaging in face-to-face work with young people by the growth in administrative chores and, in particular, the burden of constantly applying for funding
to maintain the work. The need to ensure transparency is seen as damaging
workers' ability to work instinctively. The sheer quantity of administration has
tended to result in the most experienced workers securing management-level
posts which removed them from direct work with young people. As in many
comparable areas of work, the most challenging work is often undertaken by
the least experienced workers. Decreased finances during the second decade of
the twenty-first century appear likely to impact on the middle management
tier, removing a tier of skill whose departure will remove potential models of
good practice, although on the other hand they may be those whose zest has
been exhausted.

It is worth acknowledging that writers critical of current developments
sometimes overlook the weaknesses of youth work in the past. During the 1970s
some youth work was characterized by an arrogance and anti-intellectualism
which tended to regard formal education with distrust. There was suspicion to
the point of antagonism towards a range of professionals such as school teachers, the police and social workers whose work also brought them into contact
with young people. This attitude did not support young people and generated
widespread negativity towards youth workers (most of whom were male) who
were seen as spending their time playing pool with disaffected youth (most of
whom were also male). The work, albeit undertaken by qualified workers, was
also characterized by a paucity of record keeping which resulted in a seeming
lack of accountability. The apparent spontaneity of 40 years ago, where a group
of young people and a worker might go for an unexpected, unplanned day out
without having completed parental permission forms, without having a bus
equipped with seatbelts (or even seats!), without having completed a risk assessment and without an appropriate ratio of adults to young people was potentially
dangerous for all concerned.

Conclusion

While youth work has become a graduate profession, the future of state sponsored youth work in England during a period of financial constraints is far from
clear. Moreover, there are vexed debates concerning whether the future will
see "youth work" or simply a bastardized generic "work with young people" as
the primary direction. Recent policies have called on youth workers' skills, values and knowledge in service of a range of goals and, in particular, to support
the attempt to tackle the range of intractable problems seen as generating social
exclusion. Targeting specific groups of young people has led to the dilution of
work once aspired to be universal.

The extent to which the unstructured, unrecorded youth work which once
took place in many youth clubs was successful for many young people is uncer-

tain but it is definitely no longer a feasible model across the statutory sector where accountability is required. Many youth workers continue to work as informal educators with groups of young people in traditional informal settings in youth clubs and on street corners, nowadays monitoring and evaluating their work in line with their employers' systems. Some youth workers are optimistic about the introduction of organized programs of positive activities for young people, which engage targeted groups who might otherwise engage in anti-social behavior. Others are happy to work in school settings, running alternative forms of accreditation for pupils who have been excluded and supporting mainstream educators through informal means. Faith-based work, with youth workers linked to mosques, synagogues and churches, is an expanding area. Housing associations, drugs programs, prisons and other specifically themed work also involve qualified professional youth workers.

Despite the role played by many unpaid volunteers, it is clear that in England youth work has achieved the status of being a profession. It has a statement of ethics, a professional qualification that maintains its currency and quality and is required by many employers and a burgeoning body of specialist knowledge. The concept of state registration or similar is under consideration and is regarded as important by many involved in the field: a significant number of current youth workers would welcome the establishment of such a system.

For youth work's iconoclastic pessimists, core values are being forgotten in the rush towards the establishment of integrated youth support services, with diluted forms of generalized work with young people taking precedence in services managed by people who lack an appreciation of youth work's core. For the optimists, the range of concerns about the direction which youth work is taking notwithstanding, there is plenty to celebrate about youth work in England in the early decades of the twenty-first century. For them, the integration of services is generating a need for professionals versed in a range of skills embedded in the cherished values of voluntarism, association, informality and education. However, within three months of their election in 2010, the Conservative government had introduced massive cuts in public expenditure, which are widely predicted to have a potentially catastrophic impact on work with young people.

References

Banks, S. (1999). Ethics and the youth worker. In S. Banks (Ed.), *Ethical issues in youth work* (pp. 93–109). London: Routledge.

Board of Education. (1944) *Teachers and youth leaders. Report of the committee appointed by the President of the Board of Education to consider the supply, recruitment and training of teachers and youth leaders.* London: HMSO. Retrieved from http://www.infed.org/archives/e-texts/mcnair_part_two.htm

Bradford, S. (2007). The 'good youth leader': Constructions of professionalism in English youth work, 1939–45. *Ethics and Social Welfare, 1,* 293–309.

Department for Education and Employment (DfEE). (2000). *Connexions. The best start in life for every young person*. London: Author.

Department for Education and Skills (DfES). (2003). *Every child matters*. London: Author.

Department for Education and Skills (DfES). (2005). *Youth matters*. London: Author.

Hoyle, D. (2008). *Problematizing every child matters. The encyclopedia of informal education*. Retrieved February, 10, 2010, from http://www.infed.org/socialwork/every_child_matters_a_critique.htm

Jeffs, T., & Smith, M. K. (2010). Introducing youth work. In T. Jeffs & M. K. Smith (Eds.), *Youth work practice* (pp. 1–14). London: Macmillan.

Jeffs, T., & Spence, J. (2008). Farewell to all that? The uncertain future of youth and community work education. *Youth and Policy, 97-8*, 135–166.

Kolb, D. (1984). *Experiential learning*. Upper Saddle River, NJ: Prentice Hall.

Lifelong Learning UK (LLUK). (2008, February 2008). Professional and National Occupational Standards for Youth Work. Retrieved February 12, 2010, from http://www.ukstandards.co.uk/Find_Occupational_Standards.aspx?NosFindID=4&FormMode=ViewModeSuite&SuiteID=1431

Ministry of Education. (1960). *The youth service in England and Wales* (The Albemarle Report). London: HMSO.

National Youth Agency (NYA). (2000). *Ethical conduct in youth work*. Leicester, UK: National Youth Agency.

Qureshi, Y. (2009, April). Youth work in custody: Behind bars. *Youth Work Now*. Retrieved. January 5, 2011, from http://www.cypnow.co.uk/news/895598/Youth-Work-Custody-Behind-bars/?DCMP=ILC-SEARCH

Robertson, S. (2008). Changing patterns in recruiting youth workers. *Youth and Policy, 97-8*, 91–104.

Smith, M. K. (2007). What future for youth work? Retrieved February, 10, 2010, from http://www.rankyouthwork.org/briefings/developments_in_youth_work.pdf

Social Exclusion Unit. (1999). *Bridging the gap: new opportunities for 16–18 year olds not in education, employment or training*. London: HMSO.

Taylor, T. (2009) In defence of youth work. Retrieved February 10, 2010, from http://indefenceofyouthwork.wordpress.com/2009/03/11/the-open-letter-in-defence-of-youth-work/

Youth Advisory Council. (1945). *The purpose and content of youth work*. Retrieved February, 10, 2010, from http://www.infed.org/archives/e-texts/minofed_purpose_youth_service.htm

Yorkshire Association of Girls' Clubs. (1937). *Annual Report 1937* (unpublished). Leeds, UK: Author.

13

YOUTH WORK AS ENGAGEMENT

Ross VeLure Roholt and Judie Cutler

In this chapter, youth work as process of engagement is discussed in two contexts: first through what the first author, Ross VeLure Roholt, calls "civic youth work" and second through a description by Judie Cutler of youth work on a reservation. Two distinct domains where youth work is practiced challenge the reader and the field to ask how and if both require the same set of competencies, credentials, and curricula.

Civic Youth Work: A Beginning Description

Civic youth work is both a way to name a type of youth work practice and to pay tribute to youth workers who have sought to make real opportunities available to young people to be citizens, to be seen as such, and see themselves as such. This practice philosophy and model has been in existence for decades, if not longer (e.g., Chilcoat & Ligon, 1998). Our scholarly work has been both to study and name this practice philosophy. By naming this practice, we hope to bring it into view, begin to make it widely available and to have it used by those working with youth all over the world. Civic youth work is thus neither a current invention nor a North and West creation; it has flourished worldwide for at least several decades. Civic youth work are our words, our way of naming and illuminating what we have found to be an important and unique type of youth work practice; one that can be used to better understand and recognize co-creative, participatory community work with young people. It provides a framework for research, practice and training/education for both youth and youth workers. This chapter will focus on describing civic youth work in practice. We draw on several years of research in the United States,

Northern Ireland and Palestine, and an emergent project on civic youth work in Morocco, to describe conceptual and theoretical understandings that have been found to deepen and enrich this youth work practice (VeLure Roholt, 2007; VeLure Roholt, Hildreth, & Baizerman, 2009).

Three Central Ideas of Civic Youth Work

Civic youth work is a conceptual practice field that focuses on democratic space-making with young people by working with them to address public issues of personal and group concern. It takes place in schools, community centers, parks, museums, and on the street—anywhere. It is framed by three ideas: lived citizenship, youth as citizens now, and lived-citizen(ship) as vocation. Lived citizen is a conceptual definition of citizenship that emerged from watching and talking to young people involved in youth civic engagement, community development, community building, and public work (Boyte, 2004). Unlike other discourses of citizenship, which focus on citizenship-as-legal-status, citizenship-as-desired-activity, and citizenship-as-identity (Kymlicka & Norman, 1995), lived citizenship "approaches politics from the inside out" (VeLure Roholt et al., 2009, p. 162). It understands that any situation can be understood as political and civic. It joins direct action in public settings to experiential education pedagogies. It moves against operational definitions of citizenship and instead focuses on how citizenship is a living process that brings together engagement in the work of democracy, in all its forms, naming and understanding self as community contributor now and in the future. Their active involvement in organization and community change challenges typical conceptions of young people and youth development.

Second, civic youth work brings a new understanding of young people into view—young people as citizens, now. Often young people are seen as deficient. Some agree that young people lack maturity (James & Prout, 1997) or that they lack knowledge, skills, and attitudes (Bennette, 1997). A consequence of this deficiency conception of youth is that typical youth work aims to increase young people's knowledge and skills and change their attitudes. In clear contrast, civic youth work begins with an understanding that young people are resources, people who can engage in the work of democracy without much further training. Often a barrier to their involvement in democracy is inadequate invitation and support to remain engaged. Yates and Youniss (1999) argue, "youth can surmount great odds and make significant contributions, but it is not reasonable to expect them to become civically engaged in communities and societies that fail to support them" (p. 273). This moves us from attention primarily on youth to including sociopolitical structures and the culture about youth as citizens, e.g., youthhood—the available and typical ways of growing up here, now. Civic youth work co-creates new forms of youthhood, in part by supporting young people to publicly present their work.

In this and similar ways, civic youth work illuminates and challenges the community's definition of young person engagement and, specifically, young person as citizen. When invited and supported, young people's accomplishments go beyond what most adults expect. They build libraries, work to enhance human rights, educate peers and community about important issues, and make improvements to the local community (e.g., building a rain garden, cleaning up a local park, etc.). Civic youth work contextualizes and minimizes the perceived deficiencies of young people by showing them as active citizens, as competent persons. Put simply, when the community refuses to see young people's potential and actual talents and hence does not see them, as civic workers, citizens, youth become invisible. Civic youth work serves to make young people and their talents visible.

Finally, civic youth work also focuses on vocational discernment. Young people involved talk about their work as who they are; it adds to their self-portrait. They develop an understanding of how they want to be in the world. When done skillfully, civic youth work makes the world available to young people in new ways. They stop doing service and begin to talk about their work as an expression of who they are; thus, not to do the work would be to deny a part of self.

Civic Youth Work Practice

Civic youth work practice is at once clear, simple and subtle. One way to think about doing this youth work practice is to imagine a youth worker who comes to each group session as a question: "what are we going to do today?" To this worker, the task is not given priority, nor is the young person's development; rather the civic youth worker creates a space for engagement. The civic youth worker does this by inviting young people to be creative, imaginative, and practical—all at the same time. The civic youth worker invites young people to express what they care about and to figure out if they want to do something about this and how. This practice draws together both practice craft knowledge (Higgs & Titchen, 2001), often documented in curriculum models and practice guides (e.g., Fierce, 2010; Hildreth & Erlanson, 1998; VeLure Roholt et.al., 2009) and scholarly work on youth civic engagement (Battistoni & Hudson, 1997; VeLure Roholt et al., 2009; Youniss & Yates, 1997): youth participatory action research (Cammarota & Fine, 2008); youth participatory evaluation (Sabo-Flores, 2008); youth activism (Delgado & Staples, 2008); and community building with youth (Checkoway et al., 2003).

Civic youth work is oriented to co-developing processes and these drive group outcomes. This is an ongoing and processional outcome because it is not a space that can be created and then forgotten. It only remains as a space of invitation and practice when it is the focus of the group: It is time-bound. Nor is it a space a youth worker can create by herself. Instead space-opening and space sustaining requires the ongoing involvement and support of young people too. For example, one group in Palestine initially began by responding to the lack of space available after school to study and learn. They initially came up with the idea of building a local library. After meeting initial resistance to this idea, the group analyzed the political and social situation and came up with alternative solutions. In the end, they organized a book donation drive, receiving thousands of books from around the world, sought out the assistance of a local carpenter, who donated not only his time but also much of the supplies to build shelves for the books, and negotiated with a local youth center to have one room designated as a library. With this initial success and publicity, they are continuing to work on building a new library while they use the temporary one. Civic youth work does not follow a rigid curriculum, but rather responses to the situations that arise as the group works on the project it has chosen.

Civic youth work practiced as we propose does not promote individual projects or accomplishments. Rather, civic youth workers facilitate and support *groups* of individuals to develop, plan and undertake a civic project. It is unlikely that a single individual in these groups could accomplish the projects typically chosen. Instead, these accomplishments are possible because a group of young people worked together. For example, a group in Belfast, Northern Ireland, wanted to develop a website connecting young people to their local public servant. By the time they had finished the first phase, they had created a monitored youth portal to local and regional government thereby not only gathering young people's concerns across the region but also ensuring public servants responded to their questions.

From this example, we can begin to understand what young people indicate are the benefits of civic youth work. First, it supports young people in getting done something they care about. This is often more that task completion. Getting something done also means they learn how to get something done, around here, now and then later, again. Whether they are working in their community, school, or in an after-school program, they learn how to navigate these institutions and contacts (e.g., they learn who and by when in order to bring about a particular change). Thus, this is about their civic project, and also about their lives at school, home, and at work.

Second civic youth work provides rehearsal time and open space where they work at developing their political and civic voices. In these spaces, they are supported while they investigate and discuss and plan around civic and political issues. This is a safe space where mistakes can be made and intuition and ideas said and responded to: They are invited into dialogue (Burbules, 1993) or civic discourse (Arnett & Arneson, 1999). By having enough group rehearsal time, they are able to speak smartly on political and civic issues, to develop and use their voice. The group provides a safe space to give and receive critique of ideas and how to express these. For example, a group in Kansas City, Kansas, decided to work on getting updated textbook in their classes and enough so that every high school student could have one for the year. They quickly learned that they would need to present to the school board if the project was to succeed. The group watched school board proceedings to learn how to make an appropriate argument, drafted what they would say, and then practiced their statement in the group eliciting critique and feedback from other group members, their teachers, and their group facilitator. When they had to speak publicly, they were ready.

Finally, civic youth work benefits young people by providing an avenue to develop and improve interpersonal skills. They learn how to work well with others—even those who are not friends or the same age or race or sex. Elsewhere, they are rarely asked to and supported in working with people different from them, both within their age group and especially those younger or older, with different interests, talents and capacities.

The Reservation: A Domain of Youth Work with American Indian Youth

On each of the 18 American Indian reservations located in the northern woodlands of Minnesota and Wisconsin, there are multiple small and isolated communities. Nationally, the Native population makes up only 1.1% of the total U.S. population, but across 12 counties of Minnesota, Wisconsin, North Dakota and South Dakota, American Indians are the majority of the population. The Native young people living on these reservations and in these counties attend the usual array of public schools as well as locally run Tribal schools. Many of the Native students attending public schools take advantage of community education, out of school time and 21st-century programs for after school activities. Several larger Tribes provide afterschool and summer activities for young people through the Boys and Girls Clubs that are often located on the reservation and supported in part by the Tribe. The activities run the usual menu of homework clubs to gym time and arts and craft time. Often the Clubs are perceived to be a place for kids to go after school until their parents are home from work; it's a place to be safe, hang out and stay out of trouble and serves as childcare. These same Tribes, in an effort to provide their young people with regular exposure to traditional cultural activities, have created Tribal youth programs staffed by a respected Tribal member, developed separately from the Boys & Girls Clubs and schools. Smaller Tribes rely on grants or limited tribal dollars to fund youth workers to organize and run cultural programs. Tribes often employ a cultural leader who qualifies for the position by virtue of being Native or a respected member of the Tribe who gets along well with young people. The programs usually include time for elders to interact with youth, a language component, and will usually include a drum and dance component. The summer program may include a camp designed around ancestral ways of doing and providing for daily living.

Youth work on the reservation as seen through the eyes of a visitor to the Tribe or a non-Indian supporter, is often about creating opportunities for young people to experience things that would otherwise be limited by virtue of poverty and isolation. They think it's all about providing opportunities for young people to see beyond the boundary of the reservation. Many outsiders consider it important to give young Natives a glimpse of the American dream of individual economic success, perhaps by attending a Twins baseball game. On the other hand, youth work as seen through the eyes of the collective members of Tribal nations is about creating the opportunity to make connections between deeply held cultural traditions and the development of each young Native as a whole and complete person: mentally, physically, emotionally and spiritually. It's about supporting the development of the young person to become tomorrow's Tribal leader—the leader who understands the Tribes link to the past and the future.

American Indian youth workers in the Ojibwe and Dakota communities today struggle to maintain a traditional influence in what could be called a contemporary model of Native youth engagement. Decades ago young people developed courage, skills and character while hunting and trapping at a young age with family members; bringing food home to give to elders. While this continues today to a degree, the norm is to engage a youth worker to take a small group of young Natives on an expedition into the Boundary Waters Canoe Area where they will learn to appreciate nature, practice team work, develop an understanding of natural consequences while honing their skills with a canoe. They have the experience of living off the land, fishing for their dinner, for a defined period of time. On the reservation, the year-round after-school program might entail weekly gatherings to learn the intricacies of Tribal dance, singing on the big drum or using hand drums, learning how to make one's own regalia. This is where young people learn the Tribal songs and rituals of celebration. The Tribal schools of the Midwest universally incorporate these activities into their out-of-school time for young people as well as into their daily curriculum. Currently, only a small number of public schools include such activities, often because they don't have the human resources but also because of curriculum mandates. During Tribal summer camps, young people will experience cooking over a fire-pit, thrashing wild rice, or boiling down maple syrup. They'll learn how to do beadwork and quillwork, or go fishing and canoeing. An elder would perhaps be engaged to tell traditional stories around the campfire if it was the appropriate season—stories that invite the listener to enter the story to find meanings that could be applied to their personal lives.

As more and more youth workers are engaged with young Natives on our reservations and wherever they reside, it is important that they are equipped with a deep understanding of youth development principles. Tribes have the tools for youth workers to use if they have the blessing of Tribal cultural leaders and, most importantly, the understanding and knowledge to use it effectively. Virtually every Tribe has a version of the medicine wheel that can accommodate the integration of standard youth development principles described for the Western world as Erikson's eight stages of human development. The medicine wheel is a visual learning tool that describes the physical, emotional and psychological stages of human development in a way that engages young people in their own learning. The elders of each community continue to be the source of and inspiration for Indigenous knowledge and wisdom. They are a sought after resource for passing on the language, ceremony and rituals of hundreds of generations to the Native youth of today—passing on the rituals that continue to feed the communal soul of Tribal people. It is living this ancestral way of thought and action with shared beliefs, ritual and ceremonies that Tribal communities continue to exist.

Conclusion

Civic youth work in the North and West is about an ethos of co-creation and negotiation and related practices. It is embedded in political and social institutions and in their culture, where the meaning of citizen is illuminated, challenged, and re-negotiated when young people effectively demonstrate through their civic engagement their interest, caring, talents, and calling to be citizens now. Civic youth workers invite young people to be responsible for civic issues, to work together to address a public issue they care about, to begin to be the people they understand themselves as becoming, and to care about individuals, issues and problems and others they may or may not have met. In doing all of this, civic youth work supports the co-creation with young people of democratic living-citizen. When done well, civic youth worker and young people experience what it means to live as democratic citizens. Contrarily, youth work on the reservation relies on the indigenous knowledge of the tribes' elders. Rather than flipping power arrangements between adult-youth, the traditional elder-youth relationship is revered. Yet, what each have in common is that which is hoped for.

LeMoine LaPointe, an American Indian experiential educator, so wisely said at the Annual Gathering of MN Tribal Leaders on June 16, 2009, "If we want our young people to do extraordinary things, we have to give them extraordinary experiences. It is up to us."

References

Arnett, R., & Arneson, P. (1999). *Dialogic civility in a cynical age: Community, hope and interpersonal relationships.* Albany: State University of New York Press.

Battistoni, R., & Hudson, W. (1997). *Experiencing citizenship: Concepts and models for service learning in political science.* Washington DC: American Association for Higher Education.

Bennette, S. (1997). Why young Americans hate politics, and what we should do about it. *Political Science and Politics, 30*, 47–52.

Boyte, H. (2004). The necessity of politics. *Journal of Public Affairs, 7*, 75–85.

Burbules, N. (1993). *Dialogue in teaching: Theory and practice.* New York: Teachers College Press.

Cammarota, J., & Fine, M. (2008). *Revolutionizing education.* New York: Taylor and Francis.

Checkoway, B., Richards-Schuster, K., Abdullah, S., Aragon, M., Facio, E., Figueroa, L., Reddy, E., Welsh, M., & White, A. (2003). Young people as competent citizens. *Community Development Journal, 38*, 298–309.

Chilcoat, G., & Ligon, J. (1998). "We talk here. This is a school for talking." Participatory democracy from the classroom out into the community: How discussion was used in the Mississippi Freedom Schools. *Curriculum Inquiry, 28*, 165–194.

Delgado, M. ,& Staples, L. (2008). *Youth-led community organizing: Theory and practice.* Oxford, UK: Oxford University Press.

Fierce (2010). *Coming out, stepping up: Organizing to build the power of LGBTQ youth.* New York: Author.

Higgs, J., & Titchen, A. (2001). *Practice knowledge and expertise in the health professions.* Oxford, UK: Butterworth Heinemann.

Hildreth, R., & Erlanson, M. (1998). *Building worlds, transforming lives, making history: A guide to public achievement.* Minneapolis, MN: The Center for Democracy and Citizenship.

James, A., & Prout, A. (1997). *Constructing and reconstructing childhood: Contemporary issues in the sociological study of childhood.* New York: Falmer Press.

Kymlicka, W., & Norman, W. (1995). Return of the citizen: A survey of recent work on citizenship theory. *Ethics, 104*, 352–381.

Sabo-Flores, K. (2008). *Youth participatory evaluation: Strategies for engaging young people.* San Francisco: Jossey-Bass.

VeLure Roholt, R. (2007). *Democratic civic practice: Building democratic communities together.* Available On-Line at: http://www.publicachievement.com/Publications.aspx

VeLure Roholt, R., Hildreth, R., & Baizerman, M. (2009). *Becoming citizens: Deepening the craft of youth civic engagement.* New York: Routledge.

Youniss, J., & Yates, M. (1997). *Community service and social responsibility in youth.* Chicago: University of Chicago Press.

Yates, M., & Youniss, J. (1999). *Roots of civic identity: International perspectives on community service and activism in youth.* Cambridge, UK: Cambridge University Press.

14

YOUTH WORK ACROSS TWO DIVERSE DOMAINS OF PRACTICE

Jim Sibthorp, M. Deborah Bialeschki, Carol Stuart, and Jack Phelan

Here again two distinct domains of practice are presented side by side: parks and recreation (presented by Jim Sibthorp and M. Deborah Bialeschki) and child/youth care in Canada (presented by Carol Stuart and Jack Phelan). Both come from a tradition of supporting the well-being of children and youth but that's where the similarity ends, at least at first glance. These two profiles of what youth work is and what a youth worker aims to do offer a comparison that seems beyond logic. Each has its own competencies, credentialing, and curriculum and there is little overlap between the two. The reader is stretched in imagining how a field as diverse as is represented in these two domains can both be considered "youth work."

Youth Work as Parks and Recreation

Since the beginning of the recreation movement, issues concerning youth have always been central. Recreation services in the late 19th century and into the early 20th century were begun largely because of a concern for youth. The development of recreation in both the public and the not-for-profit sectors were a direct result of the social welfare movement with philanthropists helping to create agencies and services for children and youth. Jane Addams, often considered the "Mother of Recreation," is a good example of a social reformist interested in youth recreation. She was involved with the Playground Movement and started the first public playground in Chicago at Hull House. This settlement house was the site for a variety of youth and recreation services that she started including the early development of the Chicago Park District. She believed that youth's instincts for play were a vital force and that play contained the seeds of culture and democracy (Wellman et al., 2008). She felt that "to fail to provide for the recreation of youth is not only to deprive all of them of their natural form of expression but is certain to subject some of them to the overwhelming temptation of illicit and soul destroying pleasures" (Henderson, 1982, p. 43). Jane's plans for democratic urban areas were clearly tied to issues of equity and dignity through recreation and cultural opportunities for youth.

As recreation continued to professionalize, it became a part of public, nonprofit, and commercial sectors. Youth services were found in all sectors and primarily focused on organized activities offered for youth during their free time for personal and social benefits. The professionals who worked in recreation services were dedicated to a life of service with the belief that their work in recreation contributed to the health and well-being of their participants. For recreation professionals interested in youth, the professional focus shifted from diversionary activities that provided constructive structured activities to keep youth off the streets to youth programs focused on positive developmental youth outcomes. Today, youth recreation professionals are involved with health and wellness, mentoring, civic engagement, youth leadership, as well as using recreation as a context for identity development and formation.

The Core of Recreation Curricula

The core content of most academic programs in parks and recreation ties to three fundamental areas: (1) the foundations of the profession, (2) design and delivery, and (3) management and administration. Foundational content typically includes history, philosophy, and the use of social and behavioral science to improve health and wellness through parks and recreation. Design and delivery is focused on the design, implementation, and evaluation of programs and the design and evaluation of facilities to provide recreational opportunities. Management and administration content typically addresses the necessary operational strategies to succeed in the variety of public, nonprofit, and commercial sectors involved in parks and recreation; content coverage includes human resource management, financial management, staffing, marketing, and public administration. Many of the undergraduate programs in Canada are accredited by the Council on Accreditation of Parks, Recreation, Tourism, and Related Professions.

In addition to the core content provided to undergraduate majors in parks and recreation, students specifically interested in working with youth are required to take additional coursework. Such coursework is commonly interdisciplinary and addresses topics ranging from psychosocial youth development and youth programming to youth sports and family recreation. In addition, students often take courses specific to the setting in which they plan to work. Such courses might focus on community recreation, public and non-profit administration, grant writing, or adventure and outdoor education.

While the nature of the professional preparation for youth-specific workers is interdisciplinary, a positive youth development approach (Witt & Caldwell, 2005) is typical. Course content often focuses on concepts around youth program quality, provision of supports and opportunities, and engagement of youth at the point of service. While outcome-based programming is common (e.g., how to foster a caring community at an afterschool program), unstructured recreation is also addressed (e.g., how can and should a drop-in community center best meet the needs of youth).

Many academic programs in parks and recreation place a premium on experiential education, service learning, and learning by doing. Collaborative projects and assignments that bridge theory and practice are typical. Students must complete both small and large internships, or cooperative education experiences, prior to graduation. Internship placements at summer camps, afterschool programs, outdoor education centers, and local nonprofits such as Boys and Girls Clubs or the Girl Scouts are common.

Employment Options in Parks and Recreation

Employment options afforded students after graduation are highly diverse. Some students find employment at urban recreation centers that provide necessary supervision for children during non-school hours. Others go into youth sports, either with a community recreation center or local nonprofits. Many programs for youth are offered by national youth-serving nonprofits such as Girls Scouts, Boy Scouts, 4-H, Boys and Girls clubs, Big Brothers-Big Sisters, and a host of similar organizations. Some find work in summer camps, which themselves vary from urban nonprofits to large commercial enterprises. Students interested in outdoor or adventure education might work as wilderness instructors for organizations like National Outdoor Leadership School (NOLS) or Outward Bound. While many of these employment options may begin as part-time or seasonal, all have the potential for permanent employment. However, this will often necessitate successfully utilizing the full range of skills acquired through one's undergraduate program. Management, marketing, finance, and grant writing all become more relevant as students move up in an organization. Ideal philosophies and program ideas get vetted by fiscal and structural realities.

Students are encouraged to find an internship that may segue into a permanent position after graduation. So, the student who interned at the local community recreation center as a seasonal employee for the summer sports leagues might transition into full time placement as a program supervisor. Within public parks and recreation, these entry level positions can lead to movement within the facility, within the broader municipal parks and recreation department, or within the field of parks and recreation. It is relatively common for students to begin at a smaller center and through several years advance to a position of responsibility within larger departments and municipalities. Students also find employment as seasonal summer camp staff and move into organized camping as a full time profession, most commonly as a camp director. Outdoor education centers, schools with outdoor education programs, afterschool programs, wilderness programs, and non-profits have all offered graduates focused on working with youth rewarding and sustainable careers.

Evolution of Professional Practice

As students leave the academy for the workplace, much of their professional preparation knowledge is immediately applied in their youth work jobs. For many new youth workers, they have an opportunity to put their newly acquired knowledge of positive youth development, program implementation, and management skills to work as they match their organizations mission and goals with actions that make a difference in the lives of the young people with whom they work. As youth workers continue in their positions, there is a constant need to stay current on translations of research findings and the "best practices" that result from applied research. Professional development through conferences, trainings, online courses, webinars, and other types of resources are a constant factor for professionals. To stay current and relevant, professionals constantly seek information that helps address issues ranging from sportsmanship, abuse, wellness, leadership development, mentoring to service delivery issues such as quality programming, outcomes, and effective staff training. Sessions on evaluation and assessment as well as logic models and program theories illustrate the intentionality that many park and recreation providers have embraced. In addition, many youth-serving organizations have developed youth worker competencies that are addressed through varied professional development opportunities that serve as a framework for accreditation and certification programs. Ultimately, to make youth professional development successful, cooperation is necessary between higher education, professional associations, and professional practice.

Regardless of medium, it is clear from the number of sessions, interests, and youth related topics, that the parks and recreation profession is embracing the movement toward more intentional and developmental youth services. Much of this interest is driven by the next generation of professional leaders who are passionate about the both the profession and the increasingly complex community needs served through recreation related professions. Increasingly park and recreation professionals are expected to provide developmental programs for youth, foster active and healthy lifestyles, instill lifelong recreation and leisure skills, and reconnect kids with each other, their families, the environment, and their communities.

Discussions about professionalization of youth work are a common theme within many youth-serving organizations and professional gatherings. This emerging interest is an outgrowth of several issues such as legitimacy of the work, salaries, promotion/advancement, the competencies/skills/knowledge needed to offer high quality programs with intentional outcomes, and the focus on the need for continuing education opportunities through professional development. With the growing body of knowledge built upon solid research, the employment opportunities offered as a way to address the growing needs of children and youth, and the academic community responding to the needs for research, knowledge, and training future professionals, the professionalization of youth work is well underway.

Child and Youth Care in Canada

Child and Youth Care practice (CYC) is the generally accepted term for professional work with children, youth, and families in Canada. The post-secondary system has over 50 diploma or degree programs of two to four years in length that are specifically titled Child and Youth Care or Child and Youth Work. These programs make no professional distinction among practitioners who work with children of different ages or within different types of service. The first diploma and degree programs in Canada were created in the early 1970s in response to the need for qualified staff in residential care (see Stuart, 2009, for a history of education and professional development in Canada). Current organizational hiring practices may require a specific diploma, degree, or professional certification from the provincial CYC professional association but CYC practitioners are hired for a variety of positions with varied titles including Child and Youth Worker, Child and Youth Counselor, Youth Worker, Family Support Worker, Youth Justice Worker, Case Worker, Prevention Worker, etc. CYC practitioners can be found in a variety of settings such as group homes and residential treatment centers, hospitals and community mental health clinics, community-based outreach and school-based programs, parent education and family support programs, as well as in private practice and juvenile justice programs.

The Canadian Council of Child and Youth Care Associations (CCCYCA), the national body representing provincial CYC professional associations, adopted the following scope of practice statement in 2008: "The practice of Child and Youth Care occurs within the context of therapeutic relationships with children and youth who are experiencing difficulties in their lives. Intervention takes place within the family, the community and other social institutions, and centres on promoting emotional, social and behavioural change and well-being within the context of daily living." The CCCYCA offers a definition of Child and Youth Care consistent with the definition provided by the Association of Child and Youth Care Practice (ACYCP) in the United States: "Practitioners design and implement programs but the practice is focused on the therapeutic relationship; the application of theory and research about human growth and development to promote the optimal physical, psycho-social, spiritual, cognitive, and emotional development of young people towards a healthy and productive adulthood; and a focus on strengths and assets rather than pathology (CCCYCA, 2008).

Since post-secondary education for CYC is well established in Canada, curriculum has been defined and revised over the last 30 years and many programs use specific competencies defined by provincial certification expectations or their own curriculum reviews. Recent research in Ontario (Stuart & Carty, 2006) reviewed these documents as well as the Child and Youth Care Certification Board Inc. (CYCBC) competencies (Mattingly, Stuart, & VanderVen, 2010) and developed seven inter-related domains of practice which are essential in any setting (youth justice, residential, family support, recreation, youth employment, schools, etc.) and with clientele that come to those settings for varied reasons (abuse, criminal activity, physical or cognitive delays, symptoms of mental illness, homelessness, financial need, etc.). These domains of practice are illustrated in Figure 14.1.

The four central domains emphasize that the focus of practice is the child or youth and the intent of the practitioner is to assist young people with optimal development through the creation of relationships and the application of interventions both with the young person and with and within the systems that young people exist. CYC practitioners are concerned about problems from the perspective of the young person and work to optimize physical and mental health within a holistic health perspective (Stuart, 2009). Practitioners express a professional demeanour and skill through advanced communication

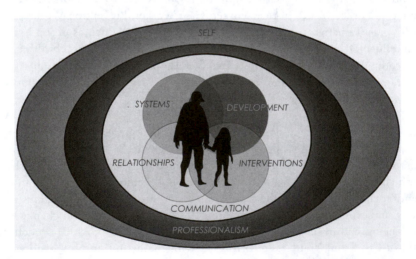

FIGURE 14.1 The domains of Child and Youth Care practice. From *Foundations of Child and Youth Care Practice* by Carol Stuart. Copyright © 2009. Reprinted with permission of Kendall Hunt Publishing Co.

techniques, and professional practice values are consistent with the Self, which forms the foundation for all practice with young people. The Self is the instrument through which the practitioner offers help.

The importance of Self in CYC practice is evident in the core characteristics of practice described by many Canadian authors. CYC work occurs at a molecular level, it doesn't occur at arm's length or in a sterilized environment. The worker has an intense and often intimate presence, which removes any possibility of detachment and distance. Creating a shared life-space with young people in the same space and time creates a shared connection, in spite of the natural tendency of both people in the helping equation to push away and keep a safe distance. Workers are present by choice, and their behavior is purposeful and responsive to the other person. CYC work is a process of experiencing life alongside others and supporting them to use this experience to change. CYC practice involves arranging experiences that are helpful, or using the experiences that emerge as we go through the day in a strategic way to support young people to change. The everydayness of the efforts can appear too simple to really be a professional task, yet the skill required to manage these experiential lessons is quite complex (Phelan, 2003).

CYC is a passion, which focuses on caring for and about children, youth and families working with them in their own milieu. Caring *for* the young person ensures that a safe and nurturing environment maximizes the developmental needs of the child for healthy growth. Caring *about* focuses on the social competence of the young person and places value on children and youth as competent members of society. We use the characteristics of the space that clients are located in and carefully adjust our timing to maximize the opportunities for change that are present within that milieu. The techniques and strategies for change used in CYC practice are unique to the moment and to the individual because timing and location are everything and this individuality allows practitioners to maximize the transfer of learning by young people to other locations in their life-space (Stuart, 2009).

Children are naturally competent, and by believing in them and valuing them as competent people CYC's help children, youth, and families learn to resolve problems as they come up, building on their skills and helping them to be ready to address the next problem. This in-the-moment approach to intervention occurs primarily within the milieu, in the place and at the time that will maximize the impact of the practitioner on the young person. CYC practitioners work to incorporate themselves into the life-space and life-story of young people and/or families so that their influence can be felt even if they are not present (Gharabaghi & Stuart, 2011). This life-space approach to the work makes the work highly experiential. Practitioners bring their own experience to the work and therefore must be very clear about how that experience might be helpful or *not* for children or families.

There is a clearly accepted knowledge base for practice, which is shared across CYC practice settings in Canada and used within the educational programs. Key knowledge areas include:

- **Relationship and connection.** Practitioners understand the nuances of relationship development and the factors that enhance relationships as well as the subtleties of the relational "in-between" (Garfat, 2008). They both develop relationships and explore the relationships and existing connections that children, youth, and families already have with knowledge about both typical and unique relationships within the human context.
- **Attachment dynamics.** Children and youth come to practitioners with damaged attachments created through loss or trauma and practitioners are knowledgeable about the effects of previous attachments on the formation of relationships and attachments in the future.
- **Systemic orientation.** Children and youth exist within a family system, which exists within a community and society. Practitioners are knowledgeable about the dynamics of systems and the influence that system dynamics have on individuals. They are able to consider these dynamics as they work with young people and their families. Regardless of whether or not the family and community are immediately present the ecology of the young person is considered.
- **Cultural competence and cultural safety.** In a global society practitioners must be knowledgeable about how to create a safe environment that is both accepting of diversity and which actively promotes an appreciation of varied cultural practices and supports young people within the context of their own culture.
- **Human growth and development** across the lifespan and from a holistic perspective has been a core knowledge area for CYC practice from early in its development. Recent knowledge about developmental theory and patterns of human growth and development recognizes that theory and research in development is culturally situated and practitioners must account for this in their practice.

A practical example of the life-space work expected of a competent practitioner may help to illustrate: A 16-year-old young woman is new to the group, and you know that she is not safe with you, an unfamiliar male. You avoid being alone with her and don't go anywhere with her unless at least one other youth is also coming. You respond to her yelling with softness and curiosity. You find ways to nurture her and care for her through favorite foods, being attentive to her comfort and responsive to her complaints. You consciously avoid any attempts to upstage her or try too hard to be liked. She needs to have you wait for her to relax her anxiety and believe in your lack of an agenda to control her or use her. You take her shopping, always with other youth, and try to get something that she needs, even a coffee or magazine. You respect her privacy, but try to create a play experience where she can relax and be a young girl. As she trusts your safeness, now you arrange "safe place" experiences where she can laugh, be childish and start to enjoy physical movement. You continue to have other people present throughout these events to prevent a panic moment, which requires you both to start all over. You know about attachment issues, abuse dynamics and developmental needs as you move into a safer relationship and create opportunities for her to be healthy.

Conclusion

The professionals who work in recreation services and in CYC, unlike their counterparts in many community agencies, have often graduated from a two- or four-year college program. There is a structured curriculum in both areas that is consistent across universities and is overseen and approved by educators and professional bodies such as the Council on Accreditation of Parks, Recreation, Tourism and Related Professions and the Child and Youth Care Educational Accreditation Board of Canada, respectively. Both professions are focused on individual change either through the use of life-space or outdoor space. Both are dedicated to a life of service with the belief that their work (and play) contributes to the health and well-being of their participants. The skills needed in residential care, school-based practice, family work, mental health, and community work are more similar than not, with the need for supervision and prior experience being somewhat different. Working in the community, street work, and working at drop in centers are all particular venues for practice, requiring a similar stance toward practice whether residential, school-based, or family support work, among others.

References

Canadian Council of Child and Youth Care Associations (CCCYCA). (2008). *Scope of practice.* Retrieved from http://www.garthgoodwin.info/Scope_of_Practice.html.

Garfat, T. (2008). The interpersonal in between: An exploration of relational child and youth care practice. In G. Bellefeuille & F. Ricks (Eds.), *Standing on the precipice: Inquiry into the creative potential of child and youth care practice* (pp. 7–34). Edmonton, Canada: MacEwan Press.

Gharabaghi, K., & Stuart, C. (2011). Right here, right now: Exploring life-space interventions for children, youth and families. Manuscript submitted for publication.

Henderson, K. (1982). Jane Addams: Pioneer in leisure services. *Journal of Physical Education, Recreation, and Dance, 53,* 42–46.

Mattingly, M., Stuart, C., & VanderVen, K. (2010). *Competencies for professional child and youth care.* Retrieved from http://www.acycp.org/standards/standards.htm.

Phelan, J. (2003). An attempt to be articulate about CYC work. Retrieved August 26, 2010, from http://www.cyc-net.org/cyc–online, October, 2003.

Stuart, C. (2009). *Foundations of child and youth care,* Dubuque, IA: Kendall Hunt.

Stuart, C., & Carty, W. (October, 2006). *The role of competence in outcomes for children and youth: An approach for mental health.* Toronto, Canada: Ryerson University.

Wellman, D., Dustin, D., Henderson, K., & Moore, R. (2008). *Service living: Building community through public parks and recreation.* State College, PA: Venture.

Witt, P. A., & Caldwell, L. L. (2005). *Recreation and youth development.* State College, PA: Venture.

15

A COMMUNITY EDUCATION APPROACH TO YOUTH WORK EDUCATION

Joel Nitzberg

Community Education offers a menu of principles and activities that through partnerships with others concerned about community life uses learning strategies to transform people's lives. It is a philosophy and an array of practices that respond to the learning needs of community members, initiating services and linkages to resources as directed by those who are impacted by such. Community Education espouses the belief that by working together formal and informal education not only enhances individual lives but also has the potential for strengthening communities and impacting society at all levels. Learning is a means for supporting change and thus preparing people for independent lives while also creating the foundation knowledge for designing productive interdependencies that must exist in civil society. Collaboration is a key strategy for community educators and so through partnering with multiple resources and stakeholders offers the means for sharing and connecting local resources to focus on humane, social, economic, and other development.

The Community Education field is broad and encompasses many incarnations, including out-of-school time and youth work programs. In fact, it offers the multiple strands of a community's learning fabric. Community educators are adept at working with community members to identify needs and resources, and then meeting those needs through weaving together formal and informal learning services. Although there is no clear launching point for our field, higher education has often been a part of its development. Whether it was sending college students to settlement houses to assist and learn from the community, providing teacher training to prepare professionals for community schools, or establishing land grant universities to address the unique needs of rural workers, higher education has often had a role in creating services based on the needs of the locale.

My own evolution as community educator began in 1987 when, as a social worker, I was managing an after school program for the community schools division of an urban district in Massachusetts. Prior to this position I had become frustrated by the limited opportunities clients were experiencing to make independent, substantial changes in their lives. I felt what I was doing as a social worker was perpetuating a dependency on service providers. My initial transformation was the result of attending a national Community Education conference in Minnesota. There I discovered like-minded people and saw the potential for making an impact on people's lives through education, and, in particular, by focusing on how community resources could be designed and adapted to the needs of learners. Ultimately, I decided that education was perhaps a field that promoted individual empowerment and that community engagement was a critical factor in people's well being. I went back to college and received a Masters Degree in Education, with a particular focus on meshing community building with learning practices. Later, I founded and became the director of a Community Education department of a college that had as its foundation the mission to provide higher education services to adults who previously lacked access.

What I present in this chapter is a brief description of some of the work of the department I directed at Cambridge College as we prepared youth workers to participate as community educators. Over many years I have experienced the value and need for educational institutions to create bridges between the professionalization of youth work and Community Education. The potential is for those who work with youth to recognize and practice the skills and knowledge of working within communities, building networks, creating relationships with multiple resources, and appreciating that learning is a lifelong and inclusive process. It is my belief that higher education has a clear and perhaps unique role in not only preparing their students for youth work, but for establishing a professionalism that incorporates Community Education practices. The examples presented below adhere to the principles of community education as espoused by the National Community Education Association (2007). These principles include:

- *Community Involvement.* Community Education promotes a sense of civic responsibility, provides leadership opportunities for community members, includes diverse populations in all aspects of community life, and encourages democratic procedures in local decision making.
- *Efficient Use of Resources.* Schools and the community's physical, financial, and human resources are used to address the community's needs. A reduction in the duplication of services is accomplished by promoting collaborative effort.
- *Lifelong Learning.* Education is viewed as a birth-to-death process and everyone in the community—individuals, businesses, public and private agencies—shares in the responsibility of educating all members of the community

and providing lifelong learning opportunities for learners of all ages, backgrounds, and needs.

- *Self-Determination.* Local people have a right and a responsibility to be involved in determining community needs and identifying community resources that can be used to address those needs.
- *Self-Help.* People are best served when their capacity to help themselves is acknowledged and developed. When people assume responsibility for their own well-being, they build independence and become part of the solution.
- *Leadership Development.* The training of local leaders in such skills as problem solving, decision-making, and group process is an essential component of successful self-help and improvement efforts.
- *Institutional Responsiveness.* Public institutions exist to serve the public and are obligated to develop programs and services that address continuously changing public needs and interests.
- *Integrated Delivery of Services.* Organizations and agencies that operate for the public good can meet their own goals and better serve the public by collaborating with organizations and agencies with similar goals.
- *Decentralization.* Services, programs, and other community involvement opportunities that are closest to people's homes have the greatest potential for high levels of public participation. Whenever possible, these activities should be available in locations with easy public access.

The Institute for Lifelong Learning and Community Building

Cambridge College is a unique learning community where students build their education on a lifetime of learning and from their experiences as members of families, communities, workplaces, networks, and peers. The college's mission is to provide academically excellent, time-efficient, and cost-effective higher education to a diverse population of working adults for whom these opportunities may have been limited or denied. Cambridge College's learning and teaching model is based on extensive experience serving adult students who thrive in non-traditional instructional environments.

In 2002, I was hired to design a comprehensive undergraduate college curriculum to teach human service majors how to be effective working in communities. The courses developed resulted from a yearlong process of interviewing education and human service practitioners concerning their requirements for community-knowledgeable and skilled workers. A collaborative planning process was formed that included an advisory group that met monthly with members representing community-based organizations, neighborhoods, and higher education. As the project unfolded and the courses were designed and implemented, an additional plan evolved. Working closely with organization practitioners and other stakeholders we created processes in which higher education could directly participate in the strengthening of communities. In 2005, the Institute for Lifelong Learning and Community Building began based on the beliefs that higher education (1) has the potential for integrating principles and practices of inclusion and real-world experiences across disciplines; (2) has an important role to play in terms of educating people at the local level, who in turn impact community life and practice; (3) can offer educational opportunities beyond those that follow traditional degree earning formats; and (4) must be flexible regarding access and program delivery models as a condition for partnering with communities.

Staff of the Institute worked in concert with community partners to customize courses, and institutionalize an affordable process for adults in the community to prepare for, and enter college, and various career pathways. There are large numbers of people unable to enter higher education as full- or part-time students due to lack of financial stability, time, and other personal accessibility issues. As a result, a range of options needs to be made available. Our plan was to provide workers, including those working with youth, with flexible opportunities to receive college coursework and other learning experiences to further their professional goals. We strongly supported the idea that higher education institutions must be committed to social justice and societal change, and therefore must design ways that are innovative, flexible and integrated with the social, economic, and workforce realities of local communities. Multiple venues for participation prior to matriculation were as important as creating financial incentives to allow students to experience college.

School-Age and Youth Development program (SAYD)

According to a report by the Wellesley Center for Women, through the past decade, the out-of-school time (OST) field has seen demand for services increase dramatically. The reality of more women entering the workforce created a greater need for adult-supervised activities after school. The emerging field of research on the benefits of OST programs to deter youth crime and improve children's social and academic skills has stimulated a greater public interest in after-school programs. Finally, the growing emphasis on educational standards and accountability favors the development of supplemental learning opportunities to support children in their academic achievements. This increased attention on OST programs has heightened the importance of appropriate training and preparation for OST staff.

To address this growing need for youth worker training, the Institute became a member of a consortia of community-based organizations (ACHIEVE Boston) that had developed a training network focusing on competencies youth workers needed for professional practice. Based on dialogues with practitioners and administrators it was agreed that community and professional recognition of the legitimacy of field required higher education involvement and partnering with youth work organizations. The following were cited as advantages of higher education's involvement:

- Community and college trainings working together would enable a sequential process resulting in professional practice.
- The alliance would offer a potential for reducing or removing competition between training programs and colleges in terms of attracting funds and participants.
- Colleges could potentially reach more people and in a sustained way as they were in the business of recruitment and offering recognized credentials.
- Higher education provides additional course offerings that broadened professional development.
- Varied and more secure resources might enable sustainability and expansion of programs that were developed.
- Training personnel working closely with college faculty could establish effective continuity between research, instruction and practice.

As a result, the Higher Education Afterschool and Youth Roundtable (HEAYR) was founded as a subcommittee of ACHIEVE. We invited many institutions to join our efforts, and a core sustained working group eventually emerged consisting of the following: North Shore Community College; Bunker Hill Community College; Lesley College; Cambridge College; University of Massachusetts, Boston; Harvard University; Northeastern University; Urban College; and Quinsigamond Community College. The process of forming HEAYR and creating a viable means for colleges and community organizations to work together took three years to develop. The complexity of the institutional differences offered multiple barriers for reaching consensus, and so passage through this maze of agendas, bureaucracies, and personalities was often daunting. Some of the early participating colleges dropped out as their administrative barriers were insurmountable. However, the core group of public and private, two and four year colleges, working with organization partners ultimately came to an agreement as to the content, classroom hours, student expectations, grading, location, instructor experience, and teaching styles. In addition, and of most significance, was the provision of college credits prior to matriculation. Introduced by Cambridge College this was an innovative model for attracting workers to this initiative. It was a major hurtle, but ultimately, I believe the most compelling aspect of this program. Students who passed the courses could transfer the credits once matriculating to any of the participating institutions.

Through careful planning, transparent communication, inclusion and tenacity of multiple members, a well-designed agreement policy, and throughout, a sense of humor, HEAYR was able to avoid and overcome major roadblocks within each college. HEAYR worked with faculty and youth work staff who had sufficient say within their organizations to implement the plan. Higher education members who taught at their respective institutions were able to assure we followed appropriate andragogical instruction. This instruction differs from pedagogy, which is geared towards children's learning. When working with adults and following the andragogical model, there is an emphasis on the student being self-directed, and using one's life experiences as part of the learning process. Malcolm Knowles' theory of instructing adults differs from that of pedagogy which he viewed to be a transmittal approach; instructors have determined in advance the knowledge and skills to be learned (Knowles, 1980, 1984). Content is developed prior to instruction and lessons are arranged in sequential and logical units. The andragogical approach also deals with content, but the model is less about the transmission of precise information and skills. Rather, it focuses on the process itself, of helping learners acquire needed information and skills and requires the instructor to be a facilitator. Instructors following adult learning theory incorporate learner's view of self, assist students in understanding their unique learning styles, and provide opportunities for learners to influence design and related activities.

An essential objective of the partnership was for courses for each cohort to be taught by different institutions. For the 2007–08 pilot, three courses were held (two development and one practice course) at a central location in Boston. Most of the participants were still at an early stage in their academic as well as professional careers. Faculty members came from the University of Massachusetts, Urban College, and Cambridge College, and were selected based on their history working directly with youth, and their interactive teaching style. The courses taught were: Early Childhood Development, Youth Development, and Principles and Practices of After School and Youth Programs.

Emerging from this process was not only the successful provision of relevant courses that were transferable to workplaces and colleges, but we had established an organization that could formalize agreements and processes for future higher education–community partnership projects. Based on evaluations from students and staff we assessed that this model of offering college level courses was an incentive for workers to continue for full degrees. It also offered an incentive for workers to remain in the field and in their current workplace. This was clearly an appetizing idea for student-starved higher education as well as organizations that experienced high turnover. However, the initial reason for providing this program remained as the prime motivator for this and potentially future expansion, professionalizing the field of youth work to support youth, and their respective organizations.

The course that I taught that was customized for this pilot provided a combination of practical skills in program development and maintenance, with concrete ways to achieve the integration of learning with experience, all connecting to principles of Community Education. Participants learned about inclusive programming, infusing academic goals and enrichment activities while engaging community resources and families. They identified meaningful strength-based strategies and activities linking the needs of youth to school and curriculum standards, while connecting to and utilizing the resources within communities. They were taught how organizational capacity building includes establishing a democratic work environment with clear philosophies and inclusive practices, and maintaining consistent beliefs and practices that encourage participants at all levels to be authentic and effective.

The design process for creating the course was inclusive. In addition to conferring with HEAYR members, those at Cambridge College were part of the design. At the time, I was teaching a course on School-Family-Community Partnerships. My students, who were a combination of education and human service majors, were engaged as co-creators integrating their own professional needs and ideas as to what they thought should be included. It is critically important to incorporate the understanding of those who practice in the same or related fields, as they bring real-world experiences and knowledge to the learning process. My students were an invaluable part of the design process (which was also a useful learning experience for them). Not only did they offer first-hand knowledge as to what it meant to be a student and worker but by being engaged in this process the connections they made between their own practice and theory coupled with project design, provided them with a real-world and useful learning experience. With the course designed and accepted by HEAYR, I brought it before the Cambridge College's curriculum committee for approval. This was a necessary step for all participating colleges, bringing to their respective decision-making structures their respective course for approval to offer college credits.

Principles and Practices of After School and Youth Programs had three major themes: (1) Fundamentals of Effective Programs; (2) Activities and Curriculum; and (3) Families, Schools and Community Partnerships. Instruction followed a highly interactive and varied model including group discussion, individual reflection, lecture, group and individual projects, hands-on learning activities, individual and small group problem solving, role-play/simulations, and a final group presentation. Out-of-class learning activities included assigned readings with written assignments, journal entries, research, and a final paper. The model was based on the understanding that people learn by assimilating multiple current and past experiences, and that they must be active players in their own knowledge process. Community educators are charged with empowering learners to be full participants, and that ultimately their learning is transferrable to their communities, making meaningful, practical contributions to families, workplaces, and communities.

The idea of providing college level work coupled with credits remains a bold concept, and yet, the successful engagement of youth workers and their commitment to study and apply their learning to day-to-day work is a testament to this approach of combining professional training with academic rigor. It remains critically important to maintain close connections and working relationships between higher education partners and youth work organizations, and we believed that for professional development of this workforce to be successful, both community resources and higher education must be unified.

Unfortunately, after the pilot ended funding sources dried up. HEAYR members remain connected, and its leadership is pursuing the plan for a sustained organization. The goal is to create a state-wide association of participating higher education institutions to include on each local consortia the following: Two- and four-year public and private colleges, and research universities; community-based organizations and schools that will support their workers' learning and practical application; other consortia and individual organizations that offer resources relevant for youth work. In addition, the plan is to offer additional courses, including those designed for program managers and other upper level administrators.

International Youth Worker Training

Starting in 2007, the Institute established close working relations with an international youth organization, Youth Entrepreneurship and Sustainability (YES Inc.) to design curricula and a training program for youth workers. YES Inc.'s mission is to build the individual capacity of youth in developing countries to enable them to move toward formal employment. The philosophy of this organization is to look beyond the current ways of thinking and doing business, to find new ideas, products, services and processes that are customized to fit local needs and conditions. YES's mission includes cultivating youth as entrepreneurs, providing them with the training and support to build on their current strengths the knowledge and skills necessary to be adaptable and enterprising. The organization was launched in 2002 in Alexandria, Egypt by 1,600 delegates from 120 countries. The Alexandria Summit was hosted by the Arab Republic of Egypt and co-chaired by Mrs. Suzanne Mubarak, First Lady of Egypt, and former President William J. Clinton as a way to develop the capacity of youth to lead.

Youth workers affiliated with the organization described how they valued higher education and that they desired all training related to professional development be provided by colleges. The status alone of receiving a certificate from a higher education institution was valued by their respective organizations, funders and governments, even when granted by a small institution such as Cambridge College. The partnership between YES and Cambridge College was a necessary step in moving the learning agenda forward.

The training that was developed provided youth workers with skills to be trainers themselves, and to teach younger people about self-employment and leadership. It was jointly decided that the theme of the training was on youth social entrepreneurship, believing that the combination of business acumen and skills supporting local populations would not only benefit the young entrepreneur but would address the needs of their communities. While social entrepreneurs often work through nonprofits and civic groups, many work in the private and governmental sectors. The theme among modern day social entrepreneurs emphasizes the enormous synergies and benefits when business principles are unified with social ventures. The work of social entrepreneurs comes from guiding principles that recognize that the development of a community needs to include decentralized collaboration, inclusive participation and multi-stakeholder partnerships. Creating an intentional planning process that incorporated the themes of humane relationships, self-actualization, economic and social justice, we were offering concepts very familiar to those in the youth development field. Joining the principles and practices of Community Education with the above themes, adding learning as a critical strategy, there is an increased potential for empowering people to initiate change for themselves and their communities.

The youth workers engaged in the training were not accustomed to being decision-makers or involved in changing local systems that impacted the work they were doing. They quickly recognized that the training would be invaluable, not only for the youth they worked with, but since the workers grew up in the same static systems, they saw the possibilities for their own growth as leaders. By creating trainers who valued localized learning as a means for community progress, we were potentially changing whole systems that had been operating in traditional, hierarchical systems where strength-based practices were not part of organizational cultures. They were also unacquainted with the notion that learning processes could be designed with learners, that it can be interactive and fun, and that all members of the community had the potential for involvement in lifelong learning. Youth could be a part of and key players in creating learning communities. With trained facilitators going back to train others, we had the potential for impacting larger populations of youth, thus potentially impacting many communities.

The training was held in the fall of 2009 in Nicaragua, outside the city of Managua, in a setting of palm trees and exotic flowers, tiny lizards and other less identifiable fauna, in a pastel colored adobe complex that had been converted into an educational center. The group of youth workers represented 20 municipalities across the country. Officials from these communities were willing to send the workers as they saw that youth poverty and the resultant social deterioration were having a disastrous impact, and had not been successful in altering this downward spiral. They believed it was a necessary strategy to have youth workers representing a cross section of Nicaragua to come together and have unified exposure to new knowledge while establishing an ongoing network. They were also intrigued by the idea of social entrepreneurship as a possible strategy for stabilization and growth that could be led by youth. Apparently, social entrepreneurship was not a known aspect of Nicaraguan community planning. Funding was secured through the University of Nicaragua, and throughout the week faculty and administrators visited the training to witness the process. This was an unusual experience for them as well, not only in terms of the instructional (androgogical) process, but supporting and participating in an educational process that was geared towards non-university students. The skepticism that apparently they had regarding this format for learning seemed to be quelled by the end of the week, as the academic representatives offered congratulations of the training and understanding of how the entire process of design and implementation took a full year and engaged multiple stakeholders. Their comments suggested an appreciation for how professional development of youth workers could be accomplished using experiential methodologies and that youth themselves had the potential for engaging in their own learning process.

I was the trainer and worked with an interpreter who had been very involved in helping me design the initial content. Working with the host organization, a customized curriculum evolved over the previous year. Adhering to adult learning methodologies, the in-class experiential instruction included small-group dialogue, self-reflection, speakers, and activities led by instructors and participants. Constant dialogue occurred throughout the week, not only of the content, but the process of training to enable participants to incorporate their ideas for changing content as well as methodologies to apply to their own situations. It was critically important that the trainees be engaged in understanding and applying principles and skills of teaching and learning while generating ideas as to changes in content and process to their own situations. One of the more seasoned youth workers reported later that, as a result of the week, she felt reinvigorated and enthusiastic about what she might be able to do in her work with young people. She had never experienced experiential learning before, and believed this style of instruction and engaging learners would revolutionize this work. Based on field notes, she was recorded saying: "We are used to lecturing our youth, not involving them in their own learning. This style of teaching will motivate them to be learners and leaders."

The training focused on three interconnected themes: leadership, community building, and social entrepreneurship. We presented the need for youth to acquire a sense of ownership of local issues, meshing individual goals with participating in the development of their communities. Regardless of their specific circumstances, youth have the potential for undertaking meaningful and responsible leadership experiences that can overcome risks and obstacles in their lives, while increasing their resiliency. The second theme of the training provided an understanding how social, economic, environmental, and political issues are interconnected as well as the respective relationships. It is by viewing community change through a systemic lens that offers strategies and opportunities for organizing people to improve conditions and reach sustained positive change. Coupling skills and knowledge with intentional engagement of residents, workers and learners contribute to the success of a community building effort. The final theme, social entrepreneurship, was to enable youth to discover and create innovative ways of filling gaps and connecting to essential life skills, while generating self-employment and local enterprises. Social entrepreneurs are not limited to any one field, nor are they limited to the for-profit world. They are in Information Technology (IT), the field of pharmaceuticals, transport and communication industries, retail, food production, real estate, tourism, publishing, textile manufacturing, and in the non-profit sector.

The training emphasized the importance of young people and others to see them as resources in their respective communities. It is critical that useful roles are developed, engaging youth as co-creators and as fellow leaders, and for them to be part of planning and implementation of programs and other meaningful activities related to governance and sustainability. When young people participate in planning and implementing their out-of-school time program or other endeavors, the program becomes more aligned with their interests, and the sense of ownership adds to participants' long-term investment. Attendance and interest increase, and the new ideas brought by the young people can result in new and exciting activities. They can begin to take on leadership and teaching roles and work in partnership with adults to maximize the opportunities for learning and growth for all participants. When we give youth the tools to be self-directed and invite them to take part in leadership activities, helping others, we communicate the message to young people that what you think and what you do matters.

Discussion and activities throughout the week focused on what it means to be part of a community and what responsibilities were expected from those benefiting from its sustainability. Trainees discussed the political and economic realities of individual need versus common good, and how the economic success of a community is also rooted in relationships and the potentials when creating a culture of caring. The economy of a community is not just about money and what it purchases, but includes people and processes often unseen or taken for granted that can contribute to its welfare. Questions were raised with the youth workers that included: Do we really understand what it means to be poor? Do we know what is required for people to have hope? How do we inspire or help people to have the desire to be part of a change process, especially if they are dealing with their own poverty? Trainees presented the need to be sensitized as to what youth experience, and what it means to ask them to become change agents.

We tackled the issue of youth working on a parallel process of achieving their own economic and social goals while working towards community sustainability; creating social enterprises that generated income for them, guided by a social purpose. This poses a challenge for those brought up in a culture where it is alien to combine economic independence with community advancement. Promoting social enterprise—helping others while helping oneself—is not the norm in societies built on monetary and competitive economics. Even in areas where there are some socially motivated businesses, owned individually or collectively, there is a need to create a new kind of social business marketplace and mentality. Young social entrepreneurs can be introduced to micro-enterprises and how they might position themselves strategically in the economic development process of their communities to impact change. They can learn how important it is to understand that people who have neither money nor marketable skills—the poor, the frail, the undereducated, the elderly, those with disabilities—can still participate as full and valued members of a community.

A number of interesting things occurred throughout the week, all a testament of how opening up a learning process to enable the learners to have some control over the process can significantly impact the learning itself. Trainees brought in activities they had experienced and led portions of the training. The bonding that occurred and the joy in being actively part of the process was clearly evident as days flew by, and people talked into the night about how to apply the learning back home. The same week a forum with disabled, young workers was occurring simultaneously. They were very interested in what we were doing and frequently were seen talking with youth workers about the training. They were invited to attend the last evening when the trainees presented skits describing social entrepreneurship with examples of what youth might do. Contact information was exchanged as the two groups recognized that they had ideas and work to share with one another.

During the week of training, we discussed the professional development of youth workers and how further training and connections to higher education were critical aspects to such advancement. Discussions with the higher education representatives who we engaged included how their institutions might engage local populations and incorporate what occurred during the week in other educational offerings. We congratulated them for supporting this endeavor and knowing that they were stepping out of their sphere of comfort by engaging in a learning process that was not campus-centered, or for university students. We talked about how to incorporate youth leadership and social entrepreneurship training in courses for university students preparing to work in communities, and to remain in contact with those who took the training. Today, those discussions are still occurring. Continued dialogue will be needed to determine ongoing involvement of Nicaraguan higher education institutions to further the professional development process that we initiated. Although having higher education as partners would be ideal, the success of the current training will be judged as to how youth workers are able to apply the knowledge and skills they acquired at their local levels.

The collaboration between higher education and community-based institutions can prepare youth workers to respond directly and inclusively to the social needs and issues of targeted locales. Through inclusive program development and strategies tailored to community learning needs, training content can reflect local development with real-world applications. The overall outcome will be well-educated youth workers with diverse knowledge and skills able to lead in establishing youth as leaders and social entrepreneurs. Since 2009, contacts have been made to bring the project to other countries, and particularly in areas that have the potential for higher education institutions to implement the training for their local youth workers. Organizations in the Democratic Republic of Congo, Kenya, Ghana, Egypt and India are engaged in discussions with their respective higher education partners as to how to incorporate key concepts that would be part of professional development. Social entrepreneurship, and specifically related to "green" employment, appears as a central theme of such discussions, but corresponding training issues such as practical application, equitable opportunity of access, flexibility in curriculum and teaching methodology, and individual and community transformation have been included in content discussions.

Recommendation for a Community Education Associate

Community Education creates a mutually interdependent relationship among home, school, and community resources and incorporates three overarching components—lifelong learning opportunities, community involvement with schools and other learning institutions, and efficient use of resources. It is critical that staff who provide education and related services are well trained and adept at responding to the multiple goals of education and community development. Here I wish to interject a concrete plan that supports the professional development of youth workers creating a bridge between institutions of higher education and Community Education: a certification process that offers training for frontline workers resulting in a Community Education Associate (CEA). A national organization, or several, would most likely need to oversee this process as this would further the legitimacy and transferability of such professional development. The following CEA youth work competency standards and training define the skills needed by providers and strategies necessary to demonstrate their ability to work effectively with their young charges. Overall, the purpose of the CEA is to:

- Recognize professional practice, and in this case, one that is nationally accepted.
- Improve the quality of learning for those receiving services.
- Exhibit evidence of training and resultant competencies.
- Connect across disciplines to reinforce knowledge and practice of Community Education partnered with Youth Work.

Credentials would have the following nine content areas:

- Community Education principles and practices
- Developmental theory and applications
- Organizational and instructional delivery models
- Safe and healthy environments
- Cultural competency

- Professional relationships
- Organization, individual and community capacity building
- Community collaboration
- Commitment to professional standards

The CEA process would include 90 hours of education, training or course-work, completed within three years. Training may be completed at one institution/agency or through a combination of sources such as colleges, universities, and technical colleges, workforce development agencies, workshops, etc. Training must apply to actual work experiences with youth. Training must fit into the nine specific content areas, with at least five hours in each area. There should be 300 hours of supervised work experience within the three years, working with the specific population of the credential. Assessment is to be done through a combination of observation, opinion questionnaires, and written and oral evaluation including:

- Observation/interview by a qualified Community Education, and/or Youth Work advisor.
- Evaluation by participants in programs of the candidate.
- Compilation of a professional resource file, including an autobiography and written statements of competence in the nine CEA competency areas.
- Written and oral assessment by a representative of the certifying organization.

Upon review of the candidate's training and assessment, the certifying organization will either award the credential or invite the applicant to reapply for assessment. The CEA credential is to be valid for three years after the initial award, and for five years after that, based on a renewal process. In addition, participating higher education institutions will provide the opportunity for those who complete the initial phase of the program to matriculate and receive up to nine college credits.

Conclusion

The potential is for youth workers, in their quest for high quality and professional recognition, while learning how to work in communities, to adopt Community Education principles and practices. Universities and colleges can have a major role in making this happen, and to continue an historic commitment to responding to communities and their challenges. Assistance could include such functions as training youth workers to be community-change specialists, providing them with the skills to assist community leaders to become educators, or helping to establish better patterns of communication and cooperation among residents, workers, education officials, and leaders in communities. The Community Education movement through the years has received important contributions from higher education, and this relationship offers continued possibilities. Higher education is well positioned to respond to the ever increasing complexities of community life and what is facing our nation and planet with a role in professionalizing the field of youth work and supporting a bridge to Community Education for these professionals, to offer the potential to strengthen our communities through innovative learning services and the creation of a culture of lifelong learning and interdependency.

References

Knowles, M. (1980). *The modern practice of adult education: From pedagogy to andragogy* (2nd ed.). Englewood Cliffs, NJ: Prentice Hall/Cambridge.

Knowles, M. (Ed.). (1984). *Andragogy in action. Applying modern principles of adult education.* San Francisco: Jossey Bass.

National Community Education Association (2007). Retrieved November 17, 2009. from http://www.ncea.com/nceavaluemission.aspx.

SECTION IV

Conclusion

16

ADVANCING YOUTH WORK

Opportunities and Challenges

Jane Quinn

History as Prologue

Perhaps the best way to start is by offering a brief bit of history, because it's easy to become discouraged unless we contemplate how far we have come in a very short period of time. At this point in our history of youth work and youth work education in the United States, we see largely a patchwork of efforts—some based in direct service organizations, others in intermediaries; some at community colleges and others at universities. But these efforts are much more robust and coherent than they were 20 years ago, when I conducted a study of American youth organizations for the Carnegie Council on Adolescent Development (Carnegie Council, 1992). At that time, the Carnegie Task Force on Youth Development and Community Programs struggled to define some of the basic concepts around which there is now general consensus—for example, what we mean by the terms "youth development" and "youth worker;" how our efforts in the nonschool hours relate to (are similar to and yet different from) the work of schools; and the variety of practice settings in which youth workers operate. As part of that study, we convened a consultation with experts on the professional development of youth workers, recognizing the importance of this issue in relation to quality of and access to youth development programs. The consultation consisted of a pre-meeting survey and a day-long convening of 19 experts from across the youth development field, including representatives from national and local youth-serving organizations, researchers from several universities and staff leaders from several national intermediary organizations (Center for Early Adolescence, United Way of America, Wellesley School Age Child Care Project—now the National Institute on Out-of-School Time). The results of the day-long meeting were summarized in a written report, which was distributed widely within the youth development field (Carnegie Council on Adolescent Development, 1991). Preparing this chapter provided me with the impetus to revisit that document, and to assess the field's progress on the 10 overarching recommendations made by the panel of experts convened during this field-wide consultation:

Recommendation #1: Establish agreements on the basic definitions and philosophies around which this vocation can cooperatively operate. Based on what we have read in the preceding chapters and what I know about our collective efforts in the field, I think we have made excellent progress on this recommendation. In my view, there is general agreement on the basic definition of youth development as a strengths-based approach to promoting positive growth in all of the basic domains (cognitive, social, emotional, physical and moral), and also general agreement that the role of adults is to partner with young people in this developmental process, in recognition of the idea that young people are active agents of their own development. Most of the authors in this volume voice agreement with these basic ideas and also concur that youth development professionals can work in multiple settings—including youth organizations, schools, after-school programs, camps, museums, libraries and religious organizations. Some authors take an even broader view, observing that workers in juvenile justice, residential treatment and child welfare settings also play a key role in promoting positive youth development, along with an ameliorative role.

Recommendation #2: Greatly expand the availability of appropriate training for direct service workers. Again, based on what we have read in the previous chapters as well as what we know from other efforts in the field, we have made good progress on this front. We read about systems of professional development implemented by local and national organizations, which move beyond training to include orientation, on-site coaching and ongoing supervision; about point-of-service program quality assessment tools that include a major focus on staff quality; and about partnerships between direct service organizations and higher education institutions that create cohort groups and networks of direct service workers.

Recommendation #3: Advocate for the importance of adequate support for professional development service, training, and supervision with national and local funding sources in both public and private sectors. My assessment is that our collective progress has been somewhat spotty on this score. Some national and local funders—most notably the Wallace Foundation, the Marion Ewing Kauffman Foundation and the William Penn Foundation—have made major investments in professional development of youth workers. And some public funding streams—especially the 21st Century Community Learning Centers—have created a set-aside for professional development, evaluation and program administration. But overall, many of the efforts we read about in this volume are supported by fragile, unstable and inadequate funding. Professional development continues to be viewed largely as "nice but not necessary," and as an expense rather than an investment.

Recommendation #4: Develop collaborative approaches to in-service training that encourage agencies to tap one another's strengths and cooperate to tackle weaknesses. This volume offers many examples of exemplary collaborations between direct service organizations and institutions of higher education; and between intermediary organizations and direct service organizations. Untapped opportunities abound in this arena, however. For example, wouldn't it be great to read about collaborations between Girls Incorporated and Boys & Girls Clubs of America around gender-specific programming, or between Big Brothers/Big Sisters and other mentoring organizations? It was heartening to read that many colleges and universities are hiring youth development practitioners as adjunct faculty in their youth work education courses. This is a great example of tapping into strengths and tackling weaknesses at the same time.

Recommendation #5: Recruit youth workers early during youth development programming. Although I did not find examples of this strategy cited in the previous chapters, I do know from my work as part of the Next Generation Coalition that many organizations have adopted this strategy by creating a "career ladder" that enables young people to move from program participant to junior counselor to youth worker. This strategy has been a mainstay of the YMCA and Boys & Girls Clubs for decades, and has proven successful in creating a powerful staff and volunteer pipeline for these major national organizations.

Recommendation #6: Re-examine existing levels of pre-service training. Within this recommendation, the Carnegie experts envisioned a robust role for community colleges, which we are now reading about in several chapters in this volume— as partners in both pre- and in-service professional development.

Recommendation #7: Advocate to the professional schools that currently participate in the training of youth workers (social work, education, recreation, human development and theology) to increase their academic emphasis on the philosophy and knowledge base of youth development. The Carnegie consultants recommended that schools of social work reinstitute an emphasis on group work. To my knowledge, there has not been much uptake on this recommendation (a view that is affirmed by Camille Williamson, a recent graduate of the University of Chicago's School of Social Service Administration, in Chapter 8). However, elsewhere in the volume we read about explicit links between institutions of higher education and practice settings, including professional schools' field placements in youth organizations, youth work practitioners serving as adjunct faculty, youth development organizations as research sites and other examples of connections between practice and theory.

Recommendation #8: Create mechanisms that will increase communication and networking within the field of youth development, such as a professional association or a widely distributed journal. Over the past 20 years, the youth development field has created a national newspaper, Youth Today, and at least one journal, New Directions for Youth Development. The after-school field has developed at least two journals, Afterschool Matters and AfterSchool Today, and several professional associations, including the National AfterSchool Association (a membership organization) and the Afterschool Alliance (an advocacy organization). A related effort, the National Summer Learning Association, was created to work on both professional development and advocacy around summer learning. The National Community Education Association continues to provide conferences and other networking opportunities to community educators, many of whom consider themselves to be youth development professionals. And, since 1998, the Coalition for Community Schools has brought together all of the country's major education and youth-serving organizations in a network that advocates for the full integration of positive youth development into school reform (through the strategy of community schools).

Recommendation #9: Develop a set of standards for entry into and progression within the youth development field. The progress here has been largely around creating a consensus about the core competencies needed by youth workers. And that progress has been quite profound. Despite some minor differences, there is generally very broad agreement on the core competencies as they have been outlined by several national organizations, and these consensus documents are beginning to have a deep impact on the kinds of professional development offered by colleges and universities, direct service organizations and intermediary groups—as described in several of the early chapters in this volume.

Recommendation #10: Develop public information networks in the local and national media that portray service to promote youth development—volunteer and paid—as important and valuable work. To my knowledge, this has not really happened. About 10 years ago, two national Ad Council campaigns—one on after-school programs and the other, on community schools—illustrated good youth development in action. It is difficult to assess the impact of these campaigns. While polls conducted for the Afterschool Alliance indicate a high level of public support for after-school programs, it's unclear that this support is related to the value of youth work and more likely that it correlates with the public's concerns about crime and safety.

All in all, this analysis shows that the field has made rather excellent progress on these ten recommendations developed by experts from across the youth development field. Let's now turn our attention to the road ahead—both the opportunities and challenges.

Opportunities

As I read the preceding chapters, I made a running list of opportunities and challenges—and I am happy to report that the opportunities out-numbered the challenges by at least a two-to-one ratio. Here are the major opportunities, as I see them:

Engagement as the Key

New research has highlighted the role of student engagement in promoting or hindering school success and preparation for productive adulthood (the goal of all of our efforts). For example, a recent study (Yazzie-Mintz, 2010) on student engagement found that half of high school students say they are bored in school every day, citing the following reasons: material isn't interesting (over 80%), isn't relevant (over 40%), is too difficult (about 25%) or is too easy (about 33%); or lack of interaction with teachers (about 33%). Other research has documented that students' boredom and subsequent disengagement from school is the primary cause of dropping out (Balfanz & Letgers, 2004). Youth workers can help young people stay engaged in learning, and several of the ideas outlined in this volume—about professional development that is directed toward creating challenging activities, student-directed learning and apprenticeships—can build students' engagement in their own healthy development, help them stay connected to school, and help them develop career and education aspirations.

Common Core Standards

Probably the biggest event in school reform over the past five years is the development of common core standards in key academic subjects. These standards have now been adopted by all but a handful of states, and their implementation will have an enormous effect on schools across the country. The relevance of this to youth work practice is that the common core standards will provide new opportunities for youth organizations to delineate their key roles in helping young people meet those standards. For example, some of the standards call for the development of "soft skills," such as critical thinking and teamwork that youth organizations excel at (and schools generally don't). The ability of youth workers to demonstrate their value to schools in relation to the common core standards will create unparalleled opportunities over the next decade.

Recruiting Second-Career Professionals

As optimistic as I am, I don't see the pay scale for youth workers taking any gigantic leaps forward any time soon. As an alternative, I propose that we reach out to second-career professionals who can bring both experience and specialized skills—often at a reasonable price. I am enamored of the idea of an Encore Career, as advanced by Marc Freedman (2007), the President of Civic Ventures. Freedman writes about the availability of a growing cohort of older adults who are facing 30 to 40 post-retirement years and looking for socially useful venues for their time and talent. In my work, I have met retired principals who have become leaders of youth organizations and retired business leaders who want to work with children (and are often willing to volunteer their time in exchange for the knowledge that they are contributing to the betterment of others). We often think of recent college graduates when we recruit for entry-level positions in youth development, but let's not ignore another huge cadre of adults who can make important contributions to our workforce.

Creating More Demonstrations of Good Youth Work Practice

Using new technologies, including the Internet, we can demonstrate what engaged learning and strong relationships really look like. Several preceding chapters talked about advances in professional development, such as using case studies and real-life dilemmas to build the practice skills of youth workers. Videos that demonstrate the effective practices of experienced youth workers should become ubiquitous in our professional development offerings at both the pre- and in-service levels.

Building on Successful Investments

I have been impressed over the past decade-plus by the extent to which the Advancing Youth Development training curriculum has seen widespread use and has gotten into the "water supply" across our field—and into other fields. For example, I recently learned of a school district that had used these materials to train all of their school safety officers in principles of positive youth development, a use that even its original funder and authors probably had not envisioned. The many users of Advancing Youth Development (some of whom we read about in earlier chapters) would probably welcome updated and advanced versions of these very effective materials.

Thanking the Investors

As someone who helped to fund several of the initiatives described in this volume, I was heartened to read about the longevity and sustainability of these investments. Although I have not worked at the Wallace Foundation now for more than a decade, I regularly run into people who tell me they are still doing the work that Wallace supported. I always encourage them to thank the Foundation and let the current staff know what a difference Wallace support made in catalyzing their work. This advice covers all the investors whose work is cited in the preceding chapters—including the Office of Juvenile Justice and Delinquency Prevention, which supported the creation of Advancing Youth Development. A well-placed note of appreciation might actually spur additional investments; and, even if it doesn't, it's a good business practice.

Building Stronger Bridges Between Higher Education and Employers

I am genuinely excited to read about the growing number of higher education institutions that are involved in youth worker education. This represents a major change from 20, and even 10, years ago. As these programs grow, it is imperative to build strong linkages with employers—both to elicit their viewpoints about the knowledge and skills that are valued in the marketplace and to gain their agreement that they will give serious consideration to the programs' graduates. Higher education institutions can also help to build strong linkages by conducting in-service professional development for employers. These are the kinds of "new institutional arrangements" that can achieve durability and can create win-win situations for both parties.

Challenges

The Economic Outlook

Most of the innovations we read about in the preceding chapters are dependent on outside funding, and the outlook for discretionary dollars in the years ahead is bleak. As long as professional development is seen as an expense, rather than an investment, innovators will have to scramble for needed resources. As we seek to build stronger bridges between youth workers and institutions of higher education, it is important to recognize that both groups are experiencing serious financial problems. The organizations that employ youth workers are facing serious cutbacks, and colleges and universities are challenged to raise tuition and develop additional "cash cows" (revenue-generating programs), which are unlikely to include youth work education.

Claiming the "Orphan"

Many observers believe that the multiple entry points to youth work as a profession represents a strength; similarly, a plausible argument can be made that the multiple homes for youth work education also constitute a strength. In the preceding chapters we read about schools of education, social work, human services and human development that sponsored youth work education. My own view is that this situation is really not tenable, and that youth work education deserves a real home in academia. But this current situation has been going on for a very long time, and the outlook for a satisfactory resolution appears increasingly dim. At one time, I had hopes that my own discipline, social work, would claim youth work as one of its sub-specialty fields. The argument for this approach is strong: social work, like youth work, is inherently multi-disciplinary and draws much of its understanding from long-standing theories of human development. Social work, like youth work, is an applied discipline, with a strong emphasis on connecting practice with theory. But, as a field, social work has gotten distracted by the lure of third-party payments and is directing much of its attention to preparing the next generation of psychotherapists.

Extended Learning Time

The current education policy discussions about increasing "time on task" have assiduously avoided asking, "what is the task?" As youth developers, we would likely agree that young people need more time to engage in high-yield learning activities and in building positive relationships with peers and adults. But there is a seductive quality to the idea of "extending learning time" because it seems simple and straightforward to many policy makers. There is a real danger that new policies around "extended learning time" will result in more of the kind of schooling that is not working for many young people now. And this, of course, will mean that youth workers will have less access to young people's time and attention.

The Romance of International Comparisons

I love reading about the National Youth Service in England as much as anyone. It gives us an idea of what is possible—there. Youth work veterans in the United States, including Karen Pittman and *Youth Today* founder Bill Treanor, have written extensively about the British approach, including its long history, clear philosophy and strong infrastructure (see Pittman, 2004). But my experience with school reform leads me to understand that international comparisons will get us only so far. For example, my current work involves community schools—an approach to school reform that addresses students' academic and non-academic needs through long-term partnerships between schools and community resources. We have struggled mightily to get this common-sense strategy to become the norm in the United States—and the struggle continues. Meanwhile, the British Parliament created a national education policy several years ago that every school would become an "extended school" by 2012 and, within just a few years, schools across that country made rapid progress toward achieving their stated national goal. The notable absence of an overarching youth policy in our country is a long-standing and serious impediment to achieving coherence in our approach to supporting the positive development of America's young people. While there is much we can learn from other countries (and the chapters in this volume about England and Australia are both interesting and useful), I see a challenge in trying to extract more nuggets than is warranted by the policy landscape in our own country at this time.

Conclusion

From where I sit, the case for investing in quality youth development programs and opportunities has never been stronger. As several authors have rightly pointed out, the 2002 publication by the National Research Council and Institute of Medicine of *Community Programs to Promote Youth Development* was a game-changer—by making an unimpeachable research-based case for the value of youth work (Eccles & Gootman, 2002). We stand on strong shoulders as we work together to remind policy makers and the general public about the needs and strengths of the "whole child," as we create strategies to bridge the gaps between theory and practice, and as we seek to convince funders that professional development is an investment, a legitimate cost of doing business in our very important business of supporting young people on the road to productive adulthood.

References

Balfanz, R., & Letgers, N. (2004, September). *Locating the dropout crisis: Which high schools produce the nation's dropouts? Where are they located? Who attends them?* Baltimore, MD: Johns Hopkins University Press.

Carnegie Council on Adolescent Development. (1991, May 13). *Task Force on Youth Development and Community Programs, Carnegie Council on Adolescent Development. Report on the consultation on professional development of youthworkers.* New York: Carnegie Corporation of New York.

Carnegie Council on Adolescent Development. (1992). *Task Force on Youth Development and Community Programs, Carnegie Council on Adolescent Development. A matter of time: Risk and opportunity in the nonschool hours.* New York: Carnegie Corporation of New York.

Eccles, J., & Gootman, J. A. (Eds.). (2002). *Community programs to promote youth development.* National Research Council and Institute of Medicine, Committee on Community-Level Programs for Youth, Board on Children, Youth, and Families, Division of Behavioral Health and Social Sciences and Education. Washington, DC: National Academy Press.

Freedman, M. (2007). *Encore: Finding work that matters in the second half of life.* New York: Public Affairs.

Pittman, K. J. (2004, Winter). Reflections on the road not (yet) taken: How a centralized public strategy can help youth work focus on youth. *New Directions for Youth Development, 104,* 87–99.

Yazzie-Mintz, E. (2010). *Charting the path from engagement to achievement: A report on the 2009 high school survey of student engagement.* Bloomington: Indiana University.

17

FRAMING TRENDS, POSING QUESTIONS

Dana Fusco

This volume brings together a wide variety of perspectives and practices for Advancing Youth Work. The goal was not to tell one story but to tell many stories both within and outside of the United States. Collectively, the authors present a broad spectrum of field-building activities already underway. While it is safe to say that the authors of this volume agree that advancing youth work is critical to giving young people access to the types of opportunities that will enhance their lives and their futures, it is also clear that we are not always in agreement on how to get there. Will defining a set of competencies needed for staff enhance quality youth work or undermine professionalism and autonomy? Will a credential offer organizations sufficient criteria for hiring qualified staff or serve as a gate to maintaining a diverse workforce? Are there ways to think about professional development that support critical and situated reasoning above and beyond competencies? Where should such professional development occur, led by whom, and what should be the role of higher education in the arrangement? Would a degree in youth studies serve as the right basis for developing practitioner expertise? Is there a unified discipline of youth studies that transcends contexts of practice? Should there be?

I am not advocating that agreement on these and other questions is a necessary prerequisite for advancing youth work. In fact, in the spirit of strengthening our collective voice, this volume is meant to highlight the areas of agreement as well as the tensions in order to stimulate healthy dialogue and debate. It begins from the position that whether one agrees or disagrees that a credentialing process is needed or that a baccalaureate degree should be an entry point to practice, there are leaders in the field working in these and other directions. As such we can assume there is inherent value in each of these activities. Whether we agree or disagree, we can and should assess both the intended value as well as the potential risk of these activities as the next step in advancing youth work as a field, a profession and a discipline. Bringing together different viewpoints and efforts under one roof helps us to examine the current meta-narrative for the field.

The intent of this chapter then is not to add new content, but to locate and then name this meta-narrative. In the first two sections three current trends for advancing youth work were discussed: competencies, credentials, and curriculum. In Section III the contributions captured additional contexts of youth work in order to help ground the discussion in real domains of practice. The contexts are geographically dissimilar in terms of their location in the world (i.e., England, Canada, Northern Ireland, Nicaragua, an Indian reservation), in the community (on the street, in residence, in tribe, in a park), and in their positioning of youth work (as civic engagement, as recreation, as community development, as social reform). As such they help us flesh out some central and critical questions in the field as a whole. In this chapter, I will frame the trends in advancing youth work and take the liberty of highlighting some of the critical questions that the authors of this volume implicitly or explicitly ask as well as posing some of my own. Hopefully, these questions (here italicized for added emphasis) can serve as triggers for continued conversations in the classroom, in the boardroom, and in the multipurpose/rec room. I will then attempt to cull from the volume several meta-themes and then look at what such an analysis offers up for advancing youth work and youth work education.

Current Trends, Critical Questions

Competencies and Credentials

The volume begins with several chapters that help us address the question: *What is the intended value of developing competencies and credentials for Advancing Youth Work?* Competency frameworks are benchmarks for what youth workers should know and be able to do. Interestingly, most professions are now utilizing the language of competencies. For instance, in 2005 all four national associations for the professional education of physician assistants endorsed a set of competencies modeled after medical education. In the area of youth work, competencies have been articulated by various states and organizations seeking to develop system-wide approaches to professional development at the city, state, national and even intercontinental levels. In fact, there exist an estimated hundred competency frameworks for youth workers to date in the United States. According to Starr, Yohalem, and Gannett (2009), who recently compiled and analyzed some of these frameworks, "articulating the core competencies that youth workers need to be effective is an important step in strengthening the quality and stability of the workforce" (p. 3). Once endorsed, competency frameworks can be a driver of change in the field. As Jonas helps us to see in

Chapter 2, at a micro or organizational level, core competencies help staff set goals, provide direction for professional development activities, and organize hiring and staff evaluation processes in relation to an agreed-upon set of criteria that defines quality practice. At a macro level, a competency framework can also help guide in the development of credentialing systems for youth workers. About half of the competency frameworks developed are linked to a credential, often at the local or state level, and most recently, as Curry and colleagues discuss in Chapter 3, on a national level.

One value of a credentialing exam is that it gives youth workers a credential that signifies respect for the work they do. It also brings public acknowledgement and visibility to the field. Several workforce studies have found that youth workers while satisfied with their jobs feel "invisible" or not recognized for the work they do (Fusco, 2003; Yohalem & Pittman, 2006). Earning a credential is a public display of achievement. On the other hand, "unless credentialing brings higher compensation or provides a distinct advantage in hiring, it is questionable whether individuals would seek certification or coursework" (Foundations, Inc., 2010, p. 10).

Another stated value of the national certification exam is that it is one of the few initiatives aimed at creating a unified field of youth work to include: early care and education, community-based child and youth development programs, parent education and family support, school-based programs, community mental health, group homes, day and residential treatment centers, early intervention, home-based care and treatment, psychiatric centers, pediatric health care, and juvenile justice programs. As Gannett in Chapter 1 of this volume states, "the strength of this field has got to be that we think of ourselves in a very broad-based way." It is clear that many of us view the field in broad terms seeing the commonalities (and the uniqueness) across youth-serving sectors. For others, the advantage of a unified movement may be outweighed by the restriction of articulating and measuring discrete competencies. That is, not everyone is comfortable with the language of competencies, or what it suggests about the forthcoming constriction imposed by a professional movement. While competencies and credentials have practical benefits, some ask: *What do we risk in reducing youth work to a series of discrete skills? Will increased accountability and bureaucracy undermine the creative wisdom and capacity of youth workers?* Critics view competencies as antithetical to the creation of a professional identity.

In Chapter 4, Walker and Walker argue that quality practice requires an understanding of youth work as complex and dynamic, and practitioner development as supporting complex and situational reasoning; reasoning that perhaps is not to be found in an isolated skill set, either in a competency framework or on a credentialing exam. If we believe that practitioner development requires not just knowing or knowing about, but knowing how (and I would argue, knowing when) then we might delve into the tension further and pursue the question: *What kinds of activities, strategies and experiences contribute to the development of practitioner expertise and are they different from those that contribute to the development of competencies?* Walker and Walker present several models of professional development, within and outside of the university that they deem have promise in supporting practitioner expertise, or phronesis. The models share important features—they promote reflective practice; require sustained practice; and do not avoid the messiness of practice but rely on real-world dilemmas of practice. In short, they share a view of practitioner development that is based not on isolated bits of knowledge or skills but on the 'knotty' situations that emerge when working with young people. They help us to celebrate the youth worker as professional, engaged in thinking in authentic and powerful ways.

Similarly, in Chapter 5, Judith Bessant describes the struggle in Australia for youth work to develop a professional identity and sees core competencies as an impediment to moving in this direction. She advocates for higher education as a means for youth workers to develop the intellectual capacities associated with a highly effective professional. However, there is also a deeper posturing that Bessant invites the reader into; namely, that of problematizing not just youth work education and how it is approached, but the very ways in which youth and youth work practice have been situated in Western, normative, pragmatic understandings and empiricism. By extension, the unintended risk in articulating a set of competencies lies not in what is included but in what is also excluded. Competencies and credentials are by definition based on a set of knowledge and skills that relies on the value judgment of those who defined the set to be inclusive, valid, valuable, and critically able to determine how it qualifies someone to work with youth. For instance, by virtue of including legal policies in the knowledge set, have we excluded other non-Western, non-normative ways that youth workers may judge their actions such as through moral, spiritual or cultural compasses? We must ask: *What is included and excluded in our valued knowledge sets? Who decides and why? And what groups, if any, might be marginalized in the process?* It seems obvious that the work of Curry and colleagues has taken such issues to heart in developing an assessment framework that triangulates knowledge and how knowledge might best be assessed (e.g., through a traditional exam, a portfolio of practice, and a supervisor assessment of performance). Care to issues of validity can be complemented by care to issues of access by asking questions such as: *What are the unintended consequences of requiring credentials of youth workers? To what extent do professionalization efforts create gateways rather than opportunities for ensuring a diverse workforce?*

Collectively, the chapters in Sections I highlight the pragmatic value of competency frameworks particularly when linked to credentialing, pay raises, and ultimately a career trajectory for youth workers; they also point to the potential limitations of these trends in advancing youth work as a profession and youth workers as professionals and help us examine more critically how to encourage the emergent expertise of youth workers in more fluid, problem-posing learning environments and networks. While the discussion between competencies versus expertise seems to be a point of tension, occasionally airing the points of disagreement uncovers areas of unforeseen convergence. That is, in practice there may be less difference than can be seen through description alone. Jonas helps us to understand how when an organization puts into practice a competency framework those competencies become a living and valued part of the organizational culture. In stressing specific "competencies," youth workers were given a lens from which to gauge, reflect and refine their actions with youth. As Jonas articulates, the entry-level worker needs some guideposts, which become a part of how s/he thinks about the work. The competencies on paper might read as a list of discrete skills but in practice were embedded in real actions and contexts. Maybe it is not competencies per se that is the issue but how those competencies come into being, e.g., whether they emerge and continue to re-emerge organically from practice, and then how they are used thereafter e.g., as a trigger for conversations, reflections, actions, and revision. In fact, this would seem to have been the case in the Youth Development Network presented by Davis-Manigaulte in Chapter 11. Interestingly, it was this group of practitioners who themselves thought defining competencies was important but then used those competencies as a guide for framing discussions, giving feedback, and for refining their practice based on their reflections, for creating a commentary of practice. Important to the Network were not the competencies per se but what creating them fostered in terms of dialogue, feedback, and the creation of a professional identity and community. I think we could agree that competencies to the exclusion of situated reasoning and expertise is problematic in any profession and to any philosophy of professional education. In the end, we can ponder further: *Are competencies and expertise competing tendencies? Can someone be an incompetent expert? A competent novice? To whom is expertise entrusted: scholars? practitioners? youth? What else is required in the development of expertise not included in our current reliance on cognitive models of professional education?* These questions allow us to consider what the role of "good" youth work education might be and the multiple pathways towards becoming a master practitioner.

Curriculum

Until recently, practitioner development consisted mostly of workshops and trainings. Often necessitated by a part-time and unstable workforce, keeping workshops brief was considered necessary. However, research has revealed that programs staffed by workers with more advanced education show higher staff retention rates (Russell et al., 2006). Many colleges have developed programs geared towards youth practitioners. In fact, courses and degree programs are rapidly emerging within institutions of higher education (Bowie & Bronte-Tinkew, 2006). Seven states have credential programs with links to higher education. Section II of this volume asks: *How can community agencies and institutions of higher education collaborate in the professional development of youth workers?* In Chapter 6, Pete Watkins presented an example of a college-based program discussing some of the lessons learned, obstacles overcome and challenges that remain after 10 years of educating youth workers at an urban community college in Philadelphia. In Chapter 7, Michael Heathfield presented a second example in the city of Chicago. Both examples are success stories of how to create effective partnerships between community agencies and higher education. Each has adapted its curriculum to the needs of the youth workers and the community and points to the value of higher education in helping to advance the field. In Chapter 8, Camille Williamson, a student of many disciplines (psychology, social work, education) before finding a youth studies program, drives home the point that youth studies has a knowledge base (and a methodology for teaching it) that cannot be substituted by courses in other disciplines.

Many college programs for youth workers pull from education, psychology, social work, recreation, health, leisure studies, and the like. Certainly there are valuable nuggets of knowledge to be gleaned from these areas. However, particularly in the past five years, the field of youth studies and its allied areas of OST, CYC, youth and community development, civic youth work, and afterschool education have amassed a literature base that should also be included in any curriculum. This literature base speaks to the multiple contexts of youth work and what it means to work with diverse groups of young people in ways that are often not found in most normative theories of human development and psychology. In 2006, the National Institute on Out-of-School Time reviewed professional development systems to assess the value of credentialing programs (Cornerstone for Kids, 2006). According to the report, "colleges are struggling to keep the credentials and degree programs running due to lack of enrollment" (p. 15). The lack of steady demand makes offering courses a challenge for higher education. In instances where enrollment is low, students may be re-directed towards existing classes in psychology or education, rather than in courses designed for their field. In such instances, participants may not see the relevance of what they are learning as reflected in statements such as, "The class doesn't relate clearly to what we're doing in after school" (Vile et al., 2008, p. 18).

Thus, there exists a tension in answering the question of whether higher education will continue to serve as a good partner for supporting youth work, particularly without a more central role in the academy. In Chapter 9, Fusco asks: *What do we risk by focusing on the development of the profession without an equal focus on the development of the discipline?* As Fusco points out, without a distinct discipline grounded in our theoretical and practical understandings of youth and youth work, we will continue to sit on the periphery of academia pulling from existing coursework that has minimal connection to our actual work with young people in the many contexts in which we interact with them. Fusco argues that part of developing a unique body of knowledge that will have greater relevancy will require developing the next generation of youth work scholars. In Chapter 10, Ross VeLure Roholt and Michael Baizerman explore the contested space of youth, youth work, and youth studies. They critically examine the question: *Are institutions of higher learning the best site and faculty the best people to prepare masters in youth studies and youth work?* They wonder aloud how the ever-changing purpose and structure of higher education will serve a disciplinary home to youth studies, as proposed by Fusco. These chapters sit in dialectic with interesting questions and tensions to be explored by the reader. They provoke us to entertain alternate models of developing practitioner expertise, perhaps one led by practitioners themselves. As Hill, Matloff-Nieves, and Townsend (2009) argue, "We should acknowledge the expertise of OST practitioners, recognizing that they are not merely passive receivers of research and policy but also actors who engage in making sense of their experiences" (p. 47). Thus, we might ask: *What might be explored differently in relation to one's professional development when the matter of study and how it is studied is led by practitioners themselves?* In Chapter 11, Jackie Davis-Manigaulte explores how a network of practitioners mirrored the principles of Wenger's "communities of practice" including participation, mutual engagement, identify and reification. Her research revealed that the Network provided a unique learning opportunity for the participants and showed how that learning was put into practice.

Such a view of engaging practitioners as active participants in the teaching/learning process is not outside the realm of what is possible or even recommended in professional education. Examples provided here by Walker and Walker (Chapter 4), Watkins (Chapter 6), Heathfield (Chapter 7), and VeLure Roholt and Baizerman (Chapter 10) provide strong cases for the types of active and reflective engagement of practitioner expertise in the college classroom. With some agreement on how professional development should occur (the essential features of the learning environment), we still have not reached consensus on what should be taught. To understand the knowledge base of youth work, we must understand the many contexts in which youth work occurs. In this next section, I explicate some of the principles that stand out as part of this volume's meta-narrative.

Contexts

In the recent book, *What is Youth Work?*, editors Janet Batsleer and Bernard Davies (2010) presented compelling narratives on youth work as partnership, empowerment, boundary crossing, and chartering of (un)gendered and anti-racist spaces in which young people can claim their identities and create new ones. The rhetoric on youth work abroad is about helping young people navigate and challenge internalized views from mainstream society in order to break through the chains that bind them to an identity of detachment and oppression. It also has a civic component. Youth work is not only about supporting individual development, it is about using the tatters of individual woes to challenge and change power dynamics in society to better the lives of all. It is about leaving behind, through the made transgressions of youth and youth workers, a better world.

Comparing ourselves to international interpretations of youth work is fascinating both in what it tells us about youth work elsewhere and in what it reveals about the focus of youth work in the United States. As such, there are at least three distinctions worth articulating up front. First, in the United States, the recent predominant dialogue on youth work has emerged in relation to the rhetoric of school. Popular conversation about education has come to recognize that there is no "off" button for learning; learning occurs throughout the day and the year. With this frame in mind, we begin to notice that school accounts for less than 17% of a young person's non-sleeping hours. This leaves 63% of a young person's potential learning time unaccounted for. It is through the construct of time (or non-school time) that most current discourse on youth work appears. Youth work becomes defined by when it occurs—*not* during school. The current focus on school/nonschool owes some of its development to the federal government's 21st Century Community Learning Centers. These centers, first funded by President Clinton in the 1990s, continue to receive government support in high poverty (rural and urban) areas to provide academic enrichment during non-school hours. Since their inception, they have quadrupled the numbers of afterschool programs and also led to a growth in research on afterschool education. However, some urged that "afterschool" did not account for programs occurring before school, on weekends, during holidays, and during summer hence, the emergence of the more current terminology, Out-of-School Time (OST). Still, time becomes the demarcation for defining youth work (or what happens out-of-school). In the same, uncontested breath, youth work now encapsulated by the language of education becomes the supplement to school or opportunity for "extended learning."

The idea of supplementing education during non-school hours receives enormous public support, particularly from working parents. Parents are well aware of the need to fill (un)structured time with (con)structive activities. With origins as far back as the Bible, an idle mind was, and still is, considered the "devil's playground." Parents particularly keen on ensuring their child's acceptance into the finest academic institutions from nursery school to graduate school, enrich their child's time with trips to museums and libraries, summer vacations, music lessons, science fairs, camp, sports, and the like. Children whose parents are not able, financially or otherwise, to coordinate out-of-school time begin the school year further and further behind their more affluent peers. The importance of quality out-of-school time learning opportunities shaped and led by youth workers are in the spotlight now more than ever. They have become the great social equalizer—a role that the American public school system was to play but failed.

A second dominant discourse in the United States is Positive Youth Development (PYD). Youth development as a practice should be available for *all* young people, not only those considered disadvantaged or at-risk. The change in nomenclature was heavily influenced by newer ideologies that repositioned human development from a biological and normative paradigm to an ecological and cultural one. Perhaps an oversimplified but nonetheless useful interpretation of this ideology suggests reframing development from the need to fill a young person's deficits (what was missing if one looked at a "disadvantaged" young person against the benchmark of "normal" development) towards a view that development begins with identifying existing strengths and building assets that serve as a protective factor against risk. That is, focusing on problems (and trying to prevent them) does not ensure that a young person has the competencies and capabilities to succeed in life hence the PYD mantra: "Problem free is not fully prepared" (Pittman, 1991).

The third issue is that in the United States there is a distinct focus on defining youth work by what it aims to achieve and less on what it means to engage with or work with youth. There is an actor with no action. Unlike the teacher who teaches, the accountant who accounts for, or the nurse who nurses, youth workers, well, they work with youth. In New Zealand, a youth worker is a person who provides a service to build relationships with young people in order to foster well-being (Barwick, 2006). Batsleer (2008) states that youth work is "about making and developing a sense of meaning with young people, based on increasing commitment to searching out truthful information and understandings" (p. 7). In the United States, the central tenets of youth work and what it aims to achieve are not articulated with consistency. *Is youth work a supplement to education, a way to build community, a way to support individual development? Is it the same across contexts such as afterschool, residential, foster care, juvenile centers, youth ministry, and peace corps? Is there an essence of principle that defines what it means to professionally interact with a young person in the context of being a youth worker?*

Principles That Cut Across Contexts

While the most public narrative in the United States for youth work has become school-linked, framed by positive development, and outcome oriented, the narratives presented in this volume offer some additional insights into the nature of youth work. Drawing from the chapters in Section III, there are several principles that thread through this volume as part of the meta-narrative of youth work. These principles cut across the specific contexts of youth work. The first principle is that "youth" refers to the years from school age through early adulthood. It has been argued by some that youth work should remain focused on adolescence, as is the case in much of the United Kingdom. However, this limitation to adolescence no longer defines who we are have become. This shifting of "adolescence" closer into "childhood" has occurred for two reasons. First, youth work has come to be associated with school-age care, child and youth care, afterschool, summer camp, and other practices that serve children during pre-adolescent years. Second, young people are experiencing "adolescence" earlier. Not only has the onset of puberty shifted downward, but Western society expects more from its children than it once did. Longer school days, less time for free play, more homework, more chores, and the assumption that children can handle the bombardment of messages aired during "family hour" television are but a few examples. The preponderance with sexual identity and "adult" behaviors can be witnessed in children as young as five years of age in some communities. Children are exposed to a much broader and richer array of adult messages through television, movies, the Internet, and daily conversations. Such shifts mean that youth workers cannot wait until the onset of even the pre-teenage years any longer.

The second principle that emerges here is that youth work is a contextualized practice. It is not a focus on the individual in silo. Rather, youth are viewed in context (in association, in community, in space, in nature and spirit, in tribe, en milieu, in relationship). Context not only refers to collective or communal space but to time and history, i.e., the girl-in-club in the 1950s versus the girl-in-club in the 1990s. Constructs of identity (youth, boys, girls, Black boys, Asian girls, queers, gangs) have different meanings in different communities and at different points in history. Youth workers are keenly aware of the social conditions within which they work. In England, while association is a central tenet of youth work, legislation under conservative governments has reinforced an ideological shift with the focus on individuals, not communities (see Jones, Chapter 12). The shift is also occurring in the United States created, in part, by the assessment and accountability movement. Youth work, once about wholes, relations, and perspectives, is difficult to accomplish in a sociopolitical environment that supports parts, individuals, and "truths" (i.e., evidence-based practices). Youth workers encouraged to track individual growth will find it difficult to stay true to the idea that growth is in the creation of the collective or the relationship. The implication for youth work education will mean engaging youth workers in deep analysis of the times in which they are working, understanding the profession through a historical lens and deciding where to situate oneself professionally. Some youth workers will decide to push back; others will accept the current context and be content to work within it. Either way, one should be aware of the difference and make the choice explicitly.

Third, youth work is a developmental practice and as such is fluid and unpredictable. Unlike a plant that consistently requires a certain amount of water, lighting, and the right temperature to achieve maximum potential, human development is less predictable in part because human beings have the capacity to plan, change course, make decisions, and ultimately are active agents in their own development. This fluidity makes it difficult to come up with the fundamental rules of practice in youth work. We certainly can make recommendations such as, "Young people need structure;" however, as soon as we do this we must ask: What kind of structure? For whom and for how long? In what contexts and who decides? For instance, for a youth who has grown up with little to depend on, structure can be refreshing but it cannot be imposed because such a child would not trust that the one doing the imposing is doing so in his/her best interest. On the contrary, for a kid who has grown up in an over-structured world from an early age, the need may be for free play, time to create without rules and boundaries, and use the imagination. Add to this any number of other social and human factors (disability, ethnicity, talents, goals—none of which seem evident in plants), and the rules of practice change again. Complicated still, a young person may find structure to assist her during a month of relative emotional stability and in the following month decide she needs room to explore. Advancing youth work then might be less about arguing for a set of developmental rules and more about advocating for an approach that is emergent and responsive to youth. The ability to learn the craft might come through lived, applied and clinical experiences that teach such fluidity. What is learned is "the approach-as-responsiveness." Responsiveness should not be interpreted to mean there are no rules of engagement. However, it might mean that those rules are more fluid and co-created. Of course, such a responsive approach as witnessed in the most effective of youth workers also raises serious challenges for assessing outcomes. That is, effective youth workers know how to reach the most challenging of youth working "where they are at." However, today we often miss individual milestones in the requisite need for aggregated evidence. The very essence of youth work, the reasons why we engage in the work are disconnected from what funders want and are being asked for. Once we impose the need to aggregate these milestones, we ironically lose our potency. That is, how does one add Tenesha's decrease in tantrums with Mark's getting an 80 on his history test with Lisa's cutting ties with a befriended gang member? Our work focuses on relationships with individual youth who have individual needs and from which emerge amazing accomplishments. As we continue to move in the direction of assessing youth work outcomes, we must articulate this tension explicitly. What do we risk losing in the quest for statistical rigor? As soon as we introduce assessment we back into a goal that can only be met in the aggregate. That goal might be that the program helps 85% of youth improve their school attendance, self-esteem, behavior, literacy, etc. Where do individual, gradated improvements come in? This is not to say that we should not assess our work but it is to urge that we come up with methodologies that do not disguise our essence.

The final principle is that youth work is participatory. However, participation can take on many different meanings. In an afterschool program, young people may participate in hands-on activities that support learning. In a club, young people may participate in deciding what to do today (see Chapter 13). Some define participation through the lens of experience (see Chapter 14).

Valuing experience implies that "doing" facilitates learning and independence (see Chapter 15). The different interpretations of participation rest on whether the goal of participation is learning (individual development) or community development and change. Participation then is a tool for constructing knowledge, builds commentary, or civic action. The more that participation is co-constructed with young people, the greater the impact we are likely to have on building character and social and emotional growth; yet, ironically, the less we are able to measure in predictable ways what that impact is likely to be.

One can see that while youth work across contexts supports at least four principles (youth work as beginning in childhood, and as a contextualized, developmental and participatory practice), the shape these principles takes on varies. Next, I will present a typology for the principles-in-practice (see Table 17.1 for an overview). The typology offers a comparative, though precursory, glimpse of the diversity of what today we call youth work, at least in the U.S.

Principles-in-Practice

The typology focuses on four contexts of youth work: OST, empowerment, youth development and youth care. Readers are encouraged to think about additional contexts and how they might play out within this framework. Doing so will help us collectively determine whether there is value in the typology.

Out-of-School Time (OST) encompasses programs that are organized as formal as well as informal learning opportunities during nonschool hours, including summer. It includes afterschool programs but is not limited to after-school programs. Serving school-age children and adolescents, the flavor of OST is educational. However, learning in OST requires the active engagement of children and youth, and offers opportunities for enrichment complementary to traditional school curriculum. Enrichment occurs through activities after-school, before school, or during summer such as, basketball, tutoring, writing a newsletter, origami, theater, stage design, media production, baseball, music, sewing, etc. The theoretical framework that most closely embraces the field of OST is Constructivism, ranging from the individual constructivism of Piaget to the sociocultural constructivism of Vygotsky. Constructivism as a model of human learning and development positions the learner as an active constructor of knowledge. The days of sitting passively to absorb knowledge are replaced with hands–on, interactive exploration of concepts. Participants in OST are often seen engaged in discovery, experimentation, and group work for the purpose of new knowledge.

Youth empowerment programs are often designed for older children and adolescents. While also occurring during nonschool hours, they are focused on leadership, empowerment, and development. They may focus on academic goals but stress broad "soft" skills (teamwork, leadership, voice) more than content. Some that are more revolutionary in thinking can be associated with

TABLE 17.1 Typology for Principles in Action

Category of youth work	Theoretical frameworks	Youth work as contextualized	Youth work as fluid and emergent	Youth work as participatory
Out-of-School Time (OST)	Constructivism, Social Constructivism	Context as learning environment and group environment	What emerges are "teachable moments," knowledge, individual development	Participation as engagement in activities, apprenticeship
Empowerment	Critical and Emancipatory Pedagogy, Service Learning, Youth Leadership	Context as social condition	What emerges is critical awareness, consciousness	Participation as leadership and system change
Youth Development	Ecological, Developmental, Positive Psychology	Context as multi-layered (youth-in-family/school/ community)	What emerges are new developmental assets	Participation as taking on new roles and responsibilities
Youth Care	Needs, Social Work, Behavioral	Context as group	Individual progress in acceptable social behaviors	Participation in life occupation

the theoretical frameworks of critical pedagogues such as, bell hooks or Paulo Friere. In the United Kingdom, these programs may be known as Informal Learning (Batsleer, 2008), not to be confused with informal education in the United States. Informal learning is about the consciousness-raising that occurs by engaging in conversations with youth "where they are," while informal education in the United States is learning in informal settings such as, museum education, and as such would be categorized here under OST. OST programs can support the ideas of giving youth voice and choice; however, participation is from the vantage point of engagement rather than empowerment. It is a means towards an end, not the end itself.

The youth development approach embodies notions of empowerment but adds notions of competencies and care. Emerging as a conceptual framework and an approach, youth development stands in contrast to programs that focused on prevention and intervention strategies for at-risk youth. Prevention/intervention focus on a subset of adolescents needing special programs to fix problem behaviors. The failure of such efforts led to the need to envisage a new approach. By the early 1990s, the consensus was that avoiding drugs, sexual activity, and other "dangerous" behaviors did not prepare one for a successful transition into adulthood. This is consistent with research which shows that exposure to risk factors increases the likelihood of problem behaviors, while exposure to protective factors prevents problem behaviors even in spite of risk exposure (Hawkins, Catalano, & Miller, 1992; Sameroff & Seifer, 1990). Theoretical models such as that offered by Bronfenbrenner are helpful in understanding the joint influences of family, school, peers, and other social groups and point to the need for cross-institutional collaborations in creating a net of protection. Such protection comes in the form of bonding, social and emotional competence, critical thinking and decision-making, self-determination and self-efficacy, spirituality, positive identities, and prosocial norms and engagement. Youth development is more of an approach than a category. OST and empowerment programs can support elements of youth development; however, neither OST nor Empowerment programs necessarily emerged from this tradition.

Youth care is focused on the life work engaged in by youth workers that focuses on the overall well-being of children and youth. The setting can range from a residential facility to the street, but the nature of the work is to address the holistic needs of the person from hygiene to job skills. One theoretical framework that underpins models of care is Maslow's hierarchy of needs as it addresses both basic survival needs and more advanced belonging needs. The goal of the youth care worker is to help the individual reach what Maslow called self-actualization, or the full realization of one's potential. In residential and treatment programs there is a group work element to reach the goal but the focus remains on the progress of the individual (Mann-Feder & Litner, 2004). In other words, individual development is supported through the application of group principles, with the notion of self and self-in-relationship. While principles from the field of social work inform group engagement, the practice, particularly in the United States, is also informed by behavioral theories, most notably that of B.F. Skinner or some version of cognitive-behavior therapy. In some cases, behavioral contracts and modification plans are incorporated into the individual's treatment plan.

I have not captured all the faces of youth work here or expect that all programs will fall into neat categories. I put forward an analytical framework that (1) defines youth work and its underlying principles and (2) draws attention to the fact that helping youth workers develop their craft will require attention to the contexts in which they work and how youth and youth work are understood within that perspective and across domains/perspectives. That is, youth workers should be aware of the multiplicity of viewpoints on youth and youth work. Advancing youth work will mean understanding the totality of who we are including the tensions in our midst and more conscientiously striving to articulate our practice(s). Given the increased tendency caused by funding streams for youth work to take on an educational agenda and move away from broader purposes and objectives, the necessity to define who we are, what we do, and why we do it is never before more critical. If we cannot claim this field, it will be claimed for us. The authors of this volume have provided rich descriptions of youth work and what that means for youth work education and advancing the field. One theme is certain: we are not interested in "youth work" becoming another catch phrase, rather we do the work we do so that it is the lived experience of those who need it most.

References

Barwick, H. (2006). *Youth work today: A review of the issues and challenges*. Taiiohi, New Zealand: Ministry of Youth Development.

Batsleer, J. (2008). *Informal learning in youth work*. Thousand Oaks, CA: Sage.

Batsleer, J., & Davies, B. (Eds.). (2010). *What is youth work?* Exeter, UK: Learning Matters Ltd.

Bowie, L., & Bronte-Tinkew, J. (2006, December). The importance of professional development for youth workers. *Child Trends, 17*, 1–9.

Cornerstone for Kids. (2006). *Growing the next generation of youth professionals: Workforce opportunities and challenges*. Houston, TX: The Human Service Workforce Initiative, Cornerstone for Kids.

Foundations, Inc. (2010). Out-of-school time: Leveraging higher education for quality. Retrieved from http://wyafterschoolalliance.org/ Upload/File/Higher_Ed_Report_ Feb2010.pdf.

Fusco, D. (2003). *A landscape study of youth workers in out-of-school time*. New York: York College of the City University of New York, CUNY Workforce Development Initiative.

Hawkins, J. D., Catalano, R. F., & Miller, J. Y. (1992). Risk and protective factors for alcohol and other drug problems in adolescence and early adulthood: Implications for substance abuse prevention. *Psychological Bulletin, 112*, 64–105.

Hill, S. L., Matloff-Nieves, S., & Townsend, L. O. (2009, Spring). Putting our questions at the center: Afterschool matters practitioner fellowships. *Afterschool Matters*, 46–50.

Mann-Feder, V. R., & Litner, B. (2004). A normative re-educative approach to youthwork education: Department of Applied Human Sciences, Concordia University. *Child & Youth Care Forum, 33*, 275–286.

Pittman, K. J. (1991). *Promoting youth development: Strengthening the role of youth-serving and community organizations. Report prepared for The U.S. Department of Agriculture Extension Services.* Washington, DC: Center for Youth Development and Policy Research.

Russell, C. A., Reisner, E. R., Pearson, L. M., Afolabi, K. P., Miller, T. D., & Mielke, M. B. (2006*). Evaluation of DYCD's Out-of-School Time Initiative: Report on the first year.* Washington, DC: Policy Studies Associates, Inc. Retrieved from http://www.policystudies.com/studies/youth/OST.html.

Sameroff, A. J., & Seifer, R. (1990). Early contributors to developmental risk. In J. Rolf, A. S. Masten, D. Cichetti, K. H. Nuechterlein, & S. Weintraub (Eds.), *Risk and protective factors in the development of psychopathology* (pp. 52–66). New York: Cambridge University Press.

Starr, E., Yohalem, N., & Gannett, E. (2009). *Youth work core competencies: A review of existing frameworks* (commissioned by School's Out Washington). Seattle, WA: Next Generation Youth Work Coalition.

Vile, J. D., Russell, C. A., Miller, T. D., & Reisner, E. R. (2008). *College opportunities for after-school workers: Report on the first-year implementation of the Center for After-School Excellence certificate programs.* New York: Center for After-School Excellence.

Yohalem, N., & Pittman, K. (2006). *Putting youth work on the map: Key findings and implications from two major workforce studies.* Seattle, WA: Next Generation Youth Work Coalition.

ABOUT THE AUTHORS

Michael Baizerman, Ph.D., is Professor and Director of Youth Studies in the School of Social Work, University of Minnesota. He holds degrees in Political Science, Social Work, and Public Health. He has taught in youth studies since 1972 and also carried out community-consultation on youth work and youth studies locally and internationally. He has published widely in youth work and youth studies and extensively in program evaluation. Currently he is working with the National University of Laos on co-creating culturally appropriate youth work education and training.

Judith Bessant, Ph.D., is a Professor of Youth Studies and Sociology at Royal Melbourne Institute of Technology University, Australia. She has a history of curriculum writing for the state government in the area of sociology. Within the university system she has developed social science and youth studies curriculum. Professor Bessant has worked internationally and domestically to develop strategic plans and policy. She also researches, publishes and teaches in the areas of sociology, policy, youth studies, education, social theory and policy.

M. Deborah Bialeschki, Ph.D., earned a Doctor of Philosophy in Continuing and Adult Education from the University of Wisconsin-Madison. Deb was on the faculty at the University of North Carolina-Chapel Hill in the Department of Recreation and Leisure Studies for 20 years until she retired in 2005 as an Emeritus Professor. She is currently Director of Research and Chair of the Professional Development Center with the American Camp Association (ACA) where she is involved in research focused on youth development and the camp experience. She has authored 12 books, collaborated on 17 book chapters, and contributed over 100 articles and presentations in national and international journals and conferences. She received academic awards including the Tanner Faculty Award for Excellence in Undergraduate Teaching from UNC-Chapel Hill, the Society for Park and Recreation Educators (SPRE) National Award for Excellence in Teaching, and the SPRE Distinguished Colleague Award. Her research has focused on youth development through outdoor/camping experiences, staff training and development, and gender issues in leisure and outdoor recreation.

Dale Curry, Ph.D., LSW, CYC-P, is Associate Professor of Human Development and Family Studies and Director of the International Institute for Human Service Workforce Research and Development at Kent State University. Dale has over 30 years of experience in direct service, supervision, administration, education and training in child and family services. He is the Editor of the journal *Training and Development in Human Services,* Co-editor of the *Journal of Child and Youth Care Work* and the Principal Investigator of the North American Certification Project. He has published on topical areas such as professional development, worker retention, transfer of learning, trainer development, and ethics.

Judie Cutler, M.S., M.S.W., worked for the Minneapolis Public Schools for 25 years prior to returning to Webster, Wisconsin, in 2004 where she currently resides near the St. Croix Reservation. While with the school district she worked extensively in the field of multicultural education as a school social worker creating programs to support the health and wellness of families from many cultures. She is now working for policy and systems changes to improve collaborative efforts between community agencies, organizations, schools and Tribes. She co-founded Full Circle Community Institute in 1997, a consulting group focusing on cross-cultural communication, community coalition building, leadership development, research, evaluation and workshop facilitation. Most recently, Judie provides technical assistance to the Red Lake School District and Red Lake Nation in support of their long-term recovery efforts after the March 21, 2005, school shooting. Her relationship with Minnesota Tribes has expanded to include a Statewide Native Youth Initiative, Preparing Native Youth for a Lifetime of Choices Not Circumstances: Highlighting Research and Best Practice to Improve Educational, Social & Emotional Outcomes. Judie is enrolled with the Lake Superior Band of Chippewa, the St. Croix Tribe.

Jacqueline Davis-Manigaulte, Ed.D., is a Senior Extension Associate and Program Leader for Family and Youth Development Programs with Cornell University Cooperative Extension in New York City. She has extensive experience in the leadership, development and implementation of educational programs for youth and adult audiences. She recently received a doctorate from Columbia University/Teachers College in Adult Education. Her dissertation is entitled, *An Interpretive Case Study of Youth Development Network.*

Frank Eckles has been involved in the child and youth care workforce since the early 1970s and was instrumental in the formation of the Association for Child and Youth Care Practice (ACYCP), which represents child and youth care practitioners nationally. Frank currently serves on the ACYCP board of directors and for the past 10 years has worked on the national credentialing program. In 2007 when the Child and Youth Care Certification Board (CYCCB) was created by ACYCP to oversee the implementation of the national credentialing program, Frank was appointed to the Board and continues to serves as the Board President.

Dana Fusco, Ph.D., is an Associate Professor of Teacher Education and served as Acting Associate Dean of the School of Health and Behavioral Sciences at York College of the City University of New York until June 2011. As Dean she was responsible fors most of the college's professional education programs. Throughout her career, she has worked as a practitioner, researcher, and evaluator of youth development programs and developed the Certificate Program for Child and Youth Workers at York College. Her documentary, *When School Is Not Enough,* explores the role of afterschool programs in the lives of urban youth. Her most recent publications have centered on youth work education such as, *Shared Research Dialogue: One College's Model for the Professional Development of Youth Practitioners.* She holds a doctoral degree in Educational Psychology from the Graduate Center of the City University of New York.

Ellen Gannett is Director of the National Institute on Out-of-School Time (NIOST) at the Wellesley Centers for Women at Wellesley College. NIOST is a national action/research project, which for the past 30 years has provided research, evaluation, technical assistance, consultation, and specialized training on afterschool programs throughout the United States. As the director of NIOST, she ensures that research bridges the fields of child care, education, and youth development in order to promote programming that addresses the development of the whole child. Ellen has co-authored many NIOST's publications including, *Youth Work Core Competencies: A Review of Existing Frameworks* and *Links to Learning: A Curriculum Planning Guide for Afterschool Programs.* She also contributed to the writing and development of ASQ: Assessing School-Age Child Care Quality, School Age and Youth Development Credential (SAYD) as well as the Afterschool Program Assessment System (APAS). She is the national co-chair of the Next Generation Youth Work Coalition and national board member of the American Camp Association.

Michael Heathfield, Ph.D., was a senior professor responsible for training youth and community workers in England. His college was the first in the United Kingdom to offer an honors degree in professional youth and community work. His doctoral research explored how to make judgments about youth work practice and he has written and published articles on the subject of professional youth work both here and in the U.K. He was the Coordinator of Training Services for the Chicago Area Project where he created a range of professional development strategies including the Youth Development Practitioner Certification Program and in 2005, an AA/AAS degree in professional youth work. In fall 2006 he became full-time faculty at Harold Washington College where he is Coordinator of Social Work and Youth Work Programs. He is also chair of the college-wide Assessment Committee and was a co-chair of the national Next Generation Youth Work Coalition.

Sarah Jonas, Ed.M., joined the Children's Aid Society in 1998 as a community school director. She was promoted to Education Coordinator for Community Schools in 1999, Director of Educational Services for Community Schools and City and Country Divisions in 2004, and Director of Regional Initiatives for the National Center for Community Schools in 2009. Ms. Jonas is a certified teacher who taught for seven years in public schools in Los Angeles and New York City. She received her bachelor's degree in English Literature from Yale University and her Ed.M. in Administration, Planning and Social Policy from the Harvard Graduate School of Education.

Helen Jones, Dip. YCW, M.Ed., Ed.D. is Course Leader for professionally validated youth and community work degrees at the University of Huddersfield, U.K. where she teaches both pre-service and in-service undergraduate and postgraduate students. She has been involved in a range of curriculum and program developments including the delivery of the degree in Zambia to two cohorts. From 2000–2005 she coordinated quality assurance for the Commonwealth Youth Programme's Diploma in Youth in Development. She is a trustee of The Youth Association whose roots lie in Leeds Association of Girls' Clubs (founded in 1904) and whose history she is currently researching.

Joel Nitzberg, M.S.W., M.Ed., has Masters degrees in Social Work and Education, and over 25 years experience working on community issues specifically related to meshing education, workforce development and community capacity building. His most recent position was with Cambridge College as senior faculty and the Director of the Institute for Lifelong Learning and Community Building where he used principles of community education and community building to create customized educational services for adult learners in low-income communities. Prior to his position at the college, he worked for the Massachusetts Department of Education. He has recently ended his role as the President of the National Community Education Association. Over the years he has been an active advocate for youth development and engaging young people as community change agents. Mr. Nitzberg has a long history as a curriculum designer, trainer, leader and program manager. Some specific activities included establishing a local youth council in a city in Massachusetts, training youth workers in the United States and overseas and presently developing a national network of young community education leaders.

Jack Phelan, MS, Certified CYCW is a Professor Emeritus at Grant MacEwan University in Edmonton, Alberta who continues to teach for the Bachelor of Child and Youth Care program. He has a 25-year record of distinguished service at MacEwan, and has spent over 40 years in the field of child and youth care. Jack was co-chair during much of the period that the child and youth care degree proposal was being developed and piloted. Jack is past president of the Child and Youth Care Association of Alberta (CYCAA) and has served on its executive board in various capacities for over twenty years. He has been an active member of the CYCAA Legislation Committee that has been advocating for CYCAA legislation under the Health Professions Act and for more formal recognition of the field by government. For the past 40 years, he has done workshops and keynote addresses on topics related to child and youth care across North America, Scotland, Ireland, Sweden, and South Africa.

Jane Quinn is a social worker and youth worker with four decades of experience that include direct service with children and families, program development, fundraising, grantmaking, research and advocacy. She currently serves as the Vice President for Community Schools at The Children's Aid Society (CAS) in New York City, where she directs the National Center for Community Schools and contributes strategic planning and sustainability expertise to The Children's Aid Society's 22 local community schools in New York City. Jane came to CAS from the Wallace-Reader's Digest Funds, where she served as Program Director for seven years. Prior to that, she directed a national study of community-based youth organizations for the Carnegie Corporation of New York, which resulted in the publication of a book entitled *A Matter of Time: Risk and Opportunity in the Nonschool Hours*. Together with Joy Dryfoos, Jane co-edited a book entitled *Community Schools in Action: Lessons from a Decade of Practice,* which was published by Oxford University Press in 2005. In addition, she writes a regular column on youth development practice issues for *Youth Today.*

Andrew J. Schneider-Muñoz, Ed.D., CYC-P, is an Associate Professor (Visiting) and certified child and youth care worker at the University of Pittsburgh School of Education where he leads the concentration in Child and Youth Care Work. The Harvard-trained child psychologist and anthropologist conducts field studies in youth work around the world with recent projects to establish a global youth development strategy for vulnerable populations in the United States, South Africa, Russia, Mexico and Samoa. His work focuses on the influences of the global economy on parenting and youth work practices. Editor of *the Journal of Child and Youth Care Work* and Co-editor of *AfterSchool Around the Globe,* Schneider-Munoz is recognized for research in setting the standards and metrics for success in after-school, national service, and after-school programs. He is also known for having guided the research agendas for leading youth-serving organizations including the Center for Youth Development, City Year, and Search Institute.

Jim Sibthorp, Ph.D., is an Associate Professor at the University of Utah in the Department of Parks, Recreation, and Tourism. He teaches courses on youth programming, outdoor education, and research methods. Much of Jim's current research involves collaborative, youth focused, projects with the American Camp Association and the National Outdoor Leadership School (NOLS).

Carol Stuart, Ph.D., began her career in Child and Youth Care in Ontario, Canada and has 30 years of experience across three Canadian provinces. Carol has taught at Ryerson University, University of Victoria, and Grant MacEwan Community College to students at all levels. Carol's research interests include professional practice standards; integrated service delivery; the relationship between child and youth care competencies and outcomes; and participatory and qualitative approaches to research. She has recently published Foundations of Child and Youth Care, an introductory textbook adopted by educational programs across Canada and is the Managing Editor for the journal, Relational Child and Youth Care Practice. Carol has had a major role in developing the competencies and certification exams for child and youth care in Alberta and North America and is a certified CYC with Alberta, Ontario, and internationally with the Child and Youth Care Certification Board (CYCCB), Inc., where she is also a founding Board member and the chair of their Competency Review committee. Carol is President of the newly formed Child and Youth Care Educational Accreditation Board of Canada with a mandate to develop a viable accreditation process for post-secondary CYC education programs.

Ross VeLure Roholt, Ph.D., is an Assistant Professor in Youth Studies, School of Social Work, at the University of Minnesota. He holds degrees in Education, Social Work, Political Science and International Relations. Since 2007, he has taught 12 different courses in Youth Studies and Youth Development Leadership programs. Before joining the Youth Studies faculty, Ross worked for two years in Belfast, Northern Ireland on issues around youth civic engagement and youth work practice. He has consulted both locally and internationally on youth work practice, especially in Jordan, Israel, and Palestine territories. Currently he is developing a youth work practice, Civic Youthwork, and also continues to consult with youth organizations and groups in Jordan and Morocco.

Joyce Walker, Ph.D., is a professor at the University of Minnesota Extension Center for Youth Development. Her focus and leadership in youth worker education, training and professional development have shaped and guided the national Building Exemplary Systems of Training Initiative (BEST), the Youth Development Leadership M.Ed. Program (University of Minnesota) and the Youth Work Institute (Extension Center for Youth Development). Community involvement includes Camp Fire USA Minnesota Council Foundation chair, Sheltering Arms Foundation executive committee and the national Next Generation Youth Work Coalition co-chair. She serves on the editorial board of the U.K. journal *Youth & Policy*.

Kate Walker, Ph.D., is a research associate at the University of Minnesota Extension Center for Youth Development where she conducts applied research and evaluation on youth development practice and programs. Her works centers on understanding, evaluating and elevating youth work practice. She is particularly interested in practitioner expertise, workforce development, program quality and ethics. Her current research explores the dilemmas that practitioners face in their everyday work with youth and their strategies for addressing these challenges. Kate received her doctoral degree in Educational Psychology from the University of Illinois at Urbana-Champaign.

Pete Watkins, M.S.W., has been in the field of youth work since the late 1980s. He has a B.A. in psychology from University of Pennsylvania and a master's degree in social work from Temple University. He is currently Assistant Professor in the Psychology, Education and Human Services department, and Coordinator of the Youth Work Certificate Program at Community College of Philadelphia. He is also an adjunct faculty member at Temple University.

Camille Williamson, M.S.W., grew up on the far south side of Chicago. She is a graduate of the Masters Program at the University of Chicago, School of Social Service Administration, with an emphasis in clinical work with youth. She also a holds a B.A. from the University of Illinois at Urbana-Champaign where she majored in psychology and minored in sociology with an emphasis in child and adolescent development. In high school she became co-founder of the Chicagoland Youth Against AIDS (CYAA) whose mission was to provide HIV/AIDS prevention education and condoms to adolescents and young adults. It was this experience that helped establish and solidify her high interest in the advancement and empowerment of youth. Currently, Camille is the Director of Educational Talent Search at Southwest Youth Collaborative, a program designed to expose low-income, first generation students to college. Throughout her career Camille has learned that support lies in the acknowledgement of the youths' expressed needs, their participation in the development of programs to meet their needs, and the belief in their ability to grow and thrive from their own set of experiences.

INDEX